The Philosophy of Interpretation

ℳ METAPHILOSOPHY

A METAPHILOSOPHY MONOGRAPH

Series Editor
Armen T. Marsoobian

The Philosophy of Interpretation

Edited by

Joseph Margolis and
Tom Rockmore

BLACKWELL
Publishers

Copyright © Blackwell Publishers 2000

First published 1999

ISBN 0–631–22047–X (Pbk)

Blackwell Publishers
108 Cowley Road
Oxford OX4 1JF, UK

Blackwell Publishers Inc
350 Main Street
Malden, Massachusetts 02148, USA

British Library Cataloguing in Publication Data has been applied for

Library of Congress Cataloging-in-Publication Data has been applied for

Typeset by Cambrian Typesetters, Frimley, Surrey
Printed in Great Britain
MPG Books, Bodmin, Cornwall

This book is printed on acid-free paper

Contents

1

INTRODUCTION: THE PHILOSOPHY OF INTERPRETATION

JOSEPH MARGOLIS AND TOM ROCKMORE

In the second half of our century, interpretation has been accorded an increasingly prominent role in the perception and understanding both of physical and cultural reality and of our own role in both. The sources of this accommodation may be traced to the following themes at least: (1) the questionable status of neutrality in the physical sciences and the cognate recovery of objectivity (without neutrality) as a critical "construction" of some sort; (2) the intentional, significative, or semiotic nature of the entire artifactual world of human culture, intrinsically apt for interpretation and essential to the work of human self-understanding; (3) the inseparability of our unique cognitive abilities in understanding the natural world and ourselves; and (4) the social formation of self-interpreting selves, the congruent formation of their conceptual powers, and the enormously puzzling fact that the exercise of those powers changes human nature and changes those powers in significant and discernible ways.

These four themes were unified and featured, philosophically, for the first time, in the interval following the French Revolution, which culminates in Hegel – the period we now call "post-Kantian." Its conceptual visions often strike us as embarrassingly grandiose, but its leading lights achieved a sense of the inclusive unity of the entire intelligible world, which notably eludes us now. Also, its principal lessons, which are barely suggested in the summary just given, provide a compelling and exceedingly lean constraint on our own philosophical labors. It would not be unreasonable to suggest that the unities the post-Kantians envisioned extended and corrected the grand unity achieved in Kant's own "Copernican revolution," which they were motivated to complete. In their best moments, the post-Kantians challenged the fixity and certainty of transcendental reason and realigned its themes in the direction of an encultured and historical process.

Inevitably, it seems, interpretation, or reason functioning in the interpretive mode, under constraints like those just collected, became the natural successor of Pure Reason in the Kantian sense – for all those inquiries that, one way or another, remained sympathetic with particular strands of the post-Kantian vision. To be sure, the analysis of interpretation is usually narrowly centered on the critical treatment of history, the fine arts, sacred and legal texts, and the like. But it is impossible to pursue these matters without speculating about their bearing on the more general analysis of culture, the human condition, and the epistemic standing of the natural sciences. You see this particularly in recent American pragmatism and European hermeneutics, and certainly in Marxist and Freudian inquiries. The specialized topics of interpretation in literature and painting, the New Testament and the Koran, feminism and radical history, still make sense, of course. But they are all tethered in some way as various modern responses to the Hegelian vision. There is, therefore, a strong motivation to link the grander and the more local themes of interpretation in a more systemic way.

The piecemeal nature of the preponderant part of Anglo-American philosophy often seems unnecessarily restricted: the thought nags that there are important discoveries to be made in reclaiming connections between seemingly disconnected inquiries, for instance, between the physical sciences and the arts. In fact, one could easily defend the thesis that Western philosophy is being increasingly polarized between those who mean to recover the post-Kantian unities and those who oppose the very idea that that is possible or worth exploring. In the American setting, the matter may be illustrated by the incipient contest between a strengthened pragmatism and the turn toward "naturalism" (or what has been termed "naturalizing" in recent analytic philosophy). Champions of the latter movement – Donald Davidson, for instance, or even Richard Rorty to the extent that Rorty is a "naturalizer" – reject interpretation (or interpretive *tertia*) in rejecting epistemic intermediaries of any sort within the scope of naturalized explanations. More equivocally, figures like Hilary Putnam and (even earlier) diminished figures like Thomas Kuhn support the inescapability of interpretive *tertia*. The implied contest may well be the single liveliest issue in the whole of Anglo-American philosophy as we move into the twenty-first century. Hence, the more familiar local questions of what to understand by the rigor of interpretive judgment in this or that discipline continue to suggest a larger puzzle.

There may be no single way to collect all the "local" questions regarding interpretation. But they tend to gather around a handful of topics:

- What can "objectivity" possibly mean, when "neutrality" is dubious or no longer assured?
- What is "objective" in the way of fixing "meaning" and related cultural structures?
- What is the structure of those things that are by nature interpretable (if indeed there are any)?

- Is the logic of interpretation significantly different from the logic of the natural sciences? If so, why or why not?
- How does the historical drift of societal experience affect what may count as an objective interpretation of an artwork or text or history?

These surely form a selection of the central cluster of questions regularly raised about interpretation among a family of well-known disciplines – those that belong to constitutional lawyers, connoisseurs of art, musicologists, historians of civilization, literary critics, guardians of sacred texts, political pundits. In a very natural way, the energy of these inquiries dovetails with the larger issues bruited. For if it turned out, for example, that such notorious theories as incommensurabilism, historicism, and relativism – which, arguably, address the fortunes of one or another interpretive *tertium* – proved to be a respectable, even vigorous, competitor in all our efforts to account for our understanding the world and ourselves, then philosophy would probably take a decisive turn toward the reclamation of the post-Kantian themes that are notably now somewhat marginalized. This is meant not as a prophecy but as a sign of the strategic importance of construing interpretation as a distinct problematic. Seen this way, the theory of interpretation has itself become a general theory of knowledge and reality.

2

INTERPRETATION AND JUSTIFICATION

DAVID NOVITZ

For the most part, we interpret in order to understand, and to have arrived, in this way, at a sound understanding is to have interpreted successfully. This suggests that some interpretations are better than others, so that whenever understanding is sought we are obliged to justify our interpretations – to demonstrate that they furnish an adequate understanding of the world and its objects. The problem is to know whether this is possible – that what we take to be conclusive justifications do not covertly appeal to other favoured interpretations or systems of explanation, thus obviating the possibility of a neutral justification.

The dispute between those who argue that there are neutral grounds in terms of which to justify interpretation (Beardsley 1970, 1992; Hirsch 1967, 1976; Iseminger 1992; Davies 1988, 1995; Stecker 1992, 1997; Novitz 1987) and those who argue that there are no such grounds – that justification, such as it is, is always relative to a preferred system of explanation (Margolis 1976, 1989, 1995a, 1995b; Shusterman 1992) – can be resolved only if we have an adequate grasp of the nature of interpretation: of what it involves, what it seeks to achieve, and how pervasive it is in human cognition. It is here that I begin.

Notes on the Nature of Interpretation

I have said that interpretation is intimately linked to understanding, and so it is. But we should not think that my ability to understand something on a particular occasion invariably depends on my own interpretative efforts. I may understand because I *already* know, or I may come to understand because you (or a dictionary, textbook, or encyclopedia) have informed me about it. We live, as Lorraine Code has argued, in an epistemic community – which is just to say that we depend for a good deal of our knowledge and understanding on the efforts and enquiries of others (Code 1987, Chap. 7). So while it may arguably be the case that all understanding depends in

4

some way on interpretation, my coming to understand on any given occasion need not involve my own interpretations.

Even so, in one basic – perhaps the primary – sense of this word, "interpretation" mentions an activity that we wittingly perform in order to fill gaps in our understanding. In this sense, interpretation is called for only when we know that we have run out of established knowledge and belief in terms of which to dispel our confusion or ignorance. Put differently, interpretation (in the primary sense) always requires knowledge of one's own lack of comprehension – knowledge, perhaps, of the fact that one is puzzled about something that one wishes to understand. And the process of coming to understand it invariably involves the imaginative formulation of hypotheses that are expressly designed to dispel one's incomprehension.

There is, though, a second sense of "interpretation" – what I have elsewhere called "elaborative interpretation" – that does not involve a self-conscious quest for understanding (Novitz 1987, 91–93). The reader of a novel, for instance, may subjectively elaborate the author's words by filling in the indeterminacies of the text – in ways, say, that give Elizabeth Bennet auburn hair, high cheekbones, and a husky voice, without it being the case either that Jane Austen has specified these qualities or that the reader is aware of his or her ignorance of them. Without reflecting on it, and perhaps without even realising what is being done, the reader fleshes out the novel along particular lines and does so by imagining that Elizabeth Bennet has certain qualities – ones that are consistent with the text but that are not specified by it. In the same way, a pianist's performance of a musical work could be an elaborative interpretation, and will be if the pianist unreflectively fills in the indeterminacies of the score and does so without attempting to solve particular puzzles, believing that his performance is obvious or else unproblematic.

Although elaborative interpretations obviously affect one's understanding of cultural objects, they are not designed to secure understanding and are not embarked upon because of any awareness of one's own ignorance. They sometimes seem obvious to the interpreter, and there need be no awareness of having imaginatively imputed properties to a fictional character or a natural object, still less of having done so without obvious warrant.

Questions regarding the adequacy of elaborative interpretations do not usually arise and will do so only if they contradict certain other beliefs that are held about the object of interpretation. Since in the ordinary course of events elaborative interpretations are confined to the indeterminacies of a work, a character, or a state of affairs, there are a large range of possible elaborations, all equally plausible, but not always compatible with one another. The Irishman who elaboratively imputes reddish hair to Elizabeth Bennet is not mistaken, but neither is the Italian who imagines her hair to be a darker shade. Nor is either of them correct about her hair colour if it is also the case that *Pride and Prejudice* does not stipulate this. Of course, if the text tells us that she had no hair, then any elaborative interpretation to the effect that her hair was red or black or auburn would be false, but false only because it transgresses the authorial prescriptions that help constitute the character.

What I call elaborative interpretation has a good deal in common with what Roland Barthes calls a "writerly" response to a cultural object and with what Michael Krausz regards as "imputational interpretation" (Barthes 1974, 4; Krausz 1993, Chap. 3). For according to both, our "imputational" or "writerly" interpretation helps constitute the object of interpretation – or, as Barthes calls it, the "text." It constructs the text by imputing properties to it – properties that then actually form part of it. But Barthes would be well advised to proceed with caution here. Unlike Krausz, he does not appear to countenance any constraints at all on writerly responses to the text, for, as he tells us, he wants the reader to have more than "the poor freedom either to accept or reject the text"; he wants the reader to have the writerly power to construct or constitute the text. While the text, on Barthes's view, is to be distinguished from the work, where the latter is a concrete object that occupies space and time and the former is a constructed "methodological field," it is nonetheless the case that for Barthes the text is the bearer of meaning and other intentional properties. However, since cultural objects are partly identified and reidentified in terms of their intentional properties, and not merely in terms of the spatio-temporal location of the physical object that embodies them, there do need to be constraints on the ways in which readers construct (or elaborate) texts and other cultural objects – just in order to permit their reidentification across time and to ensure that those who speak of what they take to be the same cultural object remain part of the same conversation. In order to make sense of a writerly response to a cultural object, therefore, we have to introduce constraints on that response – constraints that include particular inscriptions on paper, in paint, specific images on the moving screen, and, of course, the cultural conventions that mediate these within a society at a given time (Margolis 1995a, 36, 39).[1] How precisely such constraints operate is something that I return to presently.

There can be no doubt that our elaborative interpretations, like any writerly response to a cultural object, will be coloured by our own experiences and our own culturally acquired beliefs, expectations, and values. How one applies all of these becomes a mark of how imaginative one is, but is not directed at the acquisition of an adequate understanding; it is

---

[1]   Joseph Margolis (1995a) supposes that because Barthes regards the work of art as an enduring physical object, reference is secured. But reference is secured only to the physical object that embodies the text, not to the "text" or cultural object itself (since on Barthes's account a physical object may embody more than one cultural object).

what is sometimes called ludic (or playful) interpretation – which, while explorative in the sense that it realises different possibilities, is nonetheless gratuitous in that it has no particular aim and does not seriously attempt to dispel ignorance or impart understanding. Hence, there is no question of justifying such interpretations or of attempting to discover whether they are true or false. If we assess them at all, we do so for their imaginative prowess – or, as Joseph Margolis once termed it, for their virtuosity.

Clearly, then, elaborative interpretations need to be distinguished from those that seek, self-consciously, to add to our understanding – that is, from what I have elsewhere called "elucidatory interpretations" (Novitz 1987, 91–93). Since the latter attempt to dispel ignorance, solve puzzles, and so render comprehensible what was previously incomprehensible, we constantly want to know of them whether they are justified, whether they do the job required of them – namely, promote an adequate understanding of the world or its objects and so place us in an epistemically stronger position regarding them.

The Epistemic Structure of Elucidatory Interpretation

Even though elucidatory interpretation can be and often is influenced by its elaborative ("writerly" or "imputational") counterpart, we can now see that it is conceptually independent of it. It seeks self-consciously to understand, in a way that elaborative interpretation does not – and so can reflect on and modify prior writerly assumptions, elaborations, or imputations if they impede a successful understanding. At every turn, one could say, elucidatory trumps elaborative interpretation – for, provided that one wishes to understand, any elaboration that is not conducive to an overall understanding is simply modified until it is conducive to this goal. Elucidatory interpretation is the *only* means of coming to make reliable sense of whatever it is that confounds us – the only way, that is, of coming to an adequate understanding whenever our existing bodies of belief and knowledge fail to guide us.

Elucidatory interpretations, we can now see, have a very definite epistemic structure since they require that interpreters be aware of their own ignorance, which they then wittingly seek to dispel by imaginatively formulating hypotheses that function as tentative solutions to some question. It is, moreover, in terms of their distinctive epistemic structure that (elucidatory) interpretations may best be distinguished from descriptions. For, as we have seen, in order to interpret in this sense, one must believe that one lacks the requisite knowledge or beliefs in terms of which to advance one's understanding. Hence Robert Matthews is entirely correct when, in writing of interpretation in this sense, he says that it is epistemically weaker than description, for description (unlike interpretation) proceeds firmly in the belief that one knows and can make sense of the object of one's description (Matthews 1977, 5–14; Novitz 1987, 93–97).

Even so, it is reasonable to suppose that much of what we now take ourselves to know, and of what we now apply linguistically in descriptions, was once the object of some person's bemusement and required acts of interpretation in order to render the unintelligible intelligible. Such acts consist in more or less well informed imaginative conjectures, guesses, or fanciful construals, all of which result in the formulation of particular explanatory hypotheses. Those guesses, hypotheses, or construals that fail to make proper sense of a particular puzzle will be rejected and modified in the light of our knowledge of at least one failure, so that, as a result of successive trial-and-error modifications – what Hans-Georg Gadamer has elsewhere called "to-and-fro movements" (1988, 93) – we will eventually arrive at construals that work to ease our confusion, that enable us to make sense of and negotiate a text, a social situation, or the physical world more adequately than we could otherwise have done. For as long as they continue to do this, we will assent to and believe them, and provided that they continue to work, we will eventually come to regard them as knowledge.

It is at this point that what we take to be the knowledge derived from earlier interpretations is or can be applied in descriptions – but this is not to say that today's description is really just a covert interpretation.[2] It is not. It is a confirmed interpretation that not only renders something intelligible but that also promotes a reliable understanding – one, at the very least, that has predictive utility and is consistent with other well-established core understandings. As a result, it places us in an epistemically stronger position regarding the world than any unconfirmed interpretation can do – something that we discover through our successful interaction with, or our actions in, the world around us.[3]

If all of this is right, the activity of interpreting may be distinguished from that of describing in terms of their respective epistemic structures. People interpret when they acknowledge their own ignorance, when they believe that they do not understand, and when they seek to understand by formulating and tentatively projecting hypotheses onto the object of their bemusement. By contrast, people describe when they believe that they know or understand and when they seek to apply their knowledge or understanding linguistically in an informative way to the world around them.

Margolis's approach to this distinction is very different. Initially, he tried to ground it ontologically in terms of the relative stability of the

---

[2]   In what follows, I will mean by "interpretation" *elucidatory interpretation* and will use the adjective "elucidatory" only when there is a risk of confusion.

[3]   I discuss below the question whether natural objects are properly described as objects of *interpretation*.

objects of interpretation and description. We describe stable objects, he maintains, and interpret unstable ones "whose properties pose something of a puzzle" (1980, 111).[4] But any such move, I once argued, has to be problematic since our perception of stabilities is itself unstable (Novitz 1987, 95). How we see the world depends importantly on the beliefs that we bring to perception, so that objects are only taken to have certain properties for as long as our beliefs (and theories) about them endure. Since empirical beliefs do change, there can be no way in which Margolis can discern which properties of an object – whether it be natural or cultural – are stable. Hence, I argued, Margolis runs the risk of reducing all empirical descriptions to interpretations.

But it has since become apparent that Margolis is entirely willing to embrace this consequence. This is so because, on his view, there is no way at all of knowing how things are – reality, he tells us, is not cognitively transparent – so that there is no way of discerning what properties an object, whether cultural or natural, actually has (1995a, 2). Nor can we tell, he thinks, what the mind contributes to our grasp of the world's real structure, especially because the ways in which we think and construe are themselves historically produced (1995a, 3). Here he seems to be in agreement with Richard Shusterman, who writes that

> any distinction between describing and interpreting (as between understanding and interpreting) can only be relative and formal. It must be a pragmatic, shifting, heuristic distinction, not an unchanging one which provides a firm and incorruptible core of determinate truth for simple and final description. In other words, . . . the descriptive facts are simply whatever we all strongly agree upon, while interpretations are simply what commands less consensus and displays (and tolerates) wider divergence. (1992, 71–72)

At its best, then, Margolis and Shusterman think that the sort of knowledge that I deem necessary to a true description – knowledge, say, about the properties that inhere in objects – is not available to us independently of interpretation; "instability" or Nietzschean "flux," it would seem, is endemic and ubiquitous. At most, then, the distinction between interpretation and description, as I have drawn it, is not "principled" and depends on certain "regularized interpretations" being construed as descriptions for certain preferred purposes, so that, as Margolis tells us, "interpretations may be descriptions and descriptions may or may not be interpretations" (1995a, 12).

---

[4]   It sometimes seems that Margolis believes that only those objects that embody intentional properties – what he regards as cultural objects – are the proper objects of interpretation. I dispute this presently.

The Doctrine of Cognitive Intransparency

It is true that the imaginative construals involved in interpretation play a vital role in the acquisition and growth of knowledge (Novitz 1987, Chap. 2). Even so, recent work in evolutionary psychology and cognitive science suggests that by no means are all of our cognitive states a function of such construals – nor could they be (Barkow, Cosmides, and Tooby 1992). However, even if it were the case that all of what we take to be empirical knowledge depends at some level on interpretation, it still would not be true that the external world is somehow occluded by the concepts or the discourse in terms of which we construe our experience.

Suppose that a particular set of interpretations about the nature of the physical and social environment serves us well, enables us to negotiate the world or our environment adequately, and continues to do so over a reasonable period of time. As a result, and not unreasonably, we rely on these interpretations, assent to and so believe them, and provided that they continue to work, we will not just assert their truth but will claim to know the propositions that they embody. We do so on pragmatic grounds: the interpretations work; they enable us to make sense, explain, predict, navigate, control, and manipulate. In light of this, it would be seriously misleading to entertain the higher-order interpretation that successful first-order interpretations about our world somehow prevent cognitive access to the furniture and the properties of the world or else fail to "cut the world at its joints." If it is assented to, this higher-order interpretation would not just undermine our initially successful interpretation, but would also, if sincerely entertained and relied upon, starkly limit our capacity to act in and negotiate the world around us. Such a higher-order interpretation (which is what the doctrine of cognitive intransparency amounts to) would not place us in an epistemically stronger position regarding our physical or social environment. It would not facilitate understanding, and for this reason – and on the basis once again of pragmatist criteria – it would be a wholly unsuccessful interpretation.

We would do better, therefore, to construe those interpretations that serve us well as revealing, in all salient respects, the way an object is. In other words, where we successfully interpret the object as having the property XYZ – "successful" in the sense that it enables us to cope with the object – the best higher-order interpretation concerning it is that it successfully isolates the property XYZ in the object. But since this is the higher-order interpretation that works best, and since it withstands the tests of experience and time, there is good reason to assent to it, hence to say that we *know* and have access to the fact that the object has property XYZ.

Certainly our knowledge of the world in this case is a function of interpretative discourse and does not leap into our minds independently of some discursive means of discovering it. But this does not entail that the world is cognitively intransparent. On the contrary, interpretation is the very process that makes the world cognitively accessible and, when successful, renders the world cognitively transparent – not in the sense that it affords direct, unmediated access to it, but in the sense that, as soon as the interpretation works, and for so long as it continues to work, there is no good reason to doubt, and considerable reason to maintain, that one does have cognitive access to those aspects of the world that it purports to reveal. As we know the world, so it is.

It is true, as David Hume never tires of telling us, that empirical knowledge-claims are fallible, so that it may indeed turn out that experience shows our knowledge-claims to be mistaken, hence that the interpretation on which a particular claim to knowledge was based was inadequate from the start, that it was misleading rather than helpful. But for so long as we have no reason to suppose this, and as long as there is reason to suppose the contrary, we remain justified in believing it and in basing claims to knowledge on it. We are justified, that is, in claiming to know how the world is. Any future interpretation will have to be consistent with this claim to knowledge, and in some cases conform to it, before we will be in a position to rely on it, believe it, and eventually treat it as knowledge.

The claim that the world is cognitively intransparent is not just misleading; it is also paradoxical. For any assertion to the effect that our so-called knowledge of the world is an interpretative construct that cannot be known to correspond to how things *really* are prompts the question, Is this something that can be known by those who assert it or is it similarly a construct? If it is just an interpretative construct, why should we take it as revealing how things are with respect to knowledge and the world? For anything that would count as a reason for believing it would also count as a reason for saying that it is something about the world that is not cognitively intransparent to us. If, on the other hand, the doctrine that the world is cognitively intransparent is not just a construct but is a known fact about our cognitive capacities, then at least one aspect of the world – that which has to do with human cognition – is not cognitively intransparent. But if *it* is epistemically accessible to us, why should other aspects of the world remain cognitively occluded? Until these questions are answered, there is no reason to believe the claim that the world is cognitively intransparent and considerable reason to believe otherwise.

Crucially, doctrines of cognitive intransparency are deeply subversive of rational justification. For if our interpretations and descriptions really are cognitively insulated from the facts that they claim to report, there is no possibility of appealing to those facts in order, rationally, to defend our descriptions and interpretations. Even worse, if the way things are has no rational bearing on the interpretations in question, then those interpretations cannot be known to be about anything in the real world. But we interpret in the elucidatory sense precisely because we wish to understand how things *are*, and because we know that we do not understand how they are. If there is no way (as someone like Richard Rorty would have) in which things actually are, and no way of coming to know how they are, then there is no point to (elucidatory) interpretation (Rorty 1998, 389–94).[5] And, with appropriate adjustments, exactly the same is true of description.

Since there is, as I have argued, good reason to believe that we can have knowledge of how things are in the world, there is also good reason to believe that our descriptions (which involve the linguistic application of such knowledge) can be distinguished from and can serve, rationally, to confirm or justify particular interpretations. It is futile to claim, as Margolis and Shusterman do, that the distinction between description and interpretation is not "principled" or "firm." A well-founded conceptual distinction can be and has to be drawn between the two. Certainly the distinction is not founded on *de re* necessity; it is founded on human cognitive practice, but this does not make it any the less firm or principled.

The Historicity of Interpretation

The claim that we can rely on past successful interpretations, and so on our knowledge of the way the world is, in order to justify a particular interpretation will doubtlessly be challenged on the ground that it overlooks the extent to which each particular interpretation is shaped by historical and social circumstance (Goldstein 1976; Margolis 1976, 1980, 1995a; Rorty 1989, Part I; Krausz 1993, Chap. 6). We are all reared within cultures, the argument goes, and we adopt specific sets of beliefs, world views, myths, and values on account of our cultural location. These, we are told, mediate the way in which we interpret or construe the world, and this is why two people from different cultures may very well construe natural or cultural objects differently.

Since it would seem that two incompatible interpretations can both enable us to negotiate the world or certain of its objects satisfactorily, it is always possible (so the argument goes) that there should be two or more interpretations that impute different and exclusive properties to the same object. Moreover, these interpretations may both work, may both facilitate our understanding, and may both enable us to cope in the world. Since this is so, it is argued, the fact that any particular interpretation is adjudged successful in pragmatist terms cannot ensure that it "cuts the world at its joints" – that it reveals the world to us as it is.

This, moreover, is why Margolis thinks that there are no grounds for saying of an interpretation that it is true, for this would require some culturally neutral terrain from which to tell how things really are (Margolis 1976, 37, 44; 1995b, 2). But since we are importantly (albeit contingently) a product of our respective cultures, since the systems of

---

[5]   It is important to note that Margolis (1995a, 21) does not wish to dispense with what I call elucidatory interpretation.

belief that shape our respective worlds help shape our experience, our interpretations partially create the properties of the objects that we interpret; they are "writerly" or "imputational" or "elaborative" interpretations that create epistemic and ontological "flux" – cognitive and ontic variations that depend on a range of cultural and historical contingencies. This is why there is and can be no neutral way of adjudicating between competing interpretations (McDowell 1994).[6] Moreover, since two incompatible interpretations cannot both be true but can both be regarded as plausible, Margolis contends that interpretations are to be assessed for degrees of plausibility, not their truth (1976, 37). Where interpretation is concerned, a bivalent logic should be replaced by a many-valued logic.

As against this, however, it is often argued that to say that a proposition is plausible is just to say that it is likely to be true, so that any reason one gives for its plausibility would also count as a reason for its truth (Beardsley 1992, 37). In order to avoid this sort of criticism, Margolis contends that interpretations are judged plausible not in virtue of their truth-likelihood but "in virtue of their use of preferred explanatory models in any given domain," where such preferences are presumably a function of historical or cultural circumstance (1980, 159). In this way, Margolis introduces a new and different sense of "plausible": one that has nothing to do with the likelihood of a proposition's being true and everything to do with what people want – with their *preferred* methods of explanation. The cognitive, on Margolis's view, can no longer be distinguished in any decisive way from the conative. Hence, to judge a proposition as plausible is to express a particular attitude toward it: that one would prefer it and the system of explanation it subtends to some alternative proposition or system of explanation. The claim, then, that an interpretation is plausible says nothing at all about the likelihood of its telling us how the world is or how things hang together in the world – unless, of course, the explanatory model that it subtends is preferred for its capacity to do so; but that option plainly is not open to anyone who defends the doctrine of cognitive intransparency.

It is of course true that we are all historically located and, in some measure, historically shaped beings – reared within cultures that impart particular beliefs, values, and world views at particular times. It is also the case that our cultural inheritance is, and has to be, an obvious port of call when trying to understand something that puzzles and bemuses us. But it does not follow from this that interpretations cannot be true; nor does it follow that interpretations cannot furnish us with knowledge about the world.

For although our thinking is historically shaped, it is wrong to suppose that we are constrained by history in ways that prevent us from

---

[6] For a recent defence of a related view, see McDowell (1994), who regards experience as inherently conceptual. For a critique of this view, see Brandom (1998).

adopting new or different ways of construing the world.[7] Even though our attempts to understand through interpretation are initially framed in terms of current beliefs and values – many of which reflect our cultural allegiances – only those who are closed in their thinking, who believe that their cultural beliefs are either natural or else sacrosanct and invariably correct, will be limited in the way that a strong historicist thinks we all are.

Whenever an interpretation that is couched in terms of our cultural beliefs and values fails to promote an adequate understanding, we can construe its failure in one of two ways. We can either adhere steadfastly to those beliefs, or we can treat our failure to understand as the result of the limitations of our own perspective (Gadamer 1988, 239 ff.; Gadamer 1976, 9; Bernstein 1983, 129). If we suppose the correctness of our own perspective, the source of our failure to comprehend will be located in the nature of whatever it is that puzzles us, and we may consider it at fault – as "irrational," "stupid," "unnatural," "beyond comprehension," or whatever. If, however, we locate the problem in ourselves, we will seek tentatively to modify certain of the beliefs in terms of which we normally seek to understand. These are the beliefs, in Gadamer's words, that help constitute our "horizons," that in some sense make us the people that we are and afford us our greatest certainty. We modify these beliefs through trial and error, through "play" or a "to-and-fro movement" of successive cognitive adjustments, until we secure what Donald Davidson would call the best "holistic fit" – thereby securing an adequate understanding of whatever it is that puzzles us (Davidson 1973, 313–27).

These adjustments, as well as what Gadamer calls the "fusion of horizons," suggest that while our thinking is historically shaped, it is not bound to its historical and cultural origins. As Gadamer puts it:

> The historical movement of human life consists in the fact that it is never utterly bound to any one standpoint, and hence can never have a truly closed horizon. The horizon is, rather, something into which we move and that moves with us. Horizons change for a person who is moving. (1988, 271)

So while it is true that we bring certain cultural allegiances in the form of beliefs and values to the interpretation of various objects, these may be modified when they fail to do service, until, through the successive trial-and-error formulation of alternative hypotheses, we arrive at an interpretation that promotes an adequate understanding.

---

[7]   Joseph Margolis seems to support precisely this point of view, partly because of his adherence to the doctrine of cognitive intransparency, but also in his earlier writings. See Margolis 1965, 88; 1980, 148–49.

Interpretation and Bivalence

All that the argument of the previous section shows, however, is that our interpretations and our thinking are not strongly determined by our cultural affiliations. What it does not and cannot show is that it is impossible to have two incompatible interpretations that both promote an adequate understanding – in the sense that both enable us to predict, manipulate, control, negotiate the world and its objects with a high degree of success. A strong historicism is not needed for this to be the case. And if it is the case, then it is simply wrong to maintain that an interpretative statement is the sort of thing that can be true. Since "almost no one denies that incompatible interpretations of artworks may be jointly defended," and since "almost no one denies that many-valued logics are viable," Margolis contends that "anyone who wishes to construe interpretative judgements as truth-claims would be well advised . . . to replace (in the sector of inquiry in question) bivalence with a many-valued logic" (1995b, 2–3).

In what follows, I assume that the notion of a many-valued logic is coherent. I also assume that there are genuinely incompatible interpretations that one and the same person may find acceptable.[8] All that this requires, after all, is the capacity to be inconsistent. What I deny is that "incompatible interpretations can be jointly defended" if this is taken to entail that there are occasions when it is in principle impossible to resolve the incompatible claims of competing interpretations about one and the same cultural or natural object. I concede, of course, that there may be contingent difficulties that prevent such resolutions; what I deny is that it is ever impossible to do so.[9] Rather, on the view that I defend, it is always possible to show, of two apparently competing interpretations, either (1) that they do not really compete or (2) that if they do, both are false, or that the one is true, the other false. Where interpretation is concerned, I argue, bivalence rules.

As I have explained it, the aim of (elucidatory) interpretation is to secure an adequate understanding of whatever it is that confuses or puzzles us. An understanding, I have said, will be adequate if and only if it enables one to negotiate the world successfully (where this includes both its natural and cultural objects, events, relations, and states of affairs). Since it is reasonable to assume that there is only one way in which the world can be at any one time (call this the singularity constraint), one normally concedes that one has not finally understood if one also recog-

---

[8]   Here I would seem to differ from Stecker (1997, 121), who argues that "many of the most likely candidates for incompatible acceptable interpretations turn out to be compatible when we carefully attend to what they each are *asserting*."

[9]   Cf. Barnes (1988, 2), who maintains that "it is possible for criticism to legitimately tolerate incompatible (*genuinely* and not seemingly incompatible) interpretations for a single work." See, as well, Goldman 1990, where he maintains that "incompatible interpretations may be equally acceptable" (207).

nises that a phenomenon or state of affairs is amenable to two conflicting interpretations: interpretations that impute different and exclusive properties to the phenomenon in question. For if there is only one way that the world is at any one time – one shape to an object, one set of semantic properties to a text, or one set of pictorial properties to a painting – this suggests that an adequate understanding has not been reached, that there is work to be done, a convergence to be sought. Of course, it may be the case that two different people are each satisfied with interpretations that exclude one another. But, given the singularity constraint, one and the same person will not consider herself to have understood for so long as she subscribes to or admits, and for so long as she cannot decide between, two conflicting interpretations.

It is important to understand what the singularity constraint commits us to. In particular, just by saying that there must be some one way that something is at a particular time, we do not commit ourselves to the view that cultural objects cannot be ambiguous, or vague, or semantically confused, or else indeterminate in their meaning or their properties. What it commits us to is a realism about cultural properties such that if a work really is vague at a certain time, then it cannot also have a precise and determinate meaning; if it is ambiguous at that time, it cannot also have a single meaning at that time. This, of course, entails that the one true interpretation of an ambiguous work will reveal that ambiguity in more or less detail; and just the same will be so for vague or semantically confused works. Again, the one true interpretation of Jastrow's duck-rabbit is that it can be seen either as a duck or as a rabbit – not that it has two equally plausible, yet incompatible, interpretations.

Nor is the singularity constraint misplaced. Notice, first, that any conjunction of two contrary or contradictory, hence conflicting, propositions about the same object or state of affairs fails to inform and so cannot ensure an adequate understanding of whatever it is that one seeks to understand. Hence, to accept two conflicting interpretations as equally plausible is effectively to concede that one does not properly understand. But elucidatory interpretations, I have said, are intended to promote understanding – and are meant to do so by placing people in an epistemically stronger position regarding whatever it is that puzzles them. In order to achieve this end, though, it is always necessary to resolve any incompatibility between two interpretations, for failing this, they cannot promote any clear understanding of the way things are.

The singularity constraint is warranted for another, related reason. For in order to judge and sincerely assert something to be the case at a certain time, one has to assume that there is some one (albeit complex) way that it is at that time; failing this, there could be no point to informative assertions about the way the world is (McDowell 1998, 365). Nor would there be any point to (elucidatory) interpretations that prepare the ground, as it were, for such assertions or judgements.

To this it could be objected that whereas the singularity constraint, and hence the principle of bivalence, apply nearly enough to all natural objects, they cannot be assumed to apply to cultural ones. In much of the literature on this topic, only cultural objects are treated as the proper – or at least as the philosophically interesting – objects of interpretation. And they are regarded as interesting because it is thought that in interpreting them one effectively imputes properties to these objects in ways that complete them. On Margolis's view, for instance, cultural objects are distinguished by the fact that they "often cannot themselves be ascribed a coherent design . . . without imputing by interpretation properties that yield a plausible" account of the work as a whole (1974, 193). "The nature of the work," he continues, "is not first fixed and then interpreted"; rather, the work is "identified *for* relevant description and appraisal *when* 'it' is interpreted" (1974, 194). It is this, he thinks, that makes it impossible for us to justify an interpretation in any noncircular way by appealing to the putatively describable properties of a literary work. And this, too, is why cultural objects (but not natural ones) can plausibly be interpreted as having incompatible properties – why a bivalent logic cannot do justice to the richness of interpretation.

Thus far, it is true, I have treated cultural and natural phenomena as equally available to interpretation. There is good reason to do so. For elucidatory interpretation, as we have seen, is an activity that involves the imaginative formulation and application of hypotheses in an attempt to dispel confusion, puzzlement, or ignorance. That there is no good reason to confine this activity to cultural objects is seen from the fact not just that we are often puzzled, confused, or ignorant about natural objects, but that there are occasions when we do not know whether the object in question is a cultural or a natural object. It is, of course, entirely arbitrary to suggest of these situations that whether or not we are engaged in the activity of interpreting depends on whether the object of our confusion or puzzlement turns out to be a cultural object. The character of our activity remains constant no matter the origins of its object.[10]

Since we may interpret both cultural and natural objects, it is not immediately obvious why the criteria for success in interpretation should differ between the two. Coming to understand a phenomenon, whether cultural or natural, requires that we somehow manage to fathom the set of properties that it possesses at any given time. To arrive at the conclusion that it is amenable to two exclusive interpretations at one and the same time is effectively to concede that one has not properly understood it.

---

[10] Joseph Margolis appears to vacillate on this point. In Margolis 1995a, he is unwilling to extend his thesis about interpretation to natural objects and insists that only those (cultural) objects with intentional properties are the proper objects of interpretation (11–15). However, in a later article (1995b, 1) he tells us that he does not believe that "interpretation can be restricted in any way to the arts, or can have a different logic from that of its alethic possibilities in history and the human sciences or (in principle) among explanatory theories in the physical sciences or in philosophy at large."

Cultural Objects and Their Properties

Certainly cultural objects do not possess all of their properties in the way that natural objects do, for whereas natural objects enjoy the material embodiment of their properties, many of the properties of cultural objects are intentional and emerge only against the background of our knowledge of specific conventions. Here I follow Margolis, who, it is well known, thinks of cultural objects as physically embodied and culturally emergent (Margolis 1974, 187–96). Their physical embodiment permits us to locate and identify such objects within a unified spatio-temporal framework, while many of their remaining properties depend for their existence on the cultural background against which they emerge.

As we have seen, it is sometimes argued that because these properties are discerned only in terms of certain historically located cultural principles, it must follow that, for any cultural object, there are as many interpretations as there are cultural principles in terms of which properties are imputed to the object. Such interpretations, it is argued, may very well be incompatible, yet since there is no way of privileging any particular set of cultural principles, it is simply inappropriate to suppose that only one can be true and that the others must all be false. All, it is contended, could be equally plausible. According to this line of argument, there is no single right interpretation; the principle of bivalence does not apply to the interpretation of cultural objects (Krausz 1993, Chaps. 3 and 4; Margolis 1980, Chap. 7).

These claims, however, are seriously misleading. Although we do discern cultural properties in terms of our knowledge of prevailing cultural conventions, this does not involve imputing such properties interpretatively in terms of just any "preferred" cultural "myths" or systems of explanation. There are important, epistemically based constraints on this activity. If puzzled, a person may interpret, and, I have said, it is true that she will often do so in terms of her own cultural understandings. The question, though, is whether such an interpretation can be shown to be true. That it can is clear from the fact that if one knows the conventions that are appropriate to the cultural object in question, interpretation is not called for at all: one can straightforwardly discern the properties of the object in terms of our extant knowledge and understanding. And such knowledge and understanding can be used to justify any particular interpretation.

When, for instance, I read the sentence "The book was lying open on the table," I discern its semantic properties without "imputing" them to the sentence, and I may do so simply because I am familiar with the conventions of English that govern them. I read and understand the sentence in terms of what I know, and I do so without imputing anything to it. In such cases, understanding is secured because of the application of past shared knowledge of the appropriate cultural conventions. Hence elucidatory interpretation is not required and does not occur – this, quite simply, because I do not fail to understand. Nor is elaborative, "writerly," or imputational interpretation the source of these semantic properties. For the properties are not the product of our imaginative "virtuosity"; nor does such virtuosity secure our recognition of these properties. It is our applied knowledge of the relevant linguistic conventions that secures this. Given that such knowledge is available, it can plainly be used in descriptions to justify any interpretation of the sentence in question – where such interpretations would normally be offered only by people who are puzzled by the sentence.

Consider this example: the sound made by uttering the word "dog." When this sound is taken in conjunction with the conventions of Hebrew, the semantic property that emerges in standard contexts is *fish*; when the sound is taken against the conventions of English, however, the semantic property that emerges is *canine animal*. Importantly, once we know that the proper conventions in terms of which to construe the sound are the conventions of English, it is true to say that (in a standard context) the utterance means *canine animal*, not *fish*. It follows that it is not as if one is free, when responding to cultural objects, to impose one's own cultural understandings or preferred systems of explanation on the object. One is bound by those conventions that are pertinent to it. And it is our sometimes hard-won knowledge of these conventions that allows us to say of anyone interpreting the object *ab initio* that his or her interpretation is either true or false, justified or unjustified.

Languages and utterances in a language are cultural objects par excellence, and what applies to them applies to cultural objects in general. It is simply false to say that a well-known English utterance, qua cultural object, is "identified *for* relevant description and appraisal *when* 'it' is interpreted" (Margolis 1974, 194). It is identified for relevant description, I have argued, in terms of our shared knowledge of it and our knowledge of the conventions that pertain to it. It is knowledge of this sort that is often mustered in order to justify an interpretation.

Certainly our culturally inspired elaborative interpretations may impute properties to a work that later influence our elucidations of it, and so may lead to different and incompatible interpretations. Let us return for a moment to Elizabeth Bennet in *Pride and Prejudice*. Someone imbued with Irish culture may unreflectingly suppose Elizabeth to be more fiery and spirited than a reader from the south of England, who might think of her as spirited but restrained in her behaviour. Because of these disparate elaborative interpretations, our Irish citizen might interpret Elizabeth's reaction to Mr Bennet's indulgent and ill-considered treatment of Lydia as angry and defiant, while someone steeped in English culture might interpret it as resigned and profoundly disappointed. Who is right? Even if we suppose (falsely, I think) that both elucidatory interpretations allow us to understand most other aspects of the novel and so have the same predictive utility, it cannot be the case that both are true. For either Elizabeth

Bennet was, or she was not, angry and defiant; alternatively, the novel is indeterminate in this respect, in which case both elucidatory interpretations in question would be false.

It is an interpretative dispute, though, that can easily be resolved. For if we know only a little about the period of the culture in which the work was produced, and hence about the beliefs and values of its envisaged readership, we also know that eighteenth- and early nineteenth-century English manners would require a restrained heroine in Elizabeth Bennet – someone who is not given to outbursts or fits of temper in the face of disappointment. Restraint would be expected in anyone to be admired; defiance would be regarded as a vice.

Of course, we appeal to more than knowledge of cultural conventions when seeking to justify interpretations. We appeal, as well, to a range of genetic factors, most especially to an agent's intentions in producing the artifact. Here we can, and in academic art criticism we sometimes do, turn to biographical accounts of authors' personal histories, events that occurred in their lives, their diaries, speeches, and so on. And where this is not available to us, we appeal to generic factors – to our knowledge of particular art forms, categories of art, or kinds of cultural objects. All can be, and often are, appealed to in the context of justification.

In the end, an interpretation of a cultural object will be deemed to have been justified if it can be shown to cohere maximally with other propositions that we claim to know about the object and its cultural setting, and if it (the interpretation) allows us to negotiate (explain, predict) other aspects of the cultural object and pertinent aspects of the world that it inhabits.

It needs to be remembered, though, that there are many different things that may puzzle us about any given cultural object. In the case of a novel, for instance, the motives of a character, the meaning of certain words, a sentence, a paragraph, a chapter, the theme of a work, the structure of its plot, its origins, or its relevance to particular cultures at particular times may all be considered legitimate objects of inquiry. Of importance here is the fact that the adequacy of any interpretation can properly be assessed only with reference to the puzzle or problem that it seeks to solve. If one is puzzled by Ammu's outburst when Rahel calls to Velutha as he walks in the march (in Arundhati Roy's *The God of Small Things*), one's interpretation must solve *this* puzzle, not some other. Relative to it, it is *true* that Ammu is frightened rather than angry, and that she is frightened because she does not wish to have attention drawn to her forbidden love for Velutha.

Understood against the background of the cultural and linguistic conventions appropriate to the work, this is an adequate – a true – account of Ammu's reaction. It coheres with our knowledge of other aspects of the work and so corresponds to its describable features, and it allows us, furthermore, to understand the rest of the novel – to negotiate it successfully, in the sense that it coheres with all of our other understandings of sequences within the novel. This is not to say that there is not more that could correctly be said of this incident. Of course there is. The important point is that what is said is true, not false – and that this is quite easily ascertained.

All of this supports my contention that the interpretation of cultural objects, as with natural objects, observes the singularity constraint, for part of what is here entailed is that it is not *also* the case that some contrary interpretation applies to this incident in *The God of Small Things* – say, that Ammu was angry because she at once understood that Velutha loved Rahel. For even if there are, or should one day be, cultural conventions relative to which the latter interpretation can be derived, these conventions would not properly apply to this work or the period of the culture in which it was produced.

On my account, then, a psychoanalytically based interpretation of *Hamlet* is admissible relative only to certain puzzles. If, for instance, one wants to know what light psychoanalysis can shed on Hamlet's indecisiveness, or if one wants to understand the psychology of the anger that he directs towards Ophelia, Freudian psychology may indeed help. But it will not tell us what Shakespeare or his contemporaries understood regarding Hamlet's treatment of Ophelia; nor will it explain (except accidentally) the sense that they saw in the play as a whole; nor will it explain the theme of the work. These are different puzzles, and here psychoanalytic theory simply does not get a grip since it was not part of the cultural milieu in terms of which these puzzles need to be solved.

All of this, I have already said, is not to deny that a novel, like any other cultural product, can be deeply and pervasively ambiguous relative to an appropriate set of cultural conventions – but if it is ambiguous, the singularity constraint requires that this ambiguity be conveyed in any true interpretation of the work. So while it may often be the case that a work can support what at first sight appear to be two incompatible interpretations, if it really does support two different and incompatible sets of meanings within the framework of the same (appropriate) set of cultural conventions, this entails that the work is ambiguous – and that a true interpretation will find it so by incorporating both sets of meanings.

Conclusion

The claim that a bivalent logic cannot apply to interpretation depends crucially on a confusion between elucidatory interpretation and its "imputational," "elaborative," or "writerly" counterpart. Certainly it is true that elaborations or imputations can affect the elucidations we offer, but it does not follow from this that elucidatory interpretation is "imputational"; nor, we have seen, does it follow that elucidatory interpretations cannot be true. For, as I have shown, if our aim in interpretation is to understand whatever it is that puzzles us, elaborations – or "writerly" interpretations – can be admitted only for so long as they actually facilitate understanding, and they cease to do this whenever they fail to take due account of the conventions that properly mediate the cultural object.

Nor is it the case, I have shown, that we become acquainted with these cultural conventions only through further interpretative acts, which again reflect our historical and cultural location. To say this is either to relativise knowledge of other cultures or to insist that there is no such thing. Either option is unsatisfactory; both make it impossible to know other cultures. Yet knowledge, I have contended, is to be accounted for and identified pragmatically: those hypotheses, conjectures, and beliefs that work and that enable us to negotiate the world successfully, we regard as knowledge. And in this sense, there certainly is knowledge of other cultures – much of which is learned from the interpretative endeavours of others.

It becomes possible, I have argued, to justify our interpretations of cultural objects in terms of existing (or newly discovered) bodies of knowledge. The main reason for denying this arises from a refusal to acknowledge any "principled" or "firm" distinction between description (which involves the linguistic application of what we know) and interpretation (which is epistemically much weaker). For if description and the alleged knowledge that it embodies are just covert interpretations, then any appeal to them in an attempt to justify an interpretation does not in fact do so; it merely privileges a set of preferred interpretations, and does so for no good reason. My argument in this regard is that there is very good reason to privilege some interpretations, for the propositions expressed by an interpretation that works – propositions that actually place one in an epistemically stronger position regarding an object – can eventually and rightly be regarded as propositions one knows. These, I have shown, can be used to justify more tentative interpretations. If this attempt to draw a distinction between interpretation and description, or between imaginative conjecture and knowledge, succeeds, then we do have a firm and principled distinction in terms of which to ground neutral justifications of any interpretation whatsoever.[11]

Department of Philosophy and Religious Studies
University of Canterbury
Private Bag 4800
Christchurch, New Zealand
d.novitz@phil.canterbury.ac.nz

References

Barkow, J. H., Leda Cosmides, and John Tooby. (1992). *The Adapted Mind: Evolutionary Psychology and the Generation of Culture.* New York: Oxford University Press.

---

[11] My thanks to Stephen Gardiner and Graham Macdonald for comments on an earlier version of this chapter.

Barnes, Annette. (1988). *On Interpretation*. Oxford: Basil Blackwell.
Barthes, Roland. (1974). *S/Z*. Translated by Richard Miller. New York: Hill and Wang.
Beardsley, Monroe C. (1970). *The Possibility of Criticism*. Detroit, MI: Wayne State University Press.
——. (1992). "The Authority of the Text." In *Intention and Interpretation*, edited by Gary Iseminger. Philadelphia: Temple University Press.
Bernstein, Richard. (1983). *Beyond Objectivism and Relativism*. Philadelphia: University of Pennsylvania Press.
Brandom, Robert. (1998). "Perception and Rational Constraint." *Philosophy and Phenomenological Research*, 58, 369–74.
Code, Lorraine. (1987). *Epistemic Responsibility*. Hanover, NH: University Press of New England.
Davidson, Donald. (1973). "Radical Interpretation." *Dialectica*, 27, 313–27.
Davies, Stephen. (1988). "True Interpretations." *Philosophy & Literature*, 12, 290–97.
——. (1995). "Relativism in Interpretation." *Journal of Aesthetics and Art Criticism*, 53, 8–13.
Gadamer, Hans-Georg. (1976). *Philosophical Hermeneutics*. Trans. and ed. David E. Linge. Berkeley: University of California Press.
——. (1988). *Truth and Method*. Trans. Garret Barden and John Cumming. New York: Crossroad.
Goldman, Alan. (1990). "Interpreting Art and Literature." *Journal of Aesthetics and Art Criticism*, 48, 205–14.
Goldstein, Leon. (1976). *Historical Knowing*. Austin: University of Texas Press.
Hirsch, E. D., Jr. (1967). *Validity in Interpretation*. New Haven, CT: Yale University Press.
——. (1976). *The Aims of Interpretation*. Chicago: University of Chicago Press.
Iseminger, Gary. (1992). "An Intentional Demonstration?" In *Intention and Interpretation*, edited by Gary Iseminger. Philadelphia: Temple University Press.
Krausz, Michael. (1993). *Rightness and Reasons: Interpretation in Cultural Practices*. Ithaca, NY: Cornell University Press.
Margolis, Joseph. (1965). *The Language of Art and Art Criticism*. Detroit, MI: Wayne State University Press.
——. (1974). "Works of Art as Physically Embodied and Culturally Emergent Entities." *British Journal of Aesthetics*, 14, 187–96.
——. (1976). "Robust Relativism." *Journal of Aesthetics and Art Criticism*, 35, 37–46.
——. (1980). *Art and Philosophy*. Atlantic Highlands, NJ: Humanities Press.
——. (1989). "Reinterpreting Interpretation." *Journal of Aesthetics and Art Criticism*, 48, 237–51.

——. (1995a). *Interpretation Radical but Not Unruly: The New Puzzle of the Arts and History*. Berkeley: University of California Press.

——. (1995b). "Plain Talk about Interpretation on a Relativistic Model." *Journal of Aesthetics and Art Criticism*, 53, 1–7.

Matthews, Robert. (1977). "Describing and Interpreting Works of Art." *Journal of Aesthetics and Art Criticism*, 36, 5–14.

McDowell, John. (1994). *Mind and World*. Cambridge: Harvard University Press.

——. (1998). "Précis of *Mind and World*." *Philosophy and Phenomenological Research*, 58, 365–68.

Novitz, David. (1987). *Knowledge, Fiction and Imagination*. Philadelphia: Temple University Press.

Rorty, Richard. (1989). *Contingency, Irony, and Solidarity*. Cambridge: Cambridge University Press.

——. (1998). "McDowell, Davidson and Spontaneity." *Philosophy and Phenomenological Research*, 58, 389–94.

Shusterman, Richard. (1992). "Interpretation, Intention and Truth." In *Intention and Interpretation*, edited by Gary Iseminger, 65–75. Philadelphia: Temple University Press.

Stecker, Robert. (1992). "Incompatible Interpretations." *Journal of Aesthetics and Art Criticism*, 50, 291–98.

——. (1997). *Artworks: Definition, Meaning, Value*. University Park: Pennsylvania State University Press.

3

CONVENTIONS AND RULES IN LITERATURE

STEIN HAUGOM OLSEN

I

Views of what role convention plays in the creation and appreciation of art works gravitate towards two extremes. One view holds that works of art can be apprehended and appreciated as well as created with no reference to convention. The other claims that conventions fully determine how works of art are apprehended and are therefore necessary conditions for the creation of works of art as well as constitutive of appreciation.

The former is a version of the Romantic view of art as something that appeals spontaneously to man's most profound emotions, to man's sentient nature, without making use of or needing mediating conventions. On this view, both the creation and the appreciation of the works of art are natural and spontaneous, because art expresses basic and central human emotions that all human beings share and recognise. This view is still widespread even in academic criticism of the arts:[1]

> Year after year, and eventually century after century, countless people are transported by a Beethoven symphony, awed by a Gothic cathedral, and touched deeply by a Rembrandt self portrait or a Shakespeare play, because these works of art speak directly to a deeply rooted understanding about the nature of being and of human relationships in a way that is indissolubly tied to aesthetic experience. This phenomenon is intimately related to questions of ethics, not in the sense that the beautiful is the good and vice versa, but rather that feelings of kindness, compassion, and love arise just as spontaneously in the human heart as does the response to great works of art. The latter, at times, may require more cultural mediation than the former, but both touch a common wellspring of human experience. (Etlin 8)

Proponents of this view even maintain that knowledge of artistic conventions can be "distracting":

---

[1] Indeed, the view seems to be making a comeback. See, for example, the emphasis on spontaneity and expression in Colin Lyas's introductory book.

> Descriptions [of works of art] drawn from knowledge of the conventions
> employed in art works are usually irrelevant or distracting and where they are
> not – that is, where they do form an integral part of an imaginative perception
> of works of art, they are optional or peripheral. (Baxter 327)

Proponents of this view do not deny that artistic conventions are employed
by artists and recognised by the audience. However, conventions are held
to be dispensable because they have no epistemic role:

> The pieces of technical vocabulary – "alliteration," "exposition and recapitu-
> lation," "chiaroscuro" and so on – commonly employed by the informed spec-
> tator and critic often, if not usually, involve reference to elements in art works
> which are conventional and hence continually recur, which is often why partic-
> ular terms have been devised to refer to them quickly and conveniently.
> However, one can notice the features to which they refer even when one is
> ignorant of there being a convention that they in fact exemplify. The classic
> sonata form, for example, is such that an awareness of the elements conven-
> tionally labelled "exposition," "development" and "recapitulation" may be
> developed by an intelligent listener familiar with a work embodying the form
> even when he is unaware of there being a conventional form articulated by
> these terms. (Baxter 327–28)

Or to take a concrete example:

> If you have not learned that the broad brimmed black hat, the reclining pose
> with the head on the hand, and the unbuttoned sleeves were all signs of
> "melancholy" well established in Western art, you certainly would miss that
> aspect of the "meaning" of Joseph Wright of Derby's portrait of Sir Brooke
> Boothby (17880–1). Yet would this lack of knowledge keep you from respond-
> ing to any of the human qualities that you might see in the face or to any of the
> so-called formal qualities derived from the disposition of shapes and colors? I
> suspect not. (Etlin 153)

Artistic conventions, according to this view, has heuristic value, but is not
integral to aesthetic appreciation. It is external to art and is of interest only
for the sociology of art and not for aesthetics (Etlin 7ff.).

If we leave aside the problematic appeal in the Romantic view to a
natural and spontaneous response to the work of art,[2] a substantial argument can be made to support the view that conventional features of a
work of art are identifiable without knowledge of the conventions in
question. This argument can be made simply by looking at an example

---

[2]   To the extent that Etlin presents an argument for this view, he relies on Susanne K.
Langer's notion that the work of art has a structure that is analogous to what she calls "the
pattern of sentience, the pattern of life itself, as it is felt and directly known" (Langer 31).
There are serious problems with Langer's notion of a parallel between the structure of a
work of art and "sentience." Indeed, as many commentators have pointed out, the notion of
sentience is itself obscure. See my own criticisms of Langer in Olsen 1978, 34–39.

of a highly conventionalised genre of literature, such as the sonnet. It can be argued that it is possible to recognise all the conventional features of a sonnet without ever knowing the name or knowing that there is a tradition of sonnet writing, though such knowledge would ease the recognition of these conventional features. Consider the following example:

> Having this day my horse, my hand, my launce
>   Guided so well, that I obtain'd the prize,
>   Both by the judgement of the English eyes,
> And of some sent from that sweet enemie *Fraunce*;
> Horsemen my skill in horsemanship advaunce;
>   Town-folkes my strength; a daintier judge applies
>   His praise to sleight, which form good use doth rise;
> Some luckie wits impute it but to chaunce;
>   Others because of both sides I do take
> My bloud from them who did excell in this,
>   Thinke Nature me a man of armes did make.
> How farre they shot awrie! the true cause is,
>   *Stella* lookt on, and from her heavenly face
> Sent forth the beames, which made so faire my race.
>   (Sir Philip Sidney, *Astrophil and Stella* 41)

Here is a critical comment on the poem that discusses the possibility of construing the poem either as an Italian or as an English sonnet:

> If we read this with the Italian structure in mind we find a contrast, in octave and sestet, between Sidney's equestrian abilities and his true motivation, between the superficial exercise of skill, strength or delight and even luck, and the real cause of his success. We sense an opposition between accidental acquired qualities (octave) and essential given qualities (sestet), enabling us to read the tercets as thus linked even in their distinction between heredity and astrology. The Italian octave fully supports this, and the sestet is indeed syntactically organized into tercets.
> But if we read the sonnet with the English structure in mind, we can see a rather different organization: a douzain (in which the first quatrain states Sidney's success, the second the views of those who attribute it to nurture and the third the views of those who attribute it to nature) and a couplet which solves the problem. One's sense that the English structure predominates is reinforced by a couplet introducing Stella (as in other sonnets) as a kind of *dea ex machina*, and by the neatness with which the misguided judges are eclipsed by Stella in the role not only of beneficent star, but of judge herself. (Fuller 18–19)

However, an alternative description could also be given of this poem, "affording the same imaginative perception of the art work," and which did not "employ a vocabulary embodying reference to the relevant conventions" (Baxter 327). In fact, such a description could be given simply by taking out the technical expressions such as "sonnet," "Italian structure,"

"English structure," "douzain," "quatrain," "sestet," "octave," and so on, and substituting for them full descriptions of the aspects of the poem to which they refer.

Two further points lend substance to the view of literary convention as external to the literary work itself. First, an artistic convention has to have a point of origin: "an *initial* adoption of a practice in art is not itself a convention, and one can have an understanding of the initial instances which *a fortiori* is not an understanding of a convention" (Baxter 329). Second, it is integral to the conception of a literary work of art that it is unique and unrepeatable. This uniqueness is created through the interrelationship between its various elements, which together form an artistic unity. Each element, which is identified in an imaginative perception, is thus motivated through the contribution it makes to the aesthetic whole: there is a *reason* for its presence that involves no reference to any convention. The recurrent regularities that are identified in imaginative perception are not identified as recurrent regularities but as features contributing to the aesthetic whole. "A literary text," says a critic remarking on the difficulty in seeing literary conventions as arbitrary, "is one we recognise because all its features are there for a reason" (Reeves 799). And the reason why a feature is there does not make any reference to convention. Though such regularities recur in work after work, they do not recur as the same *aesthetic* features.

The orphan plot occurs in a number of eighteenth- and nineteenth-century English novels. There is an orphan plot in *Joseph Andrews* as well as in *Tom Jones*, in *Jane Eyre* as well as in *Oliver Twist*, and in *Emma*, where it is an important ingredient. At a certain level of generality, these plots can be seen as similar, but an imaginative perception of each of these works necessarily goes beyond this level of generality. It is possible to describe the potential of the orphan plot in eighteenth- and nineteenth-century novels. An orphan has no determinate social position since his or her "birth" is unknown. The orphan plot thus becomes a quest for a social and economic identity that will determine whom the orphan can marry, what friends he or she can have, whether he or she will be rich or poor, and so on. However, the actual contribution made by the orphan plot to the artistic vision in a specific work, for example, *Tom Jones*, has to be determined in an appreciative interpretation of that work. The orphan plot has totally different functions in *Joseph Andrews*, *Tom Jones*, *Emma*, *Jane Eyre*, and *Oliver Twist*.

II

The conventionalist view denies that it is possible to respond spontaneously to art. All apprehension and appreciation of art are structured by conventions, and the reader/audience cannot go beyond these conventions because they *constitute* the experience of the work of art. Conventionalism comes in various forms. *Radical Conventionalism* assumes that conventions have no basis in "nature" or "reality." One cannot legitimise conventions by reference to an independently recognisable truth or norm. This is a general point about all artistic conventions, but Radical Conventionalism tends to focus on the role of convention in artistic and literary *representation*. "Literary texts, under a structuralist-conventionalist view," says Thomas G. Pavel, giving a succinct summary of this view as it appears in literary theory,

> cannot be taken to speak about states of affairs outside themselves, since any such apparent referring is regulated by rigid conventions that make those states of affairs behave like effects of a perfectly arbitrary illusionistic game. It would not make much sense to examine the structure of fictional worlds, nor the interplay between these and actual worlds; reality in fiction is just a textual convention, not so different from the compositional conventions of the rhyme pattern in sonnets, the five acts in tragedies, or the alternative between main and secondary plots in Renaissance drama and eighteenth-century epistolary novels. The literary trend that strove most conscientiously toward minute referential adequacy, realism, has repeatedly been described as a mere ensemble of discursive textual conventions. And since language and discourse cannot copy reality, the realist convention is just as arbitrary and non-referential as any other. (Pavel 114)

Realism, in Roland Barthes's words, is concerned not with reality, but merely with "*l'effet de réel*" (Barthes 1984).

Radical Conventionalism is, however, related to Romanticism. Proponents of this view hold, as did the Romantics, that conventions are arbitrary, artificial, and repressive, and that they therefore should be attacked and undermined. Radical Conventionalism as it manifests itself in structuralism, poststructuralism, and deconstruction aims to make a political point. Since conventions have no basis in nature or reason and are thus arbitrary, their function can only be ideological: conventions conserve and protect the power of the hegemonic classes in society. It is politically and morally imperative to undermine this hegemonic power, and this necessity provides a political motivation for attacking convention. At this point, Radical Conventionalism meets a problem. For if one succeeds in undermining or even eliminating artistic conventions, one is, given the premises of this view, left without art. This, however, is no serious problem for the consistent Radical Conventionalist. It is solved by recognising that the very category of the "aesthetic" is a conventional construction embodying an ideology, "the ideology of the aesthetic," that one must get beyond. On this view there are no works of art. Works of art are "texts" that can be read as can all other texts, but they have no immanent aesthetic properties. They are seen as works of art only because they legitimise and perpetuate certain repressive ideological values.

Much has been said about the role of convention in representation, and this problem will not be pursued here. However, it is worth offering a couple of comments about the rather dramatic conclusions that have been drawn by Radical Conventionalism in the discussion of the problem of the role of truth and verisimilitude in art. Most theorists today would accept that all modes of representation are conventional. It does not follow from this that sculptural, pictorial, and verbal representations do not *refer* to anything and therefore cannot be judged true or false. Second, from the conventionality of representation it does not follow that some modes of representation are not "closer" to reality and thus more "natural," in some sense of this word, than others. Indeed, it is possible to identify features of a realistic mode of representation that makes it more natural than other modes of representation. This point was made explicitly and convincingly by Ian Watt in *The Rise of the Novel*:

> There are important differences in the degree to which different literary forms imitate reality; and the Formal Realism of the novel allows a more immediate imitation of individual experience set in its temporal and spatial environment than do other literary forms. Consequently the novel's conventions make much small demands on the audience than do most literary conventions; and this surely explains why the majority of readers in the last two hundred years have found in the novel the literary form which mostly closely satisfies their wishes for a close correspondence between life and art. (Watt 33)

In *The Rise of the Novel* Ian Watt identifies and describes those aspects of the novel which make it "correspond" closely to "life": the use of real-life names instead of type names or names of heroes; the focus on ordinary middle-class characters rather than on kings or heroes; the use of localised and minutely described settings with names and features from real places; the use of a chronological time-scheme; the use of the causal chain as a structural principle for a chain of described events; and so on. In all these respects, the novel is different from, and closer to life than, other genres, such as the romance. The criteria for what constitutes "Formal Realism" define the conditions for a literary mode of representation as being more "natural" than other modes of literary representations. It is interesting to note in this connection that realism is predominantly a mode of representation used in fictional narratives, literary and others, and in personal narratives. It is not used in other intellectual activities involving writing, such as the academic discipline of history or the social sciences. In these disciplines, the emphasis is on truth and accuracy rather than on verisimilitude and naturalness. Anyone conversant with journals of psychology, psychiatry, or sociology will know how "unnatural" the modes of representation employed in these types of journals are, as are the modes of representation in publications within the natural sciences.

III

Radical Conventionalism, concerned with artistic representation, can be distinguished from *Traditional Conventionalism* which emphasises the general role of convention in literature. This view holds simply that both the creation and the appreciation of a work of art are conventional. One area where convention apparently is central is in the appreciation of a work as being of a certain kind, a certain genre. It is a widespread view among literary critics and literary theorists that genre conventions constitute the reader's or the audience's appreciation of a work. "In literary communication," says Alastair Fowler,

> genres are functional: they actively form the experience of each work of literature. If we see *The Jew of Malta* as a savage farce, our response will not be the same as if we saw it as a tragedy. When we try to decide the genre of a work, then, our aim is to discover its meaning. Generic statements are instrumentally critical, as Mario Fubini said: they serve to make an individual effect apprehended as a warp across their *trama* or weft. And when we investigate previous states of the type, it is to clarify meaningful departures that the work itself makes. It follows that genre theory, too, is properly concerned in the main with interpretation. It deals with principles of reconstruction and interpretation and (to some extent) the evaluation of meaning. It does not deal much with classification. (Fowler 38)

The point is often made more specifically with reference to dramatic conventions. It seems to be impossible to understand a play correctly if one does not know the appropriate conventions. "At the beginning of this century," says Muriel Bradbrook,

> it became clear that even Shakespeare's characters could not stand the test of modern dramatic construction, especially in comedy. There was Bassanio who behaved like a fortune-hunter and was obviously a hero; there was Helena of Narbonne who behaved like a minx and was obviously a heroine. (Bradbrook 54)

The reason why these characters were perceived in this way was, according to Bradbrook, that the nineteenth-century standards of characterisation were being applied while the Elizabethans had quite different conventions for characterisation. Their "positive standards of characterisation," she argues,

> were roughly three: the superhuman nature of heroes, the definition of character by decorum, and the theory of Humours. There were various conventions which belonged to the drama, such as the credibility of slander, the impenetrability of disguise (which had important consequences in the characters of the villain heroes) and the limitation of motives. (54)

If one does not know conventions like the credibility of slander (or what E. E. Stoll more elegantly called the "convention of the calumniator credited" [6–8]) and the impenetrability of disguise, one may draw conclusions about the naiveté of the characters or the carelessness of the characterisation that are wholly unwarranted because one's imaginative perception of the characters is wrong. In such cases the very construal of the characters is dependent upon knowledge of conventions of characterisations.

The most graphic example of this role of convention is the debate around Hamlet's delay. Hamlet's delay is a critical crux that draws the attention of all readers and theatre audiences as it is strongly focused in the play itself. *Hamlet* is, however, a revenge tragedy. Revenge tragedies present the revenge for a recently committed offence, and they come to an end when the revenge is carried out. It is thus a necessary convention of this genre that the revenge is delayed until late in the play. This delay needs no explanation or motivation: it is a convention that structures the play. In *Hamlet* the construal of the main character is dependent upon whether or not one sees the play as a revenge tragedy, or at least as depending upon that tradition:

> It is because E. E. Stoll identifies the play as a revenge tragedy that he rejects Coleridge's construction, with its psychological account of Hamlet's delay. For Stoll, the delay is an epical convention that "makes the deed momentous when it comes at the end." Hamlet's self-reproaches are not conceived dramatically in terms of psychology. For Dover Wilson, however, this is "moonshine": the delay is part of a consistently realistic portrayal of psychological weakness. The dispute is not one that will be quickly settled in all its aspects. But we can see that both parties misconceived the relation between timeless originality and generic convention. Stoll is wrong in supposing that the existence of a conventional "popular heroic revenger" prevented Shakespeare from varying this type by introducing procrastinatory traits. And Wilson is wrong to deny that Shakespeare's communication lies precisely in such departures. In other words, the revenger and malcontent type are not classes to which Hamlet belongs or does not belong. Shakespeare is free to question the values of the genre, but can only use its terms to do so. There is no temperamental irresolution in Hamlet except what decorum of character requires. Nevertheless, Hamlet's revenge is enmeshed in scruples exceptional in the genre and amounting to a comment on it. Without knowledge of revenge tragedy, then, *Hamlet* would be incomprehensible: no valid construction would be possible. (Fowler 262)

Fowler's point here is that even when it is not being followed, the existence of literary convention structures the audience's or reader's appreciation of a work. *Hamlet* can only be properly appreciated by grasping how Shakespeare deviated from the conventions of revenge tragedy.

IV

It has been customary in literary theory to employ the conception of a convention as a critical primitive, a concept that can be used in the analysis of critical and theoretical problems, but which is not itself construed as problematic and therefore not as a relevant object of analysis or reflection. It is, however, possible to ask whether the proponents of the two different views of convention presented above employ the same concept of convention in their different arguments about the way in which convention enters into the creation and appreciation of art works, and whether within one and the same argument they employ the concept consistently. Aspects of these views and arguments indicate that they attempt to address different kinds of problems, and that the concept of convention is not used consistently. Literature is undoubtedly conventional, but at the same time it seems that there is solid support for the view that conventions do not play a fundamental role in the apprehension and appreciation of literary works; this apparent contradiction may indicate that the notion of convention in the two cases is not the same.

A convention, says the *Oxford English Dictionary* (*OED*), is a

9.a. General agreement or consent, deliberate or implicit, as constituting the origin and foundation of any custom, institution, opinion, etc., or as embodied in any accepted usage, standard of behaviour, method of artistic treatment, or the like.

In this sense convention can be used negatively as

9.b. Accepted usage become artificial and formal, and felt to be repressive of the natural in conduct or art; conventionalism.

The other relevant sense is the definition of convention as

10.a. A rule or practice based upon general consent, or accepted and upheld by society at large; an arbitrary rule or practice recognised as valid in any particular art or study; a conventionalism.

According to the *OED*, then, a convention can be either the general agreement on which any custom, institution, and so on, is based, or the rule or practice *based on* this general consent. The *OED* also mentions arbitrariness as a feature of conventions and emphasises the negative connotations of the concept. "The notion of convention," says Alain Boyer in a more colourful exposition of these associations of convention, "points towards the artificial, the irrational, the fictitious, the false and the contingent" (Boyer 116). It "evokes the unnatural and unoriginal, the rote and the mechanical application of some procedure" (119). However, the definitions of the *OED* also open up for different concepts of convention, at least one of which does not have the negative connotations that the *OED* lists.

Convention, being an agreement or norm based on agreement, is as such a human artifact, and therefore artificial and opposed to what is natural. Since man makes conventions, they can also be changed by man and are in this sense contingent. As Boyer hints, because conventions are contingent and changing, they can be opposed not only to what is natural, but also to what is rational. For reason, like nature, provides a firm foundation for action. A norm based in reason would be stable and uniform, universal and immutable. It would be a norm that was not really a convention.

Historically, the opposition between convention and reason led to two different conceptions of convention. "On the one hand," says Paul Dumouchel,

> the opposition tended toward a clear antagonism; "convention" referred to superstitious traditions and unnatural customs contrary to reason. On the other hand, it tended toward an amiable accommodation. "Convention" came to designate, not what is inimical to reason, but the domain of things indifferent, a region where reason was without prescriptive force and that could thus be abandoned to the artibrariness of human will and fancy. (Dumouchel 97)

In this region, although reason does not determine the *content* of our conventions, it may determine that we may be best served by obeying a convention. It was Hobbes, argues Dumouchel, who enlarged this domain (where reason was without prescriptive force, and where action thus had to be governed by convention) "to encompass most of social life. He argued that it forces us under pain of war and disorder to agree to one convention or another" (97). Agents are thus "rationally constrained to decide upon a course of action, which is what makes their agreement rational. To forbear decision would entail damage, or failure, and a lack of rationality in view of their interests" (99).

Hobbes, then, tied convention to reason, not by maintaining that reason dictates the content of the convention, for in that case one would no longer have a convention but rather a kind of rationally grounded norm, but by arguing that where there are no rationally founded norms, reason dictates that we agree on a rule. However, rationality can also enter into the establishment of convention in another way, that is, as an agreement between rational agents. The latter position, as Dumouchel points out, "embeds the rationality of the agreement in the structure of the agents, whose rationality is postulated by the theory" (97n. 5). Dumouchel argues that this latter position defines a "more modern concept of convention" (99n. 6 and 97n. 5),[3] but already Hume assumes that "nature provides a remedy in the judgement and understanding, for what is irregular and incommodious in the affections" (Hume 489), when it comes to

---

[3]   The specific reference is to David Lewis. Says Lewis: "If I know what you believe about the matters of fact that determine the likely effects of your alternative actions, and if I know your preferences among possible outcomes and I know that you possess a modicum of practical rationality, then I can replicate your practical reasoning to figure out what you will probably do, so that I can act appropriately" (27).

agreeing on conventions that serve our common interest. Thus, when Hume sees the convention of property ("abstaining from the possession of others") as rational agreement ("we cannot better consult [our own interest or that of our nearest friends], than by such a convention, because it is by that means we maintain society, which is so necessary to their well-being and subsistence, as well as to our own" [489]), he locates the rationality in the agents involved, and it becomes a precondition for agreement on a convention.

Developing Hume's conception of convention as agreement between rational agents, David Lewis employs analyses of human agreements and interactions taken from game-theory. Lewis sees a convention as a solution to a coordination problem that can be solved in various ways. An explicit or an implicit agreement on how to solve the coordination problem is arbitrary in the sense that those who are parties to the agreement might have chosen another way to solve the problem. Arbitrariness in this sense is therefore central in Lewis's analysis. An example of a coordination problem would be the following. A group of office workers, all working in different office blocks, want to meet regularly for lunch. There exist a number of tables at which they could meet, all roughly at the same distance from their various places of work, but none of them can be observed from any of the office blocks. It does not matter to the people involved at which table they meet, nor if they meet at the same table every time. What matters is that they all meet at the same table for lunch. They thus have to agree on or develop an agreement about a meeting place or a pattern of meeting places (table A on Monday, table B on Tuesday, table C on Wednesday, etc.). The meeting place or the pattern is arbitrarily chosen, but there must be an agreement, implicit or explicit, if one is to reach the desired goal.

Both the concept of convention employed by Hobbes and the Humean/Lewisian concept of convention tie the concept indirectly to reason. As a consequence of this, the negative connotations of the concept disappear. Once convention is based on reason, the convention itself becomes the guarantee of stability and uniformity, in spite of the fact that it is in the end contingent. If convention is the result of rational agreement, as in Hobbes, this guarantees its survival and stability. If convention is agreement between rational agents, as in the Humean/Lewisian concept, it is inherently conservative. Once the problem of coordination is solved, there is no reason to open it up again. This concept of convention endows it with a strongly positive function: it guarantees the survival of civil society. At the same time conventions remain radically arbitrary. One might have reached agreement on another pattern of behaviour that would have served the same purpose.

The *OED* definition of convention also has a second element. A convention is not defined only as "a rule of practice based upon general consent," but also as a rule or practice "accepted and upheld by society at large." This is the concept of convention adopted by radical conventional-ism: agreement is replaced by power. Constraints in art are seen as imposed through the authority of those who have had the power to deter-mine what is to count as art. Artistic convention becomes a social power-game:

> Playwrights or painters who violate the conventions are not simply neglected: they are booed, ostracized, and persecuted. If people who buy unfashionable paintings are subject to sanctions by their peers, so are those who make them. On both sides of the market, in fact, we find the same interminable ballet of conformism and one-upmanship, with some individuals making the conven-tions ever more elaborate and others desperately trying to keep abreast. (Elster 34)[4]

This concept of convention assigns a role to artibrariness different from that which it has in the Hobbesian or Humean/Lewisian conception: social conventions are contingent since they might have been different, but they are not arbitrary for those on whom they are imposed since those people do not have the choice to adopt different norms.

Finally, the *OED* definitions suggest a concept of convention where the basis for a norm is neither social power nor rational or rationally founded agreement, but quite simply habit. A convention can be "an arbitrary rule or practice recognised as valid in any particular art or study; a conven-tionalism." A convention is simply a way of doing things that in some way or other has developed. It is worth noting that an arbitrary rule of this type does not have the same stability as a rule that is founded in agreement between rational agents or social power. A way of doing things can change and develop without one's having to revise an agreement, implicit or explicit, and without one's having to challenge those who wield social power. A habitual way of doing things has no rationale.

The discussion in this section has taken us beyond the concept of convention. At this stage, the concept of convention may, for the purposes of this discussion, be usefully replaced with the more general concept of "social norm". The notion of a social norm is not to the same extent conceptually wedded to "agreement" on the one hand and "arbitrariness" and "the contingent" on the other. The above discussion focused on a number of different foundations for and properties of social norms. Social norms can have their basis in nature, in reason, in mutual agreement, in social power to impose norms, and in pure habit. Norms with their basis in nature or directly in reason are not accidental, but necessary, and one can question whether they can appropriately be called "conventions." Norms that have their basis in mutual agreement are conventional in the

---

[4]   Elster, of course, does not subscribe to the view that this is all there is to artistic convention.

core sense because the agreement can change the content of the norm. The same is true of norms with their basis in pure habit. Norms based in social power might have been different, but they cannot be changed without changing the wielders of power or changing their minds.

To this list one needs to add one further conception of social norms. They can be what John Searle has called *constitutive rules*: rules that create the possibility of new behaviour by introducing concepts that name the elements of this behaviour, as well as conventions tying this behaviour to those concepts and relating the concepts in a network (Searle 1969, 33–42).[5] It is unnecessary to expound the notion of constitutive rule here as it has been much discussed in the philosophical literature of the last twenty-five years, but for the present purpose it is useful to emphasise that these constitutive rules have a double aspect. Searle has argued that such norms define social institutions, and that if one does not know these rules, one cannot identify and describe or participate in the behaviour sanctioned by the rules. The rules are thus *necessary* for the existence of the social institution that they define. However, the institution itself is contingent since it is manmade and can disappear. So these constraints appear, paradoxically, as both necessary and contingent. The point is worth stressing because of the consequences of changing the constitutive rules of an institution: one then also changes the nature of the activity defined by the rules.

V

Using as tools the distinctions made in the last section, one is better equipped to approach the question about the extent to which convention enters into the creation and appreciation of literary works of art, that is, the extent to which convention enters into the artist's and the audience's recognition and apprehension of a literary work of art as art. The discussion in section III has suggested that even what seem to be basic literary conventions in the traditional sense have no epistemic role to play in the creation and appreciation of literary works. They must therefore be understood as conventions of the Humean/Lewisian kind that are based in an implicit agreement or in pure habit. Modes of writing develop and become accepted, and because they are known and accepted, they make communication easy. At the same time, they can function as a framework which an artist can challenge and go beyond, thus producing works that break new ground and formulate new visions. However, these conventions are ultimately dispensable; they do not define what makes a text a literary work of art.

As section I suggests, it is also impossible to accept the Romantic view

---

5   The distinction between constitutive rules and regulative rules originated in Rawls. A similar idea was found in Hart. And in his 1995 Searle developed in full the application of the notion of constitutive rule in the explanation of social institutions.

of art, which makes the work of art an aesthetic object dependent on the assumption that human nature has certain universal basic features which enable man spontaneously to recognise and appreciate aesthetic objects. If one also holds the view that literary conventions in the traditional sense have no epistemic role to play in the apprehension and appreciation of works of art, it would seem that there is no way to avoid the conclusion of the Radical Conventionalist that there is no such phenomenon as literature. Literature is essentially conventional, but no convention is essential to literature.

A different conclusion may be suggested by looking again at the interpretation of Sidney's sonnet 41 from *Astrophil and Stella*, ignoring the use of the technical vocabulary and the references to the sonnet form – ignoring, that is, the role of literary convention in the traditional sense. In this interpretation it is possible to identify a number of interpretative moves which the critic employs to build up an interpretation of the poem. The critic divides up the poem by giving generalising descriptions of those situations that the poem presents:

> If we read this with the Italian structure in mind we find a contrast, in octave and sestet, between Sidney's *equestrian abilities and his true motivation*, between *the superficial exercise of skill, strength or delight and even luck, and the real cause of his success*. We sense an *opposition between accidental acquired qualities (octave) and essential given qualities (sestet)*, enabling us to read the *tercets as thus linked even in their distinction between heredity and astrology*. The Italian octave fully supports this, and the sestet is indeed syntactically organized into tercets. (Fuller 18–19; emphasis added)

The critic divides up the poem by applying to its various parts statements generalising the situation presented in these parts of the poem: "equestrian abilities" versus "true motivation," "the superficial exercise of skill, strength or delight and even luck" versus "the real cause of his success," "accidental acquired qualities (octave)" versus "essential given qualities (sestet)," "heredity" versus "astrology." It is in the light of these thematic descriptions that the formal pattern identified with the help of the technical vocabulary acquires an aesthetic significance. The formal patterns do not in themselves have any such aesthetic significance until they are apprehended (perceived) as an integral part of a work of art. There are forms of verse, like the limerick, where the formal pattern as a rule does not have such an aesthetic significance. In fact, this is true of all kinds of nonartistic verse, for example, doggerel. There is nothing in formal patterns themselves that make them aesthetic (i.e., part of the work of art). And the thematic descriptions are not "found," but result from an exercise of the imagination. The reader "finds" these contrasts only if he or she looks at the poem from a certain perspective, with certain expectations defined by certain concepts (thematic concepts) and by certain conventions for how to apply and defend the application of these concepts (and this is where the formal patterns acquire a function for the reader). The very process of imaginatively apprehending this poem is governed by a set of conventions that the reader obeys and create the possibility for apprehending this piece of verse as a work of art.

This example suggests that literature is fundamentally conventionalist in the sense that it is a social institution governed by constitutive rules and concepts that create the possibility for producing and appreciating literary works of art. This institution consists of authors and readers of various kinds who create and appreciate literary works in accordance with these rules.[6] Because they create the possibility of producing and appreciating literary works of art, these concepts and conventions are *necessary* for literature as an art-form to exist. The concept of literature can thus be seen as anchored in this framework of rules and concepts, these rules are stable, uniform, and universal. If they were changed – and it is quite possible that they should be – the concept of literature would no longer be part of the scheme of concepts that define the culture of the West. Western culture would then be without literature, and this would be true even if all the texts that one today counts as literary works remained in existence.

For what is created by such a set of constitutive rules is not the possibility of *writing texts*, but of *producing literary works*. The difference between a text and a literary work of art is that the latter is an object of a certain kind of appreciation. Appreciation is a mode of apprehension different from that of understanding, and as a mode of apprehension, it is defined by a set of expectations. These expectations can be formulated as a set of rules which a text, if it is presented to the public as a literary work, is aimed at obeying and is expected to obey. If one removes the framework of rules and concepts which defines appreciation as a mode of apprehension, those texts which have been regarded as literary works could no longer be regarded in this way. If this happened, one would, of course, be left with a large number of texts that had no clear purpose within the culture, and if this situation continued over time, no doubt they would cease to be reprinted and would be forgotten. Some of the texts might possibly begin to serve other functions, as did literary works in the Middle Ages, when some were used in language teaching while their nature as literary works of art was not attended to. It is arguable that if the method of "reading" texts that has been propagated and sometimes employed by a number of deconstructivist and poststructuralist critics – for example, by Barthes (1970) – replaced the appreciation of what in Western culture today are called literary works of art, and became the dominant way of apprehending them, this would mean that literature had come to an end in the West. For all texts could be apprehended in this way; the concept of literature would therefore have no role to play and would mark no distinc-

---

[6] I tried to formulate such a view in Chapters 4, 5, and 6 of my 1978. See also Olsen 1987 and Lamarque and Olsen.

tion. Thus, the rules of the social institution of literature are contingent from an external perspective, but necessary from a perspective internal to the social institution itself.

It is a question of more than terminological interest what one should call these norms. It is interesting to note that authors and theorists in the neoclassical period in England and France talked about "rules" rather than "conventions":

> Those RULES of old *discover'd*, not *devis'd*
> Are *Nature* still but *Nature Methodiz'd*

says Alexander Pope in *An Essay on Criticism* (lines 68–69). In this period literary norms were seen as dictated by nature and by reason. They were consequently neither contingent nor unstable, as any practice based in habit or agreement would be. They were, on the contrary, necessary and universal. It may be said that constitutive rules too are necessary and universal in the sense explained above. Constitutive rules can be contrasted with literary conventions based on habit and tradition, which do not have any epistemic role to play in the appreciation of literary works, and which can change without any consequences for the concept of literature itself. There thus appear to be good reasons for distinguishing between literary conventions of this type and literary rules that define the possibility for creating and recognising/appreciating literary works of art

The application of the notion of constitutive rule in the description of how literary works are produced and appreciated has one further advantage. If the concept of literature is construed as defined by a set of constitutive conventions and rules which creates the possibility of a literary practice, this explains how it is possible to identify a steadily changing literary tradition with a history. Constitutive rules and concepts provide a framework within which literary convention can be seen as changing, as is the case with genre:

> The earliest phase of every kind [genre] is the late phase of another, viewed from a different historical standpoint. Naturally, we find it difficult to imagine any other groupings but our own. Nevertheless, it is fundamental to the appreciation of genre to grasp this principle of continuous movement of regrouping. Literature changes, but it is the same thing. (Fowler 159)[7]

Assuming that literature is a social institution defined by a set of constitutive rules and concepts enables us to explain how literature changes, but is the same thing.

---

[7] Fowler seems to favour a family-resemblance account of the concept of literature in his not very clear discussion of the concept (11ff., 42–44). However, a family resemblance concept would not licence the statement he makes here that "Literature changes, but it is the same thing."

References

Barthes, Roland. (1970). *S/Z*. Paris.

———. (1984). "L'effet de réel." in *Le bruissement de la langue*. Paris: Seuil. Published in English as "The Reality Effect" in *The Rustle of Language*, by Roland Barthes (Oxford: Basil Blackwell, 1986).

Baxter, Brian. (1983). "Conventions and Art." *British Journal of Aesthetics*, 23 319–32.

Boyer, Alain. (1992). "Conventions and Arbitrariness." In *Rules and Conventions: Literature, Philosophy, Social Theory*, edited by Mette Hjort, 115–29. Baltimore: Johns Hopkins University Press.

Bradbrook, Muriel. (1935). *Themes and Conventions of Elizabethan Tragedy*. Cambridge: Cambridge University Press.

Dumouchel, Paul. (1992). "Hobbes on Rules and Conventions." In *Rules and Conventions: Literature, Philosophy, Social Theory*, edited by Mette Hjort, 95–114. Baltimore: Johns Hopkins University Press.

Elster, Jon. (1992). "Conventions, Creativity, Originality." In *Rules and Conventions: Literature, Philosophy, Social Theory*, edited by Mette Hjort, 32–44. Baltimore: Johns Hopkins University Press.

Etlin, Richard A. (1996). In *Defense of Humanism: Value in the Arts and Letters*. Cambridge: Cambridge University Press.

Fowler, Alastair. (1982). *Kinds of Literature: An Introduction to the Theory of Modes*. Oxford: Oxford University Press.

Fuller, John. (1972). *The Sonnet*. London: Methuen.

Hart, H. L. A. (1961). "Law as the Union of Primary and Secondary Rules." Chapter 5 of *The Concept of Law*. Oxford: Oxford University Press.

Hume, David. (1888). *A Treatise of Human Nature*. Edited by L. A. Selby-Bigge. Oxford: Oxford University Press.

Lamarque, Peter, and Stein Haugom Olsen. (1994). "Literary Practice." Chapter 10 of *Truth, Fiction, and Literature: A Philosophical Perspective*. Oxford: Oxford University Press.

Langer, Susanne K. (1953). *Feeling and Form*. London: Routledge and Kegan Paul.

Lewis, David. (1969). *Convention*. Cambridge, MA: Harvard University Press.

Lyas, Colin. (1997). *Aesthetics*. London: UCL Press.

Olsen, Stein Haugom. (1978). *The Structure of Literary Understanding*. Cambridge: Cambridge University Press.

———. (1987). "Criticism and Appreciation." In *The End of Literary Theory*. Cambridge: Cambridge University Press.

Pavel, Thomas G. (1986). *Fictional Worlds*. Cambridge, MA: Harvard University Press.

Rawls, John. (1955). "Two Concepts of Rules." *The Philosophical Review*,

64, 3–32. Reprinted in *Theories of Ethics*, edited by Philippa Foot, 144–70 (Oxford: Oxford University Press, 1967).

Reeves, Charles Eric. (1986). "Conveniency into Nature: Literary Art and Arbitrariness. *PMLA*, 101, 798–810.

Searle, J. R. (1969). *Speech Acts*. Cambridge: Cambridge University Press.

———. (1995). *The Construction of Social Reality*. London: Allan Lane/Penguin.

Stoll, E. E. (1933). *Art and Artifice in Shakespeare*. Cambridge: Cambridge University Press.

Watt, Ian, (1967). *The Rise of the Novel: Studies in Defoe, Richardson and Fielding*. London: Chatto & Windus.

4

RELATIVISM AND THE INTERPRETATION OF TEXTS

JORGE J. E. GRACIA

One frequently hears that interpretations are matters of opinion and that one interpretation is as good as any other. Indeed, sometimes the very use of the term *interpretation* signals the idea that we are speaking about something in which different and conflicting views are not just possible but legitimate. To say that something is a matter of interpretation is often taken to mean that it is a matter in which reasonable persons may disagree because no single view is regarded as the correct one. This is the way the term is used frequently in literary and aesthetic contexts and in questions of etiquette. We may have different opinions as to the aesthetic value of a Rauschenberg Combine, the literary significance of *El Cid*, or whether it is in good taste to cut vegetables with a knife or a fork. But there are areas in which such disagreement is not regarded as legitimate. For example, we do not tolerate disagreement concerning such things as the movement of the earth (it moves), the sum of two plus two (it is four and not five), or Napoleon's marriage to Josephine (it took place).

When it comes to texts too, some say that the interpretation of a text is a matter in which disagreement is legitimate because its value, even in cases of contradictory interpretations, depends on individual persons or particular groups, societies, or cultures. Those who hold this view are frequently accused of being relativists of various sorts: individual relativists, social relativists, cultural relativists, and so on.[1] Yet neither the views of those who are accused of this hermeneutical sin, nor the views of those who are the accusers, are always clear.[2] In this chapter, I try to clarify the issue at stake between the accused and the accusers and establish some parameters for relativism in the interpretation of texts.

---

[1] Relativism is a topic that has received considerable attention. For two general collections on this topic, see Krausz 1989 and Meiland and Krausz 1982. Most frequently, discussions of relativism center on truth and the possibility of contradictory truths. See, for example, Margolis 1989.

[2] An unusually lucid attempt to bring clarity to the discussion is Stout's 1986.

I begin with a discussion of texts and interpretation. These notions are then used to address the issue under scrutiny.

Texts

Differences concerning the nature of textuality abound in the discussions among philosophers who consider this topic, so it would be impossible to do justice to them in an chapter of this size. Rather than attempt such a task and fail, I adopt a conception of texts which I have defended elsewhere, and I hope that this will be sufficient for present purposes. According to this view, "A text is a group of entities, used as signs, selected, arranged, and intended by an author to convey a specific meaning to an audience in a certain context" (Gracia 1995, 4).[3]

The entities of which texts are constituted can be anything whatever. They can be lines and figures drawn on a page; they can be gestures made by a person; they can be actions; they can be glass beads; or they can be stones. A text can be made up even of mental images. There is no prima facie reason why I cannot compose a text of images I contemplate in my mind. Indeed, I can imagine the sounds uttered when one says, "Excuse me," even when no one actually says it. The only requirement concerning the entities that make up a text is that they be perceptual, either in the sense that they are capable of being perceived through the senses or in the phenomenological sense that they are capable of being experienced as precepts. Lines, figures, gestures, and actions are examples of the first; mental images corresponding to these constitute examples of the second. Apart from the perceptual character of the entities that constitute texts, there are other requirements of textuality as specified in the definition. These perceptual entities must be used as signs, that is, they must be taken in relation to meaning; and they must be selected and arranged in a certain way by an author who intends to convey some specific meaning to an audience through them in a particular context.

This conception of texts does not entail that the only thing an author intends to do through, or with, a text is to convey meaning. Texts have many uses, such as venting emotion, issuing commands, eliciting answers, making requests, causing actions, and so on. Although most texts are used to do something more than cause understanding in an audience, all texts involve the conveyance of some meaning and thus some understanding: When I say "I apologize," the apology is accomplished precisely because the interlocutor knows the meaning of "I apologize." If the interlocutor did not know this, the apology would not be understood and would not be effective.

---

[3] This is presented as a definition of text and not of work. These two notions are frequently confused in the literature, but recently some attempts have been made at disentangling them. Among pertinent sources are Nehamas 1987; Wilsmore 1987; Barthes 1979; Currie 1991; and Gracia 1995, 59–70.

Note another important implication of the definition I have given: Texts are not to be confused either with their meanings or with the understandings of those meanings. Understanding is one of the things that texts are supposed to cause. Understanding is something that happens in the author, the audience, or both, and therefore, it is ontologically distinct from the text that causes it. The text is a group of entities considered in relation to the meaning these entities are supposed to convey.[4] Understandings are acts that take place in the minds of the members of the audience, and of course also in the mind of the author.

Likewise, the meanings of texts are neither understandings nor texts. In a very general sense, meanings are whatever we understand when we are said to understand a text. Meanings are the objects of understanding, and their understanding is accomplished through the texts which are said to be understood. A text makes me understand what you want to say to me. There are no meanings without texts and understandings, but meanings should not be identified with them.[5]

In short, we have at least four possible ontologically distinct things: a text, its meaning, and the understandings of the text by an audience and an author. Keep in mind that the conception of texts provided here is quite broad. It includes such different things as a sentence, a paragraph, and a whole book. Length, complexity, or even the ontological character of the entities that constitute a text does not qualify or disqualify something as a text. Likewise, texts can be uttered, written, acted, or thought; they can be simple or complex; they can be difficult or easy to understand; and they can be ambiguous or clear. There is no reason why any of these considerations should make a difference when it comes to the classification of something as a text. Texts come in many varieties.

With this conception of texts in mind, we can now turn to the notion of interpretation. This is also a highly contested notion, so rather than go through the many understandings of it available in the pertinent literature, I present the view I have defended elsewhere in order to see how it can help us make sense of the question we are addressing here (Gracia 1995, 147ff.).[6]

---

[4] The ontology of texts involves various questions that are hotly debated in the literature. See, for example, Ricoeur 1971; Shillingsburg 1991; Tanselle 1989; McLaverty 1984; Nehamas 1987; Grigely 1991; McGann 1991; Bellemin-Noël 1972; and Gracia 1996, 8–43. The questions concern whether texts are individual or universal, physical or nonphysical, substances or features of substances, historical or nonhistorical, and the kind of existence and location they can have.

[5] For some classic signposts in the theory of meaning, see Frege 1952; Quine 1953; Grice 1989; and Putnam 1975. Controversies about meaning have in part motivated the argument that questions of interpretation are best addressed apart from meaning. see Stout 1982.

[6] For other views of interpretation, see Hirsch 1967; Nehamas 1987; Barthes 1970; Horton 1979; Currie 1991; Juhl 1980; Barnes 1988; Goodman and Elgin 1988; Eco 1990; and Abrams 1979.

Interpretations

For our purposes, there are two senses of "interpretation" that are particularly important. In one sense, an interpretation is an understanding, and since we are dealing with texts, an interpretation of a text turns out to be the understanding one has of a text. We often speak of someone's understanding of Aristotle's *Metaphysics* as his or her interpretation of it. But we also speak of certain texts as interpretations. For example, we speak of Averroës's *Commentary on Aristotle's Metaphysics* as Averroës's interpretation of Aristotle's *Metaphysics*. Interpretations in this second sense include the text under interpretation. If they did not, the interpretation would not be an interpretation of a text but rather would stand on its own, as an independent text.

Consider a situation in Mexico in which a Mexican who knows no English tells an American tourist who knows no Spanish, "Pare." Obviously, the American has no idea of what has been said to her, but there is a third party close by who knows both English and Spanish and comes to her aid. Now, if the third party simply said, "Stop," the American tourist would not be able to connect this text with the original text, unless of course the context supplied the connection. In order to be effective and communicate the message, the third party would have to say something like, "He means for you to stop," or "He means 'Stop,' " or " 'Pare' means stop." In all cases, even when the original text is not explicitly included in the second text, there is a reference to it, for without the reference, the audience, namely, the American tourist in this case, would not be able to connect the first text to the second. Now, the second text is an example of interpretation, for translations are one common kind of interpretation. Indeed, even in the case where an interpretation is not a text, but an understanding, such an understanding has to have a reference to the text under interpretation; otherwise, one could not make the connection between the text and its interpretation.

I have expressed this view elsewhere by saying that an interpretation, understood as a text, is composed of the text under interpretation (i.e., the *interpretandum*) and a text added to it (i.e., the *interpretans*) (Gracia 1995, 149–50). And when interpretations are taken to be understandings rather than texts, they consist of certain mental acts considered in relation to the text under interpretation (i.e., the *interpretandum*). In either case, the interpretation includes a necessary reference to the *interpretandum*, and therefore does not constitute an interpretation without it.

At least one aim of all interpretations, whether they are taken as understandings or as texts of the kind we have been discussing, is to cause an understanding in an audience. Interpretations are generally produced by interpreters for the benefit of an audience. Interpreters want to make an audience understand something about the text which is being interpreted. A teacher, for example, engages in this kind of procedure in class, when she lectures on Aristotle's *Metaphysics*. The teacher wants her students to understand something about Aristotle's text and that is why she provides an interpretation, that is, either an understanding of the text or a text added to the text under interpretation to cause the understanding as she wishes her students to have.

Interpretations can be divided into two kinds, depending on whether their aim is to provide an understanding of the meaning of a text or to provide an understanding of the relation of a text or its meaning to something else.[7] Let us call the first *meaning interpretations*, and the second *relational interpretations*.[8] Meaning interpretations come in various forms, depending on what one takes the meaning of a text to be. The meaning of the text can be taken in at least four different ways, which in turn generate four different kinds of meaning interpretations: the meaning as understood by the author of the text; the meaning as understood by particular audiences; the meaning as understood independently of what authors or particular audiences understand; and the meaning as including both the meaning, taken in one or more of the three ways mentioned, and its possible implications.

If the aim of the meaning interpretation is to understand what the author of a text understood by the text, it entails producing in an audience acts of understanding that are intensionally the same as those the author of the text had when he or she produced the text.[9] The interpreter seeks to produce acts of understanding in an audience that would copy those, say, Aristotle had when he composed the *Metaphysics*. Whether this is possible or not is a matter of debate in the pertinent literature, but quite immaterial for our purposes. In principle it seems possible, although in practice it might be very difficult. Historicists argue that it is impossible to reproduce similar acts of understanding in two subjects who differ in historical circumstances. Others believe that this historicist assumption is misguided.

Something similar to what has been said concerning the author can be said when we take meaning to be determined by the understanding of particular audiences.[10] In this case it is not the author's understanding that

---

[7] Other classifications in terms of aim or purpose are also possible. For example, Stout (1986, 104–14) distinguishes between interpretations whose aims are explanatory, normative, or aesthetic.

[8] Elsewhere I have called these *textual* and *nontextual* interpretations (Gracia 1995, 164–68), although other names could also be used, such as *textual* and *contextual*. I prefer the terminology proposed here because it is suggestively descriptive.

[9] In the past thirty years the notion of author has been severely questioned. Some authors reject that there is such a thing as the author of a text (Barthes 1977; Foucault 1977), whereas others have provided provocative conceptions of the author (Nehamas 1987, 1986). I discuss the controversies surrounding the author and present my own view in Gracia 1996.

[10] Like the notion of author, the notion of audience has acquired considerable importance in contemporary discussions. For the controversies surrounding this notion, see McGann 1991; Fish 1980; Eco 1990; Iser 1989; and Gracia 1996, 151–69.

is pertinent but the understanding of audiences. The interpreter does not seek to cause in his or her audience acts of understanding similar to those Aristotle had when he composed the *Metaphysics*, but rather acts of understanding similar to those that particular audiences had when they were presented with the text.

One can also speak of the meaning of a text in terms not of what the author and particular audiences of the text understood, but in terms of what the meaning of the text is independent of the understanding of the author and any particular audience. According to this view, texts have a meaning of their own which goes beyond what authors and audiences may understand. So the interpreter of Aristotle's *Metaphysics* seeks to cause in his or her audience acts of understanding that will make the audience understand the meaning of the text taken in this sense.

Finally, if one accepts the epistemic distinction between the understanding of the meaning of a text and the understanding of the implications of that meaning, one can also say that interpreters could be interested in producing in their audiences acts of understanding of the implications of the meaning of the text in addition to the understanding of the meaning, regardless of what one takes that meaning to be.[11] In the case of Aristotle's *Metaphysics*, the aim would be to produce acts of understanding in an audience that grasp not just the meaning of the text, but also the implications of the meaning, whether anyone has ever understood them or not, including Aristotle.

The second kind of interpretation mentioned above concerns one whose aim is to provide an understanding of the relation of a text, or its meaning, to something else. This interpretation was called *relational*. The aim of this kind of interpretation is not to cause an understanding of the meaning of a text in an audience, regardless of what conception of meaning is used, but rather something else. Let us look at some examples.

Consider the case of a Marxist interpretation of Thomas Aquinas's *Summa Theologiae*. In this case we have a situation in which the interpreter is not seeking to produce in the audience acts of understanding which are similar to those of Aquinas, or of any particular audience that could have been exposed to the text at the time of its production, or even subsequently. The aim of the Marxist interpreter is not historical in this sense. For him or her, the understanding of the views Aquinas thought he had presented in his treatise could not be the aim, because this interpreter believes that Aquinas's understanding was probably ideological and vitiated by factors which Aquinas himself did not grasp, since he had not read Karl Marx's analysis of the forces of history. The same can be said of what Aquinas's contemporary audience, or any other particular audience, for

---

[11] Logically, the meaning of a text includes all its implications, but epistemically one can be aware of the meaning and not of some of the implications of the meaning. For example, the meaning of "P. Q" logically implies the meaning of "P," but one can be aware of the first without being aware of the second.

that matter, thought. Nor is the Marxist interpreter interested in causing acts of understanding, in the audience, of the meaning of the text or its purported implications independent of what Aquinas or any particular audience thought. The Marxist interpreter is interested in relating the text of Aquinas and its meaning to certain Marxist principles which make clear the historical importance of the work in the overall scheme according to which Marxists believe history proceeds.

We find a somewhat different aim in a historical interpretation of Aquinas's *Summa*. The historian, unlike the Marxist, is not trying to relate the book to Marxist principles in order to understand the role it played in history – unless, of course, the historian is a Marxist – but rather to place Aquinas's book in a historical context. For this reason, this interpreter is interested in relating the book to other historical phenomena, the times in which it was written, the events in Aquinas's life, the publication of other works, the social situation at the time in which the book was produced, the ideological hegemony of the Roman Catholic Church at the time, the influence or dependence of Aquinas's work on other works, and so on. We do not have, then, a reading of the book that aims primarily at grasping its meaning, whether understood as what Aquinas and others understood by it, as something independent of these understandings, or as the meaning and its implications. The aim of the interpreter in this case is rather to understand the book in the historical context and determine its place within it. Indeed, it should be obvious that a historical interpretation cannot aim just at an understanding of a text's meaning, regardless of how one understands meaning. For example, a historical interpretation could not merely seek to provide an understanding of what the author of a text understood by it, for the historian is interested in the historical context of the text, both past and future, and many of the factors which are part of that context were beyond the knowledge and understanding of the author.

A feminist interpretation of Aquinas's *Summa*, on the other hand, will try to create in audiences an understanding of the text in terms of certain feminist principles. Perhaps the interpreter will try to make her audience see how the book is filled with masculine conceptions which affect its message, whatever that may be. The conception of God presented in it, the understanding of humans, and so on, taken from a masculine perspective and in terms of concepts which originate in that perspective, all form part of what the feminist interpreter might aim to reveal to her audience. Her point, then, is to place the *Summa* within a feminist framework that will produce the correct feminist understanding of the book. This hermeneutic framework is composed of principles of interpretation according to which certain words and terms that occur in a text are to be understood in certain ways, as symbols of certain views, attitudes, and perspectives. But the interpretive framework also contains general epistemic and metaphysical principles about the nature of knowledge and reality within which the views of Aquinas in the *Summa* need to be located.

Relational interpretations may also have further aims. This, however, does not undermine what has been said, for although many have the further aim of explanation, for example, this aim is accomplished by relating the text or its meaning to certain principles which are taken to pertain to explanations, be they Marxist, historical, or feminist.

Now, it is clear that in some relational interpretations it is necessary for the interpreter to include an interpretation of the first kind, that is, a meaning interpretation when meaning is taken in one or more of the four senses mentioned earlier, whereas in other relational interpretations this may not be necessary. For instance, it is possible that in order to have a Marxist interpretation of a text, it is not necessary, or even desirable, to have an understanding of the meaning of the text under interpretation as understood by a particular audience, for knowledge of such an understanding might be an obstacle to a proper Marxist understanding of the text. One could also imagine a situation in which the acts of understanding that the interpreter of a relational interpretation wishes to produce in an audience can be produced independently of any meaning interpretation, so that a meaning interpretation becomes superfluous.

Are All Interpretations Relativistic?

Now that we have clarified the notions of text and interpretation, we can return to the question we posed at the beginning: Are all interpretations of texts relativistic in the sense that an interpretation is a matter in which disagreement is legitimate because its value, even in cases of contradiction, depends on individual persons or particular groups, societies, or cultures?[12]

The issue to which this question points concerns the criteria according to which the value of interpretations is determined. Individual relativists argue that the value of interpretations is always determined by criteria established by individual persons. Group relativists argue in the same way but in terms of groups. And something similar can be said concerning social, cultural, and other kinds of relativists. All these relativists hold that disagreement in interpretation is legitimate, even in cases of contradiction, because the criteria used to judge interpretations are different. Thus, the same interpretation of a text can be judged to be good and bad, and different interpretations of the text can be judged equally good or equally bad, by different persons, groups, societies, or cultures.

Still, the way we have formulated the question is too complex to allow us to answer it with any degree of clarity. We must first distinguish whether the question refers to different interpretations within the same

---

[12] For purposes of this chapter, this sense of relativism is adequate, although it may not be satisfactory in other contexts. For other formulation of relativism, see the works mentioned in note 1.

kind or to different interpretations of different kinds. Do we mean to ask, for instance, whether all Marxist interpretations of a text are equally legitimate, or whether Marxist and Freudian interpretations of the same text are equally legitimate? In order to make sure that these questions are not confused, I divide the subsequent discussion into two parts, one dealing with relativism within the same particular kind of interpretation and the other dealing with relativism across different kinds of interpretations.

Relativism within Particular Kinds of Interpretations
To determine whether relativism applies within interpretations of particular kinds, we must pose the question in terms of the two broad kinds distinguished before: meaning interpretations and relational interpretations. Let us begin, then, with meaning interpretations.

Meaning Interpretations. Recall that a meaning interpretation is either (1) an understanding of the meaning of a text or (2) a text whose aim is to produce in an audience an understanding of the meaning of an *interpretandum*. And recall that meaning can be taken in at least four different senses: the meaning understood by the author; the meaning understood by a particular audience independently of what the author understood; the meaning considered independently of what the author or particular audiences understood; and the meaning taken together with the implications of the meaning. Now, if we take each of these four possibilities in turn, the value of the interpretation in each case is relative to particular criteria, but the criteria are not necessarily or always determined by individual persons, groups, and so on. This means both that these interpretations are not necessarily relativistic and that it is not always legitimate to have different and conflicting interpretations of the same text.

Consider the case in which an interpretation is supposed to be the understanding of what an author understood by a text. In this case, it is obvious that what the author understood functions as the criterion which establishes when the interpretation is correct or not.[13] An interpretation which aims to be an understanding of what an author understood but is not, clearly is not legitimate. Moreover, it should be obvious that the legitimacy of the interpretation does not depend on criteria set by anyone. The relation between the interpretation, that is, the understanding sought by the interpreter, and the understanding of the author is independent of anyone's opinion, including that of the interpreter. The interpreter may think he or she has understood the author when in fact he or she has not.

---

[13] This is in fact the reason why some make authorial interpretations paradigmatic of all interpretations. This appears in principle to be a good way of avoiding relativism, but as we shall see, one need not go to this extreme to avoid interpretational relativism. The classic defense of this position in the recent past, framed in terms of the author's intention, is found in Hirsch 1967.

Suppose, for example, that by the sentence "The existence of God cannot be demonstrated *propter quid*," Thomas Aquinas understood that the existence of God cannot be demonstrated on the basis of an understanding of the nature of God. And suppose that an interpreter (e.g., one of my students) understands it to mean that the existence of God cannot be demonstrated from God's effects. In this case, clearly the interpreter's understanding is at fault, regardless of what he or anyone else may think about it. And the same can be said when the meaning is taken in the other ways suggested earlier. In all cases, the legitimacy and value of the interpretation, that is, of the understanding, are independent of anyone's opinion and hinge solely on the relation between two understandings.

The case of the interpretation of a text when the meaning is taken as determined by the understanding of a particular audience is both similar to and different from the case in which it is taken as determined by the author's understanding. It is different because audiences may be composed of more than one person, and this implies that there may be more than one understanding in question. Obviously, this complicates matters in ways which require more attention than we can give here. The case is similar because, as with the author, the audience's understanding functions as the criterion of value and legitimacy for the interpretation.

The case with the interpretation of a text when the meaning is taken as independent of the understanding of the author of the text and any particular audience of it is different insofar as the criteria for measuring the value and legitimacy of the interpretation are not clearly identified. What is this meaning and how is it established? The answer to this question will no doubt determine whether relativism is possible or not. Elsewhere I have defended a cultural-function view of textual meaning which precludes relativism, but I have no time to defend it in this case (Gracia 1995, 123–36). Suffice it to say that there are ways to close the door on relativism here, but the matter is by no means an open-and-shut case. Moreover, the situation when the meaning of a text is taken as including both the meaning considered independently of what the author and any particular audience understood it to be, and the implications of that meaning, is parasitic on the case we just discussed. We need not take it up separately, then.

Of course, someone might want to argue that no meaning interpretation is possible, even in cases when the meaning of the text is taken as the understanding of the author or a particular audience, let alone when the meaning is considered independent of these. To produce understandings in someone similar to the understandings an author of a text had, or a particular audience had, and so on, is impossible, because all understandings are historical and, as such, they cannot be reproduced, not just numerically, but even in content. According to this view, it is necessarily the case that the sentence "$2 + 2 = 4$" means something different when Russell understood it and when I understand it, or for that matter when I understand it and you understand it, because the circumstances that accompany Russell, you, and me, when each of us considers it, are different.

This view is based on a misunderstanding between the historical occurrence of a sentence and the historical content of the sentence. I have expressed this elsewhere by calling the former the extensional historicity of sentences, and the latter, the intensional historicity of sentences (Gracia 1992, 121–22, 165–66). Every sentence – and I am speaking of individual or token sentences – by virtue of what it is, is historically located, for sentences of this sort exist only when they are said, written, or thought by someone at some time. But this does not mean that the content, namely, what the sentence says, is always historical. Many sentences make claims that are not historical, so that their content has nothing to do with historical facts, whereas others make historical claims and have a historical intensional content. "I drank a glass of wine last night" is both extensionally and intensionally historical, but "2 + 2 = 4" is only extensionally historical, not intensionally historical.

Now, if there are sentences whose intensional content is not historical, then the understanding of that content need not be subject to historical circumstances. Indeed, there are even some sentences that are intensionally historical and do not depend on particular observers or points of view. There is a difference between saying "I drank a glass of wine last night" and "I drank too much last night." In the first case, I have a sentence which is both extensionally and intensionally historical, but whose truth value does not depend on anything other than whether I drank a glass of wine last night. The case of the second sentence is different, for not only is this extensionally and intensionally historical, but what the sentence says depends on a certain view of what constitutes too much wine drinking. Perhaps it makes sense to say that the understanding of sentences that are intensionally historical depends to a certain extent on someone's opinion or perspective, but it does not make sense to say that the understanding of all sentences does.

To this, someone might object that even sentences that are not intensionally historical use historical terms, belonging to a language, and express concepts that are the products of historical forces. To this extent, so the argument goes, the understanding of all sentences depends on historical circumstances. And this is right. But to say this does not require a particular perspective as long as what the sentence in question says is not a matter of perspective or history. Nor does it entail that the understanding of the sentence is irreproducible at some other time in history. In principle, even if it poses difficulties, we could grasp with precision what someone else understood with a word and we can entertain a concept that someone else entertains or entertained. That it is difficult to do so, or perhaps even practically impossible in many cases, does not justify saying that it is so in all cases.

So far I have been speaking as if all interpretations were understandings, but interpretations can also be texts aimed to produce understanding in audiences. When interpretations are taken in the latter sense, their value is necessarily tied to their effectiveness in producing understanding in audiences and the criteria of such value must include the condition of their effectiveness. Moreover, because audiences and their circumstances vary, it is likely that the conditions of effectiveness also vary depending on the audience. To this extent, one could say that even meaning interpretations, when considered as texts, are relative to the individual persons or groups who are their audiences. This allows for very different interpretations of the same text which are equally effective with different audiences and undermines the idea of definitive interpretations.[14] However, it does not entail that these interpretations are relativistic because the criteria for their value depend not on the opinion of individual persons or groups, but on relations between the interpretations and individual persons or groups.

In short, meaning interpretations based on author or particular-audience understandings are not relativistic insofar as, in principle, there are criteria for determining the value of these interpretations, and these criteria are not determined by individual persons, social groups, or cultures, but rather derive from the aim of the interpretation: the understanding of the meaning of a text. Accordingly, the value of the interpretation is founded on a relation which is independent from what individual persons, groups, or societies may think. This implies that this kind of meaning interpretation does not in principle tolerate disagreement, even if producing understandings of the sort required by meaning interpretations may be difficult, or even factually impossible in some cases. The case with meaning interpretations that are not based on author or particular-audience understandings is different. Whether they turn out to be relativistic or not will depend on what meanings are, how they are established, and on their limits. Now let me turn to relational interpretations.

Relational Interpretations. If the claim that interpretations are relativistic is going to make sense at all, it certainly has to make sense in the case of relational interpretations. After all, we have said that the aim of these interpretations is to establish understandings based on the relations between a text, or its meaning, and something else that the interpreter brings into the picture. And this seems to suggest that, indeed, interpretations depend on what interpreters choose to bring into play and that the value of interpretations is determined by interpreters in accordance with criteria they select. A Marxist interpreter will try to relate a text and its meaning to Marxist principles, and a feminist will do likewise with feminist principles, and in doing so they will produce equally legitimate, even if different and perhaps contradictory, interpretations.

Three initial comments are in order. First, it is clear that many of those

---

[14] I have dealt with definitive interpretations in Gracia 1994, 43–53.

who put forth relational interpretations claim that their interpretations are correct, objective, and even true. Indeed, sometimes they claim that they have the only legitimate interpretation, or at least one better than all those that had been given until they offered their own. This, of course, does not mean that these interpretations are what their proponents claim them to be, or even that there are interpretations that can have these characteristics. It is possible that the proponents of these claims are wrong not only about the value of their interpretations, but also about the possibility that some kinds of relational interpretations can be correct, objective, true, or even better than others. But it does tell us that those engaged in producing these interpretations think, or at least act – and I say this because often one finds contradictions between what interpreters say they do and what they actually do – as if their aim is to produce interpretations that are better than others. This in turn would seem to suggest that they have in mind criteria of validity and legitimacy which are more than just a matter of individual opinion.

Second, it is also important to note that those who produce what I have called relational interpretations frequently act as if these interpretations could be subjected to careful scrutiny on the basis of established criteria, which can be considered and applied independently of individual interpreters. Indeed, frequently interpreters will engage in detailed discussions to show how they meet these criteria whereas other interpreters, who are trying or have tried to produce interpretations of the same sort, have failed where they themselves have succeeded. Marxists quarrel among themselves about the understanding of a particular text, as do feminists, historians, and other interpreters of texts engaged in relational interpretations. If these interpreters did not think that their kinds of interpretations were subject to established criteria, independent of particular interpreters, their actions would make very little sense. They would amount to nothing more than a power struggle between parties who are engaged in the deception of others, but who know that in fact the only thing that counts when it comes to the judgment of the value of their interpretations is to establish their own over those which differ from them. This is possible, of course, but the principle of charity dictates that we do not assume hypocrisy when there are other, more charitable ways of construing their behavior.

Third and final, although it is no doubt true that in some kinds of relational interpretations there are no well-established criteria by which to judge their value and legitimacy, and that in many cases the criteria available and used vary from group to group, or even from interpreter to interpreter, this is certainly not the case in many others. I do not think it would sit well with Marxists to tell them that there are no Marxist criteria of interpretation when it comes to texts, and that what Marxists do when they try to give an interpretation of Thomas Aquinas's *Summa Theologiae* is a matter of personal opinion, based on personal preferences, and not the result of objective principles, based on the proper understanding of history and the location of the text in question within the whole historical scheme as understood in Marxism. They will point out that history moves along certain dialectical patterns in accordance with economic forces and that, when Marxist theory is applied to a medieval text like that of Aquinas, it yields a certain understanding of the text, which is what their commentary aims to cause in the audience for which the interpretation is being provided.

But Marxists are not alone in this. Freudians will tell you something similar. They might tell you also that the science of interpretation is not exact, unlike mathematics, but they will also insist that it is not a matter of personal opinion or that all Freudian interpretations are equally legitimate. Freudians undergo rigorous training to learn the interpretive principles that they then apply, something which would not be necessary if they believed that interpretations were purely a matter of personal perspective. Indeed, according to their scheme, there are certain words that have certain meanings which they do not ordinarily have and which can be used as evidence of the psychological significance of the text.

The historian will not be far behind. Historians generally develop a strict methodology, and those devoted to the study of particular historical periods spend much time acquiring specialized skills, such as knowledge of certain languages, cultures, events, and so on. They learn to make assertions on the basis of certain evidence, to question evidence of certain kinds, and to approach texts in certain ways. This means that the conclusions of a historian are contestable, but only because there are reasons for it, perhaps because the historian in question did not follow proper procedures, because the conclusions are not supported by the evidence, and so on. All these are used as criteria to judge historical interpretations. Naturally, historians are allowed to bring – and indeed must do so – into interpretations their own particular take and viewpoint. But this take and viewpoint must be consistent with much that is based on established procedures and criteria. This is why a particular historical interpretation can be judged to be more valuable than another, or more objective than another, or even legitimate whereas another is not. If, for example, a historian claims that Thomas Aquinas borrowed a certain doctrine from another author, he or she must provide evidence to this effect. There must first be found similar statements of the doctrine in both authors, and then there must be some evidence that indicates that Aquinas was familiar with the other author's view. A historical interpretation that makes a claim like this, and does not provide evidence for it, is quickly dismissed by other historians.

All this brings us to two important points. First, relational interpretations take place within established communities, and it is within these communities that the criteria for their legitimacy and value are developed.[15] This is why, in general, relational interpretations cannot be said to be based on individual opinion. Indeed, the supervision that these commu-

[15] Fish has used the notion of interpretive communities in his 1980. See also Putnam 1975, 228.

nities exercise over their particular kinds of interpretations is often so strict that it discourages innovation and change to such a degree that they are sometimes brought about only at a great cost to those who do it. Interpretive communities tend to be conservative and set in their ways, and development is usually tolerated only within narrow parameters and at a slow pace.

The second important point is that, in many cases, the criteria of evaluation of interpretations derive from the aim identified by the interpretive community and, therefore, it is misleading to say that the value of particular interpretations always depends on the community in the same sense. Consider, for example, a historian who makes the claim that in the *Summa*, Aquinas borrows a particular view from Augustine. If the aim sanctioned by the community of historians is to determine whether Aquinas, in the *Summa*, borrowed any view from Augustine, the criterion of a historical interpretation of Aquinas's *Summa* will be to establish whether he did or not on the basis of the evidence available, and this has nothing to do with what the community of historians may think. This explains why interpretive communities have the attitudes mentioned earlier. They understand that they have a hand in choosing the aim of the interpretive game, but once the aim is established, in at least some cases the rules follow independently of what they may think. Of course, this is not so in all cases. Some interpretive communities choose aims which allow for considerable latitude, so that in those cases there can still be room for individual disagreement.

Thus far in this section, I have been speaking of relational interpretations in general, without distinguishing between interpretations conceived as understandings and interpretations conceived as texts. This distinction makes a difference, but not a substantial one, in what has been said. The difference consists in that, as with meaning interpretations, the value of relational interpretations that are texts must include criteria of effectiveness with respect to particular audiences. This introduces an element of relativity, but it does not make these interpretations relativistic.

In conclusion, relational interpretations are not generally relativistic in an individual sense because the criteria according to which their value is measured are determined by interpretive communities rather than individual persons, except in cases where the community rules otherwise. This means that, as with meaning interpretations, relational interpretations do not in principle tolerate disagreement within particular kinds, even if producing understandings of the sort required by relational interpretations may be difficult or even factually impossible. None of this, however, makes clear whether some kinds of interpretations are better or more legitimate than others. The disagreement concerning this matter ultimately concerns the status of the criteria used in determining the value of interpretations across kinds.

Relativism across Different Kinds of Interpretation

Can the value of interpretations be judged across kinds? Is it legitimate to have different and conflicting interpretations of different kinds? Can we say, for example, that a meaning interpretation, in which the meaning is identified with the author's understanding of the meaning, is better or worse than a historical interpretation when, in the first, the interpretation has as its aim the understanding of what the author understood through the text, and in the second the aim is to understand the text in its historical context? Or, in another example, can we say that an interpretation in which the aim is to understand what a particular audience understood through a text is legitimate, whereas an interpretation in which the aim is to understand the text in relation to a Freudian scheme is not?

These questions have to do with the value of different kinds of interpretations and how to measure them. Moreover, they apply regardless of whether we are dealing with interpretations conceived as understandings or as texts that cause understanding. Taken in this sense, there are at least three sources of the criteria on which the answers to the questions can be based. The first is individual: Criteria for the value of interpretations across kinds are determined by individual persons, such as the interpreter. The second is social: Criteria are established by interpretive communities, groups, societies, or cultures. The third is more general: Criteria are determined by a general aim such as the overall, encompassing understanding of the world.

Does it make sense to ask the question of the value of different kinds of interpretation in terms of the first two kinds of criteria, namely, criteria determined by particular individuals or communities? Can we say that a certain kind of interpretation is more legitimate than another when in fact the interpreter aims only to produce one of those interpretations? Yes and no. It makes no sense to say that a kind of interpretation, say kind A, is better or worse than another kind of interpretation, say kind B, when in fact the interpreter seeks kind A, although it makes sense to say that kind A is legitimate and kind B is not. If an interpreter is seeking an understanding of what an author meant by a text, then it makes no sense to compare this kind of interpretation with a historical one, because the latter does not have as a purpose the production of such an understanding, although it does make sense to say that the historical interpretation is not legitimate under the circumstances.

Likewise, if the value of interpretations is measured in terms of the social functions that texts have, then it makes very little sense to say that a particular kind of interpretation is better or worse than another, provided that the kinds in question are all allowed in terms of the social functions of the texts in question. I assume that in this case there are only certain kinds of interpretations that are allowed, and that their value is not a matter of their kind, but a matter of the criteria used within the kind. Consider the case of a will. Wills are legal documents which have a definite social function, namely, to make known the deceased's views as to how his or her estate is to be disposed of. But society also treats wills as social documents which give information about the customs of particular social groups and even about the characters of the authors of the wills. This means that there are several legitimate kinds of interpretations that can be given of a will. But these, again, will not be competing, since their purposes are different. Their value and legitimacy should be judged only within the parameters of the kind of interpretation in question, not across kinds of interpretation. In this case, it makes sense to say that interpretations are better or worse within kinds, but not across kinds.

The third set of criteria cuts across interpretation kinds. In accordance with it, the question of the value and legitimacy of different kinds of interpretations is not posed in the context of what a particular interpreter wants, a particular interpretive community accepts, or the social function a text may have within a particular society. The question becomes, for instance, Are Freudian or feminist interpretations legitimate? This brings us to a broader context, in which a judgment is sought concerning a particular kind of interpretation in terms of what it contributes to our overall understanding of the world, not just to the understanding of a particular text in certain circumstances. Thus, for example, Do Freudian interpretations of texts contribute to our overall understanding of the world? Do feminist interpretations of texts contribute to our overall understanding of the world?

These questions point to a more fundamental issue, for they do not pertain to interpretation as such, but rather to knowledge in general. They concern the value of certain theories and their usefulness in understanding the world, including particular interpretational schemes. If one holds that there are no answers to these general questions, then one must accept that ultimately there are no kinds of interpretations that are better than others or more legitimate than others. One must also accept that one kind of interpretation is as good as another and that the value of an interpretation depends ultimately on the aims of an individual or the conventions of a particular group.[16] If, on the other hand, one accepts that there are criteria whereby theoretical schemes can be judged to be better and more legitimate than others in understanding the world, then one must also grant that, in principle, there must be certain kinds of interpretation which are better and more legitimate than others and even that there are legitimate and illegitimate kinds of interpretations.

Conclusion

In conclusion, not all interpretations of texts are relativistic, and those that are relativistic are not so in the same way. Meaning interpretations based

---

[16] Rorty and Feyerabend are two of the champions of this position. For the first, see 1979; for the second, 1981.

on author and audience understandings are not relativistic in the sense that their value is measured by criteria determined by their aim and not by individual persons or groups. This is why these interpretations do not in principle tolerate disagreement. Meaning interpretations of other kinds can in principle be relativistic, depending on the conception of meaning and its limits adopted.

Relational interpretations are not relativistic in the sense that the criteria which measure their value are not determined by individual persons, and some of them are not relativistic in the sense that their aim, as with meaning interpretations, determines the criteria of their value. But some relational interpretations are relativistic insofar as their criteria of value are determined by interpretive communities, and even in those for which criteria are determined by their aim, the latter is chosen by interpretive communities. For these reasons, and in principle, relational interpretations do not tolerate individual disagreement within particular kinds, but they tolerate disagreements of other sorts.

Finally, whether relativism across different kinds of interpretations is legitimate depends in turn on whether there are criteria that measure the value of knowledge in general apart from what individual persons and particular groups may believe. Obviously, this is too large a question to be solved in passing and must be dealt with at another time. For the moment, it is sufficient that the parameters of relativism in the interpretation of texts have been made clear.[17]

References

Abrams, M. H. (1979). "The Deconstructive Angel." *Critical Inquiry*, 3, 425–38.

Barnes, Annette. (1988). *On Interpretation: A Critical Analysis*. Oxford: Basil Blackwell.

Barthes, Roland. (1970). *S/Z*. Paris: Editions du Seuil.

——. (1977). "The Death of the Author." In *Image, Music, Text*, translated by Stephen Heath, 142–48. New York: Hill and Wang.

——. (1979). "From Work to Text." Trans. Josué V. Harari. In *Textual Strategies: Perspectives in Post-Structuralist Criticism*, edited by Josué V. Harari, 73–81. Ithaca, NY: Cornell University Press.

Bellemin-Noël, Jean. (1972). *Le texte et l'avant-texte*. Paris: Larousse.

Currie, Gregory. (1991). "Work and Text." *Mind*, 100, 325–39.

Eco, Umberto. (1990). *The Limits of Interpretation*. Bloomington: Indiana University Press.

Feyerabend, Paul. (1981). *Realism, Rationalism and Scientific Method*.

[17] My gratitude goes to William Irwin, Gregory Basham, and William Fedirko. They read an early draft of this chapter and raised many questions about both its substance and its form.

Philosophical Papers, vol. 1. Cambridge: Cambridge University Press.

Foucault, Michel. (1977). "What Is an Author?" Trans. Donald F. Bouchard and Sherry Simon. In *Language, Counter-memory, Practice: Selected Essays and Interviews*, edited by Donald F. Bouchard, 113–38. Ithaca, NY: Cornell University Press.

Fish, Stanley. (1980). *Is There a Text in This Class? The Authority of Interpretive Communities*. Cambridge, MA: Harvard University Press.

Frege, Gottlob. (1952). "On Sense and Reference." In *Translations from the Philosophical Writings of Gottlob Frege*, edited and translated by P. Geach and M. Black, 56–78. Oxford: Basil Blackwell.

Goodman, Nelson, and Catherine Z. Elgin. (1988). "Interpretation and Identity." In *Reconceptions in Philosophy and Other Arts and Sciences*, 49–65. London: Routledge.

Gracia, Jorge J. E. (1992). *Philosophy and Its History: Issues in Philosophical Historiography*. Albany: State University of New York Press.

———. (1994). "Can There Be Definitive Interpretations?" In *European Philosophy and the American Academy*, edited by B. Smith, 43–53. La Salle, IL: Hegeler Institute.

———. (1995). *A Theory of Textuality: The Logic and Epistemology*. Albany: State University of New York Press.

———. (1996). *Texts: Ontological Status, Identity, Author, Audience*. Albany: State University of New York Press.

Grice, H. P. (1989). *Studies in the Way of Words*. Cambridge, MA: Harvard University Press.

Grigely, Joseph. (1991). "The Textual Event." In *Devils and Angels: Textual Editing and Literary Criticism*, edited by Philip Cohen, 167–94. Charlottesville: University Press of Virginia.

Hirsch, E. D., Jr. (1967). *Validity in Interpretation*. New Haven, CT: Yale University Press.

Horton, Susan. (1979). *Interpreting Interpreting: Interpreting Dickens' "Dombey."* Baltimore, MD: Johns Hopkins University Press.

Iser, Wolfgang. (1989). *Prospecting: From Reader-Response to Literary Anthropology*. Baltimore, MD: Johns Hopkins University Press.

Juhl, P. D. (1980). *Interpretation: An Essay in the Philosophy of Literary Criticism*. Princeton, NJ: Princeton University Press.

Krausz, M., ed. (1989). *Relativism: Interpretation and Confrontation*. Notre Dame, IN: University of Notre Dame Press.

Margolis, Joseph. (1989). "The Truth about Relativism." In *Relativism: Interpretation and Confrontation*, edited by M. Krausz, 232–55. Notre Dame, IN: University of Notre Dame Press.

McGann, Jerome J. (1991). *The Textual Condition*. Princeton, NJ: Princeton University Press.

McLaverty, James. (1984). "The Mode of Existence of Literary Works of

Art: The Case of the *Dunciad Variorum.*" *Studies in Bibliography*, 37, 82–105.

Meiland, J. W., and M. Krausz, eds. (1982). *Relativism: Cognitive and Moral*. Notre Dame, IN: Notre Dame University Press.

Nehamas, Alexander. (1986). "What an Author Is." *Journal of Philosophy*, 83, 685–91.

——. (1987). "Writer, Text, Work, Author." In *Literature and the Question of Philosophy*, edited by Anthony J. Cascardi, 267–91. Baltimore, MD: Johns Hopkins University Press.

Putnam, Hilary. (1975). "The Meaning of 'Meaning.' " In *Mind, Language and Reality*, 215–77. Cambridge: Cambridge University Press.

Quine, W. V. O. (1953). "On What There Is." In *From a Logical Point of View*, 1–19. Cambridge, MA: Harvard University Press.

Ricoeur, Paul. (1971). "The Model of the Text: Meaningful Action Considered as a Text." *Social Research*, 38, 529–62.

Rorty, Richard. (1979). *Philosophy and the Mirror of Nature*. Princeton, NJ: Princeton University Press.

Shillingsburg, Peter L. (1991). "Text as Matter, Concept, and Action." *Studies in Bibliography*, 44, 31–82.

Stout, Jeffrey. (1982). "What Is the Meaning of a Text?" *New Literary History*, 14 (1), 1–14.

——. (1986). "The Relativity of Interpretation." *The Monist*, 69, 103–18.

Tanselle, G. Thomas. (1989). *A Rationale of Textual Criticism*. Philadelphia: University of Pennsylvania Press.

Wilsmore, Susan. (1987). "The Literary Work Is Not Its Text." *Philosophy and Literature*, 11, 307–16.

5

ON CHANGING THE SUBJECT

PAUL THOM

Sticking to the point is thought to be a good thing. Changing the subject, by contrast, is regarded as a sign of a wandering mind if it is unintentional. If it is intentional, it is vilified under such titles as "tampering with the evidence," "cooking the books," or "rigging the inquiry" – and it is seen as betraying a desire to hide something. Either way, according to this prereflective view, to change the subject is to exhibit intellectual weakness. Yet, as I shall show, *interpreters* regularly replace an initial object of interpretation by a new object, thus "changing the subject." If I am right about that, and if we accept the loaded prereflective vocabulary of "tampering," "rigging," and so on, then we seem to face the consequence that interpretation itself, to the extent that it engages in topic-altering, is a tainted practice.

I shall describe four ways in which interpreters "change the subject." These involve (1) idealizing the object of interpretation, (2) resegmenting the object of interpretation, (3) reconceiving the object of interpretation, and (4) recovering an underlying object. These are all ways of altering an initially given object of interpretation; but I will argue that, far from being symptomatic of either intellectual weakness or duplicity, they are an intrinsic part of that most central of human intellectual endeavors, interpretation, and they contribute to its positive value.

Before proceeding, I should say briefly how I am using the terms "object" and "scheme" and how in general I understand the process of interpretation. By the *object of interpretation* I mean just what is being interpreted, be it a natural phenomenon, a text or other artifact, or a human action. By an *interpretative scheme* I mean a concept or set of concepts that can be used to make sense of an object of interpretation, whether by indicating what the object signifies, what it represents, or how it is to be explained. I take it that interpretation always aims to make sense of its object by finding or else constructing a scheme to which the object fits. So much seems uncontroversial.

There may, however, be controversy over the issue of whether in pursuing this aim interpreters invariably simply fit a scheme to an object. What I shall argue is that actual interpretive practices frequently depart from this simple model by adapting the object of interpretation to fit the scheme.

Idealization

When a lecturer draws a chalk circle on the blackboard, the keen eye can easily see that what is drawn falls well short of the geometrical definition of a circle. Only by idealizing do they see the drawing as a circle.

Idealization occurs in interpretation, for instance, when audiences re-interpret wrong notes and other imperfections in performers' actions. Consider a recital by the great pianist Sviatoslav Richter that took place in February 1958 in Sofia. The recital was recorded. It started with a performance of Moussorgsky's *Pictures at an Exhibition*, and Richter smudged a note in the opening "Promenade," though some listeners to the recording do not regard that as important, among them David Fanning:

> It's a performance remarkable for sheer intensity and sense of abandon. The imperfections are plain to hear, from the opening "Promenade" on. But that only serves to prove that great pianism does not consist of technical perfection plus added extras; rather it has to do with letting the music play through the artist, of abandonment to a higher force. A degree of human perfectibility is willingly traded for a glimpse of the superhuman. (Fanning 8)

This "trading" is clearly done in Fanning's imagination, where Richter's brilliant but flawed performance is replaced by that of a superhuman pianist who abandons himself to the power of an unrecognized musical master-piece. To this idealized performance Fanning assigns great significance:

> This recital not only heralded the appearance of a new colossus in the world of piano-playing, it also played a significant part in the rehabilitation of what is now a standard in the piano repertoire. (8)

Fanning is so impressed with Richter's performance that he is able to hear through its imperfections, to an idealized performance, free of slips and smudges and displaying superhuman attributes. The actual performance merely approximates to these attributes.

What idea of interpretation do practices like this betoken? At the very least, they rest on an idea of interpretation as an attempt to make sense of its objects by applying interpretive schemes to them. The failure of that attempt leads in some cases to the interpreter's substituting an idealized object in place of the original object of interpretation. Substitution is a type of representation. Thus, in cases where interpreters idealize their objects, their activity involves not just two but three terms – object, object-as-represented, and scheme. In the case under discussion, the object-as-represented is brought in because, whereas the interpretive scheme proposed ("a new colossus of the keyboard, rehabilitating an ignored masterpiece") fits the original object of interpretation (the actual performance) only roughly, it fits the object-as-represented neatly. Such is in general the motivation for idealization in interpretation. This can be seen in scientific theorizing as well as in cultural interpretation. In both fields, theory is thought to deal appropriately with idealized objects. That means that in a sense the object of interpretation (i.e., the object-*as-represented*) is in these cases fitted to the scheme (rather than the scheme to the object), to the extent that it was the scheme's failure to fit the original object neatly that led the interpreter to substitute an idealized object.

But it is important to remember that this substitution was not done without regard for the original object's features. It was, after all, an *idealization* of the original object in the context of the proposed interpretive scheme. As such, the substitution was not an unconstrained one. Two constraints had to be satisfied. First, the object-as-represented had to fit the proposed scheme. Second, the object-as-represented had to be as faithful as possible (in the context of the proposed interpretive scheme) to the original object. In the present case these constraints appear to have been satisfied. The idealizing representation of Richter's performance can indeed be brought under the proposed interpretative scheme. What the idealizing representation preserves in Richter's performance are its "superhuman" attributes and its sense of abandon before the supreme value of the work, while omitting the performance's blemishes; and these are just the right selection to make if one wants the representation to fit the scheme while remaining as close as possible to the original object.

Resegmentation

To speak generally, material that is to undergo any sort of operation needs first to be divided into parts, and the segmentation should be appropriate to the type of operation that is to be performed. Onions that are about to be cooked need first to be chopped, and the way they are chopped should be appropriate to the sort of cooking they are to undergo. The same principle applies to material for thought. The material needs first to be segmented, and the way it is carved up should be appropriate to the sort of thinking that is to be exercised on it. Plato recognized this principle for the particular case of the dialectician, whom he enjoins "not to attempt to hack off parts like a clumsy butcher" in logical divisions (Plato 265e).

What applies to thinking in general applies also to interpretation. Objects to be interpreted under a given scheme must be appropriately segmented. It's possible for interpreters of artworks to forget this fact, because the material they interpret is generally served up to them already carved. But scientists, in their efforts to interpret nature, cannot so easily forget that the first prerequisite to constructing an explanation is to properly articulate the explicandum.

Not everything can be explained. Consider an Aristotelian example:

> A man is engaged in collecting subscriptions for a feast. He would have gone to such and such a place for the purpose of getting the money, if he had known. He actually went there for another purpose, and it was only incidentally that he got his money by going there. (Aristotle 196b33–36)

The Aristotelian interpreter, wishing to apply the interpretive scheme "explained by . . . ," finds that it cannot be applied without qualification to this complex event. It is a coincidence that, just at the time when the man needs money, he goes to a place where he can get money. However, the man did not go to that particular place by chance, but for a purpose (a purpose other than getting money). So, while his-going-there-and-getting-a-subscription has no explanation as such (but only "incidentally" as Aristotle puts it), his-going-there does have an explanation. By resegmenting the object, we make it explicable.

More generally, not everything is capable of being interpreted in accordance with a given scheme of interpretation. The so-called historical books of the Old Testament (Joshua to Esther) are now thought to resist interpretation as a record of historical events. Still, *parts* of these books may be able to be subsumed under the interpretive scheme "historical record." If you can't fit a square peg into a round hole, your options, short of just giving up, are to change the peg or to change the hole. Widening and narrowing are among the types of change to consider. Whenever a proposed scheme of interpretation can't be made to fit the object, the interpreter's options are to replace the interpretative scheme or to alter the object of interpretation, maybe by widening or narrowing it. In the case of these biblical books, interpreters can either read them as, for example, a literary narrative or else abandon hope of reading them *in toto* as historical and settle for applying this scheme to selected portions of the books. The latter strategy amounts to resegmenting the object of interpretation, viewing the books as a "narrative mine out of which the skilled interpreter may dig nuggets of history" – those nuggets being comparatively unlikely to be found in certain books such as Ruth and Esther (Provan 199).

In both these examples, by a resegmentation of the object the interpreter can bring it – represented in a pared-down form – under the chosen interpretive scheme. Resegmentation involves the representation of the whole object by a part. And in these examples the representation is constrained in ways that are similar to the constraints we formulated for cases of idealization. The substitution of a pared-down object for the original object of interpretation incorporates as much as possible of the original object's features into a new object that fits the proposed interpretive scheme. By dissolving the conjunction going-to-the-marketplace-and-getting-a-subscription into its conjuncts, we produce *two* less complex objects of interpretation, each of which is capable of receiving an explanation and each of which preserves what can be preserved of the original object. By digging out the "nuggets" from Joshua to Esther, we preserve what can be preserved of those texts while producing an object of interpretation which can successfully be read as a historical record.

Reconception

One and the same material may be brought under several different concepts. It may be seen as different things. Wherever we have a shift of intension, with no shift in extension, we have reconception. Such shifts in perspective may seem quite arbitrary, as when you see the duck-rabbit now as a duck and now as a rabbit. In other cases, the shift can seem appropriate or even rational. Reconceptions of this latter sort are a stock in trade of interpreters.

The great chemist Antoine Lavoisier, in seeking an explanatory interpretation of the phenomena of combustion, calcination, and respiration, previously conceptualized in terms of the removal of phlogiston, reconceived these phenomena by thinking of them as involving the absorption of oxygen (Thagard 39–47). By doing so he was able to construct a better explanatory interpretation of the phenomena – better because it was both more coherent (being consistent with the gain of weight during calcination and combustion) and more comprehensive (applying also to phenomena such as the effervescence of metals when placed in acids).

Donald Davidson gives another example in which an interpreter reconceives the object of interpretation.

> If you see a ketch sailing by and your companion says, "Look at that handsome yawl," you may be faced with a problem of interpretation. One natural possibility is that your friend has mistaken a ketch for a yawl, and has formed a false belief. But if his vision is good and his line of sight favourable it is even more plausible that he does not use the word "yawl" quite as you do, and has made no mistake at all about the position of the jigger on the passing yacht. We do this sort of off the cuff interpretation all the time, deciding in favour of reinterpretation of words in order to preserve a reasonable theory of belief. (Davidson 196)

I take it that in this example you start off by conceiving the object of interpretation (your friend's utterance) as having been produced by a standard meaning-rule and a peculiar belief about the kind of yacht that is passing by. Because (for reasons to do with interpretive charity) the object thus conceived resists explanatory interpretation, you reconceive it as the product of a nonstandard meaning-rule together with a reasonable belief about the kind of yacht that can be seen by you and your friend. The substitute object is susceptible to an explanatory interpretation.

It's noteworthy that Davidson's description is in a certain respect value free. He is not saying that you as interpreter attribute to your companion an *imperfect grasp* of the meaning of the word "yawl." You are supposed to think merely that your friend's use of the word is *different* from yours, not that your usage is an idealization of your friend's. Nor is there any supposition on the interpreter's part that the reconceived object has *changed* into the initial object. It's just that sense can be made of the reconceived object more readily than of the initial object.

In both these examples, the interpreter's reason for substituting a reconceived object is the same: the object-as-represented, unlike the original, can be brought under the chosen interpretive scheme. The object of interpretation's extension is (pretty much) left unchanged in this representation, while its intension is altered in favour of an intension that readily accommodates the interpretive scheme. As in our examples of idealization and resegmentation, this strategy solves the problem of linking the original object to the proposed scheme, by interposing between object and scheme a substitute object that, unlike the original, accommodates the type of significance implicit in the proposed scheme while preserving the original object's features to the maximum degree possible in the context.

Recovery

Sometimes the interpretive substitution of one object for another takes the form of recovering a latent object, of which the initially given object is postulated as being a transformation. Here there are three terms: the latent object, the manifest object (to use the Freudian expressions [Freud Chap. 4]), and the transformation. While foreswearing any pretension to either exclusiveness or exhaustiveness, I shall consider three types of recovery – the recovery of origins, of intentions, and of substrata.

Origins

Historians know that texts and other artifacts undergo transformations over time, by way of damage from the weather, natural deterioration through aging, inaccurate copying by editors, or distortion at the hands of censors. Because such transformations are possible, there can be an epistemic question of discovering or hypothesizing an origin from which the artifact came. There may also be a practical question of restoring the artifact to its original state. Sometimes the practical question is subsequent to the epistemic one: only when the original plans have been discovered can the building be restored. But sometimes the epistemic question is subsequent to the practical one: only after the painting has been restored can we know what its original appearance was.

Interpreters raise these questions if they believe that the proper interpretation of an artifact depends on the discovery or recovery of its origin. In the persona of such interpreters, David Carrier poses the question: "Unless the artwork we see has been successfully conserved, how can we accurately interpret it?" (85). The idea is that, for purposes of aesthetic interpretation, we must move beyond the object as presented and regain access to the artifact's original state.

We will find such interpretive substitutions reasonable to the extent that while we find it hard to apply the given interpretive scheme to the manifest object, we can readily apply that scheme at one remove, namely, to the restored or recovered original object. Again this process is subject to a dual constraint. On one side, the latent object must fit the proposed scheme; on the other, it must represent the manifest object as faithfully as possible in the context – a context that here includes the supposed transformation of the latent into the manifest object. That transformation obviously limits the extent to which the manifest will faithfully represent the latent object. If we are speaking of the recovery of origins, and if the transformations in question include departures from that origin or accretions to it, then these transformations serve to explain why the manifest object cannot faithfully represent the latent in certain respects.

Intentions

The interpretive ascription of intentions is especially important to us folk because it is how we standardly make sense of actions within a framework of folk psychology. Interpreters sometimes correct imperfections they notice in the execution of actions they are interpreting. In this way they effectively substitute an intended action for the action as actually executed.

Let's go back to Richter's Sofia recital. We earlier considered an interpretation that took the performance's imperfections to be unimportant in a context where the significance of the occasion was seen as historic, both in terms of the appearance of a new super-pianist and in terms of the rehabilitation of a forgotten work. But there is a far simpler interpretive context that would take the performance's imperfections to be unimportant. I mean a context in which the significance that is assigned to the event is simply that of being a performance of Moussorgsky's *Pictures at an Exhibition*. In such a context, what is relevant is what Richter intended to play; and, Richter being Richter, we know that even if there are occasional discrepancies between what he intended and what he played, by and large the two are identical. Thus, the imaginative substitution of Richter's intended performance for his actual performance, while not making a huge difference, will make some difference. This difference, however, will be important to any listeners who have scruples about whether a purported performance that doesn't fully comply with the work's directives is really a performance of that work. For such listeners, it would be possible to *interpret* the actual performance as a performance of a Moussorgsky work, by imaginatively substituting the intended performance for the actual one. (Listeners who operate with a more liberal conception of the relation between performance and work can regard it as obvious, and not a matter for interpretation, that Richter was performing the Moussorgsky piece.)

To substitute an imputed intention for the executed act is again to engage in a process of substituting an object-as-represented for a manifest object; and this substitution is again subject to the dual constraints of fitting the proposed scheme while representing the manifest object as faithfully as possible. The degree of fidelity that is possible in the context is limited by the supposition that the execution of an intention may not accurately represent the intention because of various types of slip.

If an intentionalist interpretation is to function not just as an interpretation but as an explanation, two conditions must be met: the imputed intention must have existed, and differences between the executed action and the intention must be accounted for by processes of unsuccessful implementation. Our imputation of an intention to Richter would function as an explanation of what we hear, if independent confirmation could be found for imputing nerves, or sweaty fingers, to the great pianist, and for believing that a nervous pianist, or one with sweaty fingers, would make the sort of slips that Richter actually made.

Substrata
Beneath one action, another may lie. The window-cleaners may be spies. If you have ever thought so, you will be familiar with the idea that agents may dissimulate, and with the idea that interpreters may uncover such dissimulation.

Freud thought of dreams in this kind of way. Dream interpretation is, according to him, a two-stage process. First, the apparent object of interpretation (the manifest object) is read as concealing another (latent) object, from which it has been formed by processes of distortion and repression. Second, the latent object thus uncovered is interpreted as the fulfillment of a wish. In one of Freud's examples, a mother dreams that her fifteen-year-old daughter lies dead in what the mother calls a "case." In light of word associations that the mother makes, Freud interprets the dream thus:

> The child lying in the case meant an embryo in the womb. After being enlightened up to this point, she no longer denied that the dream-picture corresponded to a wish of hers. Like so many young married women, she had been far from pleased when she became pregnant; and more than once she had allowed herself to wish that the child in her womb might die. (Freud 237–38)

The image of the child dead in a case is a distortion of an underlying image – that of the child dead in the womb. And the latter image is interpreted as representing the fulfillment of the mother's wish – fifteen years earlier – that the child would die in her womb.

Not only is the manifest object of interpretation a distortion of the latent object; it is in Freud's eyes a distortion made by the dreamer herself, though not consciously. The imputed transformation is supposed to be an unconscious masking of the latent object which the dreamer makes by way of resisting acknowledgement of the wish whose fulfillment that object represents. Freud calls this action a dissimulation (Freud 222) and describes it like this:

> In cases where the wish-fulfillment . . . has been disguised, there must have existed some inclination to put up a defence against the wish; and owing to this defence the wish was unable to express itself except in a distorted shape. (Freud 223)

Freud's substitution of the latent for the manifest dream-content is again subject to the dual constraints that govern interpretive substitution of a latent for a manifest object. The latent object must fit the proposed scheme "wish fulfillment," and it must remain as faithful as possible to the manifest object in the context. But the context includes supposed distortion and repression of the latent object, and these transformations obviously limit the extent to which fidelity is possible.

A skeptic might comment that this type of interpretive substitution could be used to interpret anything at all under a given interpretive scheme. If I want to interpret O_1 as S, and, whereas O_1 cannot be readily so interpreted, O_2 can be so interpreted, then all I have to do is to regard O_2 as the proper object of interpretation and postulate a masking transformation of O_2 into O_1. I can interpret the window-cleaners' activity as masking their true identity as spies, provided that I can think up a story about who put them up to it.

We might answer the skeptic by admitting that anything can indeed be interpreted as falling under a given scheme. At the same time, the skeptic should be reminded that interpretations postulating arbitrary substrata will be entirely fanciful unless some independent confirmation can be found for the existence of the substrate O_2 and for its masking transformation into O_1. In responding thus, we would be taking a broad view of what can count as an interpretation, including fanciful as well as nonfanciful interpretations.

If Freudian dream interpretation is to be other than fanciful, then there will have to be some independent evidence supporting the existence of the underlying wish and of the masking that the interpreter postulates. Without such evidence the Freudian construal of dreams could (on a broad view) still be counted as interpretation, though it would at best have the character of a conjecture or an imaginative construction. If the best evidence that can be found is that the postulation of a masked underlying wish makes sense of the manifest object, then the interpretation might for all we know have the same standing as an interpretation that makes sense of the manifest object by attributing the object's transformation to the operation of supernatural forces. To postulate something that, if it existed, would make sense of the object is not the same as to be in possession of evidence that the postulated entity actually exists.

The situation might be compared with the proposal in Plato's *Meno* to make sense of the existence of a priori knowledge by postulating a doctrine of recollection of knowledge from a previous existence. If we have no independent evidence for that previous existence, or if we do but we have no independent evidence for the occurrence of amnesia at birth, then the doctrine of *anamnesis* cannot function as an explanation of the existence of a priori knowledge.

In the case of the mother's dream of her daughter lying dead in a case, there was independent evidence that the underlying wish existed. The mother acknowledged that during pregnancy she had experienced this wish. But is there evidence for her having unconsciously masked the existence of the wish by distorting the latent object into the manifest object? It is certainly clear that it would have been *rational* for the mother to conceal her wish. And it is clear that her old wish had been (in Freud's words) "put aside." What is lacking is any independent evidence that the underlying wish was masked by the process of distortion that Freud hypothesizes. To that extent, a question remains about whether Freud's interpretation of the mother's dream qualifies as an explanation.

Even if it doesn't count as a successful explanation of the mother's dream, Freud's interpretation may still be a successful interpretation of another sort. It's important to remember in this context that the point of the dreamer's visit to the psychoanalyst may not have been simply to arrive at an explanatory interpretation of her dream. It may have included a desire for a therapeutic reinterpretation of a wider set of her personal narratives. And the success-conditions for such a therapeutic reinterpretation may not coincide with the success-conditions for explanations.

Conclusion

Interpretive practices of idealization, resegmentation, reconception, and recovery of origins, intentions, and substrata do occur. Taken together, they betoken an idea of interpretation as a three-term process involving an object, an object-as-represented, and the fitting of the object-as-represented to an interpretive scheme or vice versa. A rational account can be given of these interpretive practices, as long as the interpretive representation meets two constraints: it must preserve what can be preserved of the object's features in the context, and it must fit the interpretive scheme.

To the extent that such an account can be given, idealization, resegmentation, reconception, and recovery of an underlying object cannot be fairly portrayed as instances of a failure of concentration. Nor can they be portrayed as dishonest practices. On the contrary, interpreters who employ these practices can be frank about doing so without compromising the success of their activity. Fanning didn't try to hide the fact that he was idealizing. Freud didn't try to conceal the fact that he was delving beneath the manifest object. Thus the prereflective view of changing the subject, according to which it issues from either a failure of concentration or a type of dishonesty, does not apply to the interpretive practices we have discussed. Interpretation's use of topic-altering practices in no way detracts from its intellectual respectability.

In saying that a rational account can be given of these practices, I mean that appropriate constraints can be stated and that in the cases discussed these conditions appear to be met. I do not mean that every instance of these practices satisfies the relevant constraints. Clearly, idealization is sometimes done ineptly. Plato's image of the incompetent butcher makes the point that resegmentation may be mismanaged. The very existence of the phlogiston theory shows that conceptions can be misconceptions. Conjectures about origins, intentions, and substrata are on occasion delusory.

A further question remains. A statement of relevance-conditions makes clear what is required in order for the representation to provide a link between object and scheme; but that still leaves us with the question of whether it would be good interpretive practice for the interpreter to apply the given interpretive scheme to the given object at all. It's hard to think of anything other than a pragmatic answer to this further question. We know that Lavoisier was justified in seeking a better explanation of the phenomena, because the phlogiston theory is evidently inadequate. And we know that Lavoisier actually produced a better theory, so of course it was good interpretive practice for him to apply his theory to the phenomena. We may conclude cautiously that in some cases at least, not only do we know what relevance-condition would be appropriate to link a given scheme with a given object, but we also know that it would be good interpretive practice to link that scheme with that object.

It would be a mistake to think that idealization and the other interpretive practices I have discussed are unusual or marginal. On the contrary, some ways of "changing the subject" are intrinsic to interpretation. These include resegmentation and reconception. It is commonly accepted that all interpretation aims to make *comprehensive* sense of its object. If this is so, then interpreters always have to consider the object's segmentation: comprehensiveness will be compromised if the object is not appropriately segmented. Equally, the reconception of the object always has to be considered by the interpreter, seeing that the whole objective of interpretation is to subsume the object comprehensively under an interpretive scheme, and that only certain ways of conceiving the object will allow it to be subsumed under the given scheme.

Finally, both idealization and the recovery of an underlying object, while they are not intrinsic to all interpretation in the way that resegmentation and reconception are, are widespread interpretive strategies. Moreover, these strategies are universal within certain types of interpretation. Idealization is the universal practice in empirical sciences such as mechanics and chemistry. And the recovery of an underlying object is the

universal aim in certain types of interpretation, including historical interpretation, intentionalist interpretations of behaviour and of artworks, and
metaphysical and psychoanalytic interpretation.

References

Aristotle. (1930). *Physics*. Translated by R. P. Hardie and R. K. Gaye. In
The Works of Aristotle, vol. 2, edited by W. D. Ross. Oxford: Clarendon
Press.

Carrier, David. (1992). "Conservation and Restoration." In *A Companion
to Aesthetics*, edited by David Cooper. Oxford: Blackwell.

Davidson, Donald. (1984). "On the Very Idea of a Conceptual Scheme." In
Inquiries into Truth and Interpretation. Oxford: Clarendon Press.

Fanning, David. (1998). "Search for Inner Truths." In liner notes to *Great
Pianists of the 20th Century*, vol. 82: Sviatoslav Richter. Philips 456
946–2.

Freud, Sigmund. (1991). *The Interpretation of Dreams*. Translated by
James Strachey. London: Penguin Books.

Plato. (1952). *Phaedrus*. Translated by R. Hackforth. In *Plato's Phaedrus*.
Translated with Introduction and Commentary. Cambridge: Cambridge
University Press.

Provan, Iain. (1998). "The Historical Books of the Old Testament." In *The
Cambridge Companion to Biblical Interpretation*, edited by John
Barton, Cambridge: Cambridge University Press.

Thagard, Paul. (1992). *Conceptual Revolutions*. Princeton, NJ: Princeton
University Press.

6

INTERPRETATION AND INTENTION: THE DEBATE BETWEEN HYPOTHETICAL AND ACTUAL INTENTIONALISM

NOËL CARROLL.

Regarded for decades as a fallacy, intentionalist interpretation is beginning to attract a following among philosophers of art (Carroll 1992, 1993, 1997; Iseminger 1992, 1996, 1998; Livingston 1998). Broadly speaking, intentionalism is the doctrine that the actual intentions of artists are relevant to the interpretation of the artworks they create. For intentionalists, interpretation is a matter of explaining why artworks have the features, including meanings, that they possess. Since artworks possess these features as a result of the actions of artists, it seems natural to explain them, as we explain the results of actions in general, with an eye to the intentions of the pertinent agents, who are, in this case, artists.

Actual intentionalism holds to the conviction that interpretation with respect to artworks is on a continuum with interpretation of intentional action in daily life. Just as in ordinary affairs we interpret with the goal of identifying the actual intentions of the words and deeds of others, so with respect to art the actual intentions of artists are relevant to our interpretations of their productions.

Actual intentionalism, however, comes in different forms. The most extreme form maintains that the meaning of an artwork is fully determined by the actual intentions of the artist (or artists) who created it (Knapp and Michaels 1982).[1] It is this extreme form of actual intentionalism that one suspects has encouraged the view that actual intentionalism is a fallacy. For this view leads to the unpalatable conclusion that the meaning of an artwork is whatever the author intends it to mean, irrespective, if we are talking about literary texts, of the word-sequence meaning of the text (the meaning of the text derivable solely by consulting dictionaries, the rules of grammar, and the conventions of literature). This variant of actual intentionalism is clearly unacceptable, since it leads to what has been called "Humpty-Dumpty-ism": the idea that an author could make a work mean

[1]   This view is criticized in Wilson 1992.

anything simply because he wills it so – as Humpty Dumpty tries to do when he says to Alice that "glory" means "there's a knockdown argument" (Iseminger 1996). Or, to advert to nonverbal art, this view would, according to Monroe Beardsley, compel us to regard a blue sculpture as pink simply because the artist says it is (Beardsley 1981, 20).

But extreme actual intentionalism is not the only sort of intentionalism abroad today, nor is it the form of actual intentionalism to be defended here. For convenience, we can call the form of actual intentionalism to be discussed "modest actual intentionalism." In contrast to extreme intentionalism, modest actual intentionalism does not hold that the correct interpretation of an artwork is fully determined by what the artist intended. Rather, modest actual intentionalism only claims that the artist's actual intentions are relevant to interpretation. Specifically, the artist's actual intentions constrain our interpretations of artworks. With reference to literary texts, the modest actual intentionalist argues that the correct interpretation of a text is the meaning of the text that is compatible with the author's actual intention (Iseminger 1996).

Modest actual intentionalism blocks Humpty-Dumpty-ism because even if Humpty Dumpty intends "glory" to mean "knockdown argument," that is not a meaning that the textual unit ("glory") can have. The intentions of authors that the modest actual intentionalist takes seriously are only those intentions of the author that the linguistic/literary unit can support (given the conventions of language and literature). But where the linguistic unit can support more than one possible meaning, the modest actual intentionalist maintains that the correct interpretation is the one that is compatible with the author's actual intention, which itself must be supportable by the language of the text.

For example, if one utters "the fish is on the bank" and intends by that to say that the fish is on the shore, and not that it is on the steps of the Citicorp Building, then the meaning of the utterance, for the modest actual intentionalist, is "the fish is on the shore." Attributions of meaning, according to the modest actual intentionalist, must be constrained not only by what possible senses the text can support (given the conventions of language and literature), but also by our best information about the actual intended meaning of the utterer or author in question. Thus, if a given story could support either the interpretation that ghosts are wreaking havoc or only that the relevant fictional characters in the story believe that ghosts are wreaking havoc *and* it is known that the author intended the story to affirm that ghosts are wreaking havoc, the modest actual intentionalist maintains that the correct interpretation of the text is that the ghosts are wreaking havoc.[2] For the modest actual intentionalist, the author's intention here must square with what he has written, but if it squares with what he has written, then the author's intention is authoritative.

[2] This example is adapted from Livingston 1998, 841–44.

One common complaint about all forms of actual intentionalism is that they divert the audience away from the proper object of its attention. Instead of focusing on the text, intentionalism sends the reader outside the text, searching for the author's intention – perhaps in the archive where his private papers are stored. This criticism, however, is misguided here, since the modest actual intentionalist freely admits that the best evidence for what an utterer, artist, or author intends to say or mean is the utterance or artwork itself. Modest actual intentionalism is not an injunction to root for authorial meaning in hidden places. Generally, we find authorial intention expressed in the artworks in question.

Most of our interpretive endeavors, even if we are actual intentionalists, are aimed at the text. The point of actual intentionalism of the modest variety is the recovery of the intentions, conscious and otherwise, of utterers and artists, but this is consistent with close attention to the text. In fact, for the modest actual intentionalist, close interpretive attention to the text is just the pursuit of the actual intentions of the artist; it is an error to think of close attention to the text and the search for actual intentions as opposed enterprises. Moreover, the modest actual intentionalist also requires that putative authorial intentions be shown to square with what is written. So the worry that modest actual intentionalism is at variance with a textually attentive reading is groundless.

In a related vein, actual intentionalism is also frequently dismissed because it allegedly commits the fallacy of paraphrase. The actual intentionalist, it might be said, behaves as though what we really want from criticism is merely what the author intends to say. But were that so, couldn't we just e-mail her for a succinct statement of her message? Why plow through hundreds of pages of a largish novel, if all we are after is her view that money corrupts? But, of course, we value the experience of navigating our way through the novel, and we would not trade it for a compact restatement of what the novelist intended to communicate by means of it. Thus, if actual intentionalism implies that all we care about is identifying the author's intended message, then it is charged that actual intentionalism woefully mischaracterizes what concerns us in reading literature.

But there is no reason to suppose that the aim of modest actual intentionalism is to substitute a paraphrase of the author's intentions for the reading of the text. Rather, the actual intentionalist is interested in the author's intentions because they will enrich the reading of the text. Grasping the author's intentions puts us in a position to appreciate the author's inventiveness (or lack thereof) in structuring the text. The aim of the modest actual intentionalist is not primarily to return home with a paraphrase of the author's intention as pithy as a Chinese fortune cookie, but to use the author's intended meaning as a resource for engaging the text. Thus, the actual intentionalist need not commit the fallacy of paraphrase. Moreover, since engaging the text is itself importantly a process of identifying the author's actual intentions, once again we see that modest

actual intentionalism is consistent with the reader's absorption in the text
and need not represent a romp outside it.

So far we have been defending modest actual intentionalism from some
of the objections leveled at it by anti-intentionalists (those for whom reference to artistic intentions commits some sort of fallacy). And, in truth,
much of the energy of actual intentionalists in the past has been spent in
neutralizing the criticisms of anti-intentionalism. But in recent years
another threat to actual intentionalism has taken shape. Called hypothetical
intentionalism or, sometimes, postulated authorism, this view maintains
that the correct interpretation or meaning of an artwork is constrained not
by the actual intentions of authors (compatible with what they wrote), but
by the best hypotheses available about what they intended.

According to the hypothetical intentionalist, the meaning of a text is
what an ideal reader, fully informed about the cultural background of the
text, the *oeuvre* of the author, the publicly available information about the
text and the author, and the text itself, would hypothesize the intended
meaning of the text to be (Tolhurst 1979; Nehamas 1981, 1987; Levinson
1996). That is, the hypothetical intentionalist claims that the meaning of
the text correlates with the hypothesized intention, not the real intention,
of the author, and that interpreters are concerned with postulated authors,
not real authors.

Epistemologically, what this comes down to is that the hypothetical
intentionalist permits the interpreter to use all the sorts of information
publicly available to the intended, appropriate reader of a text, while
debarring information not publicly available to said reader, such as interviews with the artist as well as his or her private papers. Since modest
actual intentionalism is open to the circumspective use of such information, this is where hypothetical intentionalism and modest actual intentionalism part company most dramatically.

With regard to literary texts, the hypothetical intentionalist argues that
the meaning of the text is either the meaning of the word sequences in the
text, the speaker's meaning, or the utterance meaning. The meaning
cannot be word-sequence meaning for a number of reasons, including the
phenomenon of irony. The meaning cannot be speaker's meaning, because
this would not allow for the fact that sometimes authors fail to mean by a
text what they intend to mean by it; to suppose that the meaning of the text
in such cases is speaker's meaning would be tantamount to a reversion to
Humpty-Dumpty-ism. That leaves utterance meaning as the meaning of
the text – the meaning of the text that an ideally informed reader would
attribute to the text given the context of utterance.

Utterance meaning, inasmuch as it is a speech act, requires intentions,
but the intention in question is a hypothesized intention. It may not be the
author's genuine intention, but only, in context, the most plausibly hypothesized intention thereof. Such intentions require authors, but the author is
a postulated or constructed author, that is, the author we infer in order to

explain the features of the text – where our inferences (or postulations or constructions) are based not only on the language of the text, but also on information about the genre of the text, the author's past work, and what is publicly available concerning the author's career. Determining the meaning of an utterance on a particular occasion requires more than knowledge about the dictionary meanings of the words used to make the utterance. It requires knowledge of the context of the utterance, including certain knowledge about the speaker.

By modeling literary meaning on utterance meaning, the hypothetical intentionalist acknowledges the relevance of context, bidding the ideal interpreter to heed not only word-sequence meaning, but also all the relevant contextual information, including knowledge about the art-historical context, about the genre in question, about the author's past works, and, in addition, common, publicly available information about the life of the artist (for example, that he was a freedom fighter or is a Republican). The relevant intention for purposes of interpretation is the one that the fully informed, ideal reader would hypothesize on the basis of such knowledge (while, at the same time, ignoring the author's private pronouncements about his intentions).

For example, in the concluding pages of *The Ground beneath Her Feet*, Salman Rushdie writes of the assassination of a *rai* singer who has gone into exile to escape a worldwide plot to "wipe out singing altogether." Since "Rai" is also the name of the fictional narrator of the book and since it is widely known that Rushdie himself had to go into hiding in order to evade the vengeance of fanatics, the hypothetical intentionalist, considering the language of the text and Rushdie's public biography, can plausibly hypothesize that the passage is an allusion to Rushdie's own experience.

Obviously the hypothetical intentionalist and the modest actual intentionalist appeal to much of the same evidence. Since the modest actual intentionalist is committed to discerning the author's actual intentions, he too relies on word-sequence meaning, context, the author's *oeuvre*, the author's public biography, and so on, in order to arrive at an interpretation. Thus, since the hypothetical intentionalist and the modest actual intentionalist depend on much the same evidence, they generally deliver the same interpretations.[3] However, there are imaginable cases where the results of the two methods will diverge.

---

[3]   There is, however, this difference between the evidence countenanced by the hypothetical intentionalist and that to which the modest actual intentionalist is open: the hypothetical intentionalist will not use nonpublic authorial statements of intent (as found in diaries, journals, correspondence, and the like) as grounds for his hypotheses, whereas the modest actual intentionalist will permit the cautious use of such information. Ultimately, it seems, the hypothetical intentionalist defends this limitation on the evidence on the grounds that it does not reflect our interpretive practices. In response, I will argue later that as an empirical conjecture about our practices, this is false.

Suppose I utter "The fish is on the bank" while standing on the steps of the Citicorp Building with a large trout clearly in view behind me. Here, the ideal listener will interpret the utterance as "The fish is on the financial institution." On the other hand, if the actual intentionalist learns from me that what I truly intended by my utterance was "The fish is on the shore," then the actual intentionalist will endorse that as the interpretation of the meaning of my utterance. For that *is* the intended meaning of my utterance, which is, furthermore, compatible with what I said. The hypothetical intentionalist maintains that the meaning of the utterance is the one best warranted given the context of utterance without authorial pronouncements, but the actual intentionalist argues that even the hypothesis best warranted on those grounds can be false.

What putatively recommends hypothetical intentionalism over actual intentionalism? The hypothetical intentionalist raises two considerations. The first reason is one we have already encountered: that approaches like actual intentionalism have no way to accommodate the fact that authors can fail to communicate what they intend, and that modest actual intentionalism has no way of dealing with this fact. The second consideration is more complex. It is that hypothetical intentionalism does a better job of reflecting our actual interpretive practices than does modest actual intentionalism. Jerrold Levinson writes that hypothetical intentionalism

> acknowledges the special interests, and attendant constraints of the practice or activity of *literary* communication, according to which works – provided they are interpreted with maximal attention to relevant author-specific context ... – are ultimately more important than, and distinct from, the individuals who author them and those individuals' inner lives; works of literature thus retain, in the last analysis, a certain autonomy from the mental processes of their creators during composition at least as far as resultant meaning is concerned. It is this small but crucial dimension of distinctness between agent's meaning and work's meaning ... which is obliterated by actual intentionalism but safeguarded by the hypothetical variety. (Levinson 1996, 194)

These are significant objections. However, before returning to them, I will begin to sketch the case for modest actual intentionalism against hypothetical intentionalism.

Whereas hypothetical intentionalism claims that literary interpretation and everyday interpretation are distinct, modest actual intentionalism argues that they are importantly continuous practices. Outside the literary and artistic contexts, we generally interpret utterances, gestures, and other forms of symbolic behavior with an eye to retrieving authorial intentions. Modest actual intentionalism takes literary and artistic interpretation to be on a par with ordinary interpretation.

The hypothetical intentionalist maintains that literary and artistic practices are discontinuous with our ordinary practices and says that, in consequence, our interpretations have different aims. In the ordinary course of events, the hypothetical intentionalist concedes, our interpretations aspire to discover actual intentions, but in literary and artistic contexts, hypothesized intentions, as postulated by ideal readers, suffice.

But why suppose that there is a discontinuity between ordinary interpretation and artistic interpretation? Interpretation is part and parcel of human life. We fall back on it in order to conduct our social life with conspecifics and for strategic purposes when confronting predators, prey, and human friends and enemies. Some interpretive powers are probably biologically innate, naturally selected for adaptiveness, while many others are refined and developed through enculturation where they are also ineliminably adaptive. However, these interpretive skills are all aimed at detecting the actual intentions and/or behavioral dispositions of conspecifics, predators, prey, and the like. Interpretive skills, as adaptive endowments, would make little sense otherwise. That is why our interpretive powers were and are keyed to discerning actual intentions.

The arts themselves are, among other things, celebrations of our human powers. Like the dancer, we walk, run, and leap – and sometimes we execute fancy footwork to avoid an oncoming bicycle or to scoot to the head of the line. Dancers interest us because they display these capacities (and more) at particularly high levels of accomplishment. They show us what human grace can be not only so that we can compare what they do with what we do (and, perhaps, garner some tips from them), but also so that we can contemplate the possibilities of common human powers. Since we all communicate and express ourselves through word and gesture, we admire poets, singers, and actors who exhibit human expressive possibilities operating at full throttle.

Moreover, in a similar vein, I would like to suggest that we are interested in literary and artistic interpretations because they too exemplify highly developed skills that we all deploy constantly in our everyday commerce with our conspecifics and with their communicative and expressive behaviour. And those skills, at base, are dedicated to detecting the actual intentions of our conspecifics.

Thus, the modest actual intentionalist sees literary and artistic interpretation on a continuum with ordinary interpretive practices, which are aimed at tracking actual intentions. Certainly, even the hypothetical intentionalist must agree that our practices of literary and artistic interpretation evolved from our practices of everyday interpretation – which practices, needless to say, function to detect actual intentions. Of course, the hypothetical intentionalist may claim that artistic and literary interpretation has become detached from the practices that gave rise to it. But that conjecture itself raises a number of questions.

The first question is: Why did the practices of literary and artistic interpretation become detached from the ordinary practices of interpretation? What new purposes are served that supersede the natural purposes of ordinary interpretation? Hypothetical intentionalists have not been very forthcoming about this matter. It cannot be that pursuing hypothetical intentions is more pleasurable than pursuing actual intentions, since both approaches employ much the same methodology. Sometimes, in this context, it is said that we value the activity of literary and artistic interpretation for its own sake. But that hardly seems to be an explanation; rather, it sounds like an evasion. And, as we shall see later, many literary interpreters would appear ready to resist the claims that they engage in exegesis for its own sake rather than for the sake of recovering authorial intentions.

Second, the hypothetical intentionalist is in an extremely poor position to claim that artistic and literary interpretations aim at different purposes than ordinary interpretation – for the simple reason that the interpretive considerations that the hypothetical intentionalist recommends are roughly the same as those the modest actual intentionalist recommends: attention to the text, to the author's *oeuvre*, to the culture context, to the author's publicly available biography, and so on.

Why are these the desiderata that the modest actual intentionalist emphasizes? Because they are the sorts of things that provide a reliable indication of the author's actual intentions. Attention to these factors is what enables us to track the author's actual intentions. Thus, the very methodology of hypothetical intentionalism seems predicated upon tracking actual authorial intention. Indeed, why else would it select precisely the desiderata it does? Consequently, it does not seem that hypothetical intentionalism is calibrated to satisfy different aims than is actual intentionalism, and, therefore, it does not seem to make much sense to claim that it serves a different purpose than does actual intentionalism – which purpose, of course, is identifying the actual intentions of the author, not merely his or her plausibly hypothesized intentions.

Hypothetical intentionalism identifies the correct interpretation with whatever the ideal reader identifies as the author's hypothetical intention, whereas modest actual intentionalism goes with the author's actual intention (where it is supported by the text), should that diverge from what the ideal reader hypothesizes. However, it is somewhat perplexing that hypothetical intentionalism recommends going with the ideal reader's hypothesis, since the methodology of hypothetical intentionalism is itself designed to track the author's actual intention.

Consider an analogy. We employ scientific method in order to approximate the truth. Were we to discover that our best scientific hypothesis were false – that something else were the case – would we stick with a methodologically sound but false hypothesis, or would we go with what we knew to be true? Clearly, the very aims of science would recommend that we live with the truth. Similarly, where actual intentionalism and hypothetical intentionalism diverge in their results, given the comparable aims of their methodologies, why would we stick with the results of the hypothetical intentionalist's interpretation when a true account of an author's actual intention is available?

As already observed, the desiderata the hypothetical intentionalist respects are all designed to deliver our best approximation of the author's actual intention. Thus, if we establish the author's intention by means unavailable to the hypothetical intentionalist – perhaps through the discovery of the author's notebook – isn't that the result that we should care about? Otherwise, we appear to be fetishizing our method over what the method is designed to secure.

I submit that we respect the interpretive protocols the hypothetical intentionalist cherishes because they are reliable indicators of actual intentions. The hypothetical intentionalist provides no other reasons for our acceptance of just the sorts of information he emphasizes. It is true that the hypothetical intentionalist's protocols yield hypotheses about authorial intentions, but they are plausible hypotheses about actual intentions, not hypotheses about plausible possible intentions.

The method of hypothetical intentionalism is parasitic on the aims of actual intentionalism. That is, we attend to the things to which the hypothetical intentionalist adverts because interpretation, or at least intentionalist interpretation, aims at recovering actual intentions. That is what our interpretive practices are designed to track. If those generally reliable methods are sometimes supplemented by other creditable resources – such as the author's correspondence – why should those further resources be ignored, if they supply a more effective means to our ends?

Recall that the modest actual intentionalist is not using this evidence to claim that a text means something that the written text fails to support. He employs the author's intention to fix a meaning to the text that the text could have. He simply goes beyond the evidence permitted by the method of hypothetical intentionalism – a method that is, admittedly, quite warranted. But as in science, even a well-justified methodology can fail to zero in on the truth.

Here the hypothetical intentionalist may wish to dispute the analogy with science. A realist epistemology makes sense in science, he might say, because there is a fact of the matter that is independent of the best-warranted theories. But with respect to literature, it is claimed, there is no difference between our best interpretation of the text and the meaning of the text. But this claim appears to be either false or question-begging.

It seems false, since it is eminently conceivable that our best interpretation of a text from a remote ancient civilization could diverge from the utterance meaning of the text. But if the hypothetical intentionalist responds that there can be no gap because our best hypothesis, following his protocols of interpretation, *is* the meaning of the text, then all he has done is to reaffirm the claims of hypothetical intentionalism.

In effect, what the hypothetical intentionalist has done is to substitute the notion of warranted assertibility for truth when it comes to literary interpretation. But since we need not accept this relativizing move with respect to other forms of inquiry, it is not evident that we need to make it with respect to literary texts and artworks. We are interested in warranted assertions because they generally track truth. Thus, we are interested in warranted assertions (justifiable hypotheses) about authorial intentions because they are good indications of actual authorial intentions. So, if we come upon the author's actual intention, even if it departs from our best theory of it, then that is what we should prefer. Though Sir Richard Burton's criticisms of John Hanning Speke may have been methodologically sound, nevertheless it is to Speke that we owe the discovery of the headwaters of the Nile.

Hypothetical intentionalists may attempt to advance their approach by arguing that it accurately describes what literary interpreters do. They construct *hypotheses* about authorial intentions, ones that are presumably open to revision with the onset of further information. They don't pretend to be mind readers; they don't have cerebroscopes that enable them to peer into the minds of authors. Their interpretations are hypotheses, conjectures, or constructions. And, of course, the modest actual intentionalist agrees with this, but adds that they are hypotheses about actual intentions. Thus, when literary interpreters explore texts by considering not only their language, but also their historical context, the author's *oeuvre*, the author's public biography, and the like, they are behaving exactly in the way that the modest actual intentionalist predicts. Their behavior in regard to what they typically view as their primary data base does not favor hypothetical intentionalism over modest actual intentionalism.

The book reviewer interpreting a new novel looks in all the places the hypothetical intentionalist advises and comes up with a hypothesis, rather than hiring a private detective to rifle through the author's trash for secret statements of intention. But this is a hypothesis about the author's actual intention, not about some theoretical fiction that might be called a hypothetical or constructed or postulated intention.

Reading in accordance with the protocols of hypothetical intentionalism is simply reading for actual intentions, as the hypothetical intentionalist himself admits. However, the hypothetical intentionalist regards this search for actual authorial intent as a "heuristic" (Levinson 1996, 200). And yet if hypothetical intentionalism is supposed to reflect our actual practices of interpretations, it must be noted that many pedigreed interpreters do not act as though they regard the goal of determining actual authorial intention as merely heuristic. They appear to regard it as their final goal.

Some hypothetical intentionalists speak of postulated authors rather than hypothesized intentions. The aim of interpretation on this view is to construct the most plausible author of the text, according to the interpretive protocols of hypothetical intentionalism, in order to explain why the text has the features it has. This author-construction, the postulated author

– a sort of theoretical entity – is the object of criticism, not the actual writer who composed the text. But it is difficult to see how this theoretical construct could really explain the features of a text, since this theoretical construct could not have causally influenced the text in any way (Stecker 1987, 266).

Of course, if the postulated author is to be understood as some kind of theoretical entity or construction, then it is important to remember that theoretical entities in science are designed to approximate real processes, not hypothetical processes. That is, they are hypotheses about actual processes, not hypotheses about hypothetical processes – otherwise, they would not possess genuine explanatory power. And, given this, in science we ultimately prefer the truth to postulations that are merely well warranted. Similarly, with respect to interpretation, parity of reasoning would suggest that this is why true characterizations of authorial processes should trump postulated authorial processes.

So far we have been exploring the modest actual intentionalist's reservations about hypothetical intentionalism. But now let us return to the hypothetical intentionalist's objections to modest actual intentionalism. As you may recall, they are two in number. The first charges that modest actual intentionalism has no way to deal with the fact that sometimes authors fail to realize their intentions through their texts. But though this may be an apt criticism of extreme forms of actual intentionalism, it is not a fair criticism of modest actual intentionalism.

For the modest actual intentionalist acknowledges that authors may fail to realize their intentions; this occurs when the authors fail to produce texts that support their intentions. Where the author wrote "green," but intended "black," the modest actual intentionalist will not say the text means black, since for the modest actual intentionalist meaning is not simply a function of what the author intended, but must also be supported by what the text says.

The second objection that the hypothetical intentionalist makes concerning modest actual intentionalism is doubly important, since it not only raises a potential problem for modest actual intentionalism but, in addition, suggests a way of deflecting many of the reservations that we have already expressed about hypothetical intentionalism. Many of our criticisms have been based on the observation that the methodology of hypothetical intentionalism seems on a continuum with the methodology of everyday interpretation and, consequently, that the hypothetical intentionalist, like the ordinary interpreter, should prefer the discovery of the author's actual intention (where that is consistent with the text) over our best-warranted hypothesis about it (that is, should the author's intention and the one isolated by the hypothetical intentionalist diverge).

But the hypothetical intentionalist responds that this is not the case, since the aims of literary interpretation are different in crucial ways from the aims of everyday interpretation. Thus, the modest actual intentionalist is wrong when he advances his cause by invoking a continuum between ordinary interpretation, on the one hand, and literary and artistic interpretation, on the other hand; and wrong again when he says an interpreter should prefer statements of genuine authorial intention to the best hypotheses of authorial intent. For given the nature of our literary practices – given their special interests – the hypothetical intentionalist claims that well-warranted hypotheses, derived without the benefit of authorial avowals, are, in fact, what we really care about with respect to literary communication.

For example, Jerrold Levinson writes:

> I agree that when an author proffers a text as literature to a literary audience, just as when he or she speaks to others in the ordinary setting, the author is entering a public language game, a communicative arena, but I suggest that it is one with different aims and understandings from those that apply in normal, one-on-one, or even many-on-many, conversational settings. Although in informative discourse we rightly look for intended meaning first, foremost and hindmost, in literary art we are licensed, if I am right, to consider what meanings the verbal text before us, viewed in context, *could* be being used to convey, and then to form, if we can, in accord with the practice of literary communication to which both author and reader have implicitly subscribed, our best hypothesis of what it is being used to convey, ultimately identifying that with the meaning of the work. What distinguishes our forming that hypothesis in regard to a literary work, as opposed to a piece of conversation, is that we do so for its own sake, the contextually embedded vehicle of meaning in literature being indispensable, not something to be bypassed in favor of more direct access to personal meaning when or if that is available. (Levinson 1996, 198)

That is, literary communication is a different language game than ordinary conversation, and whereas actual authorial intentions are preferred over the best hypotheses thereof in the latter, in the former we are only interested in the most plausible attribution of authorial intention. Why? Well, that's the nature of the game. (One wonders, however, why the debate over intentionalism is so intense if the rules of the game are supposedly so clear-cut).

Here the hypothetical intentionalist seems to me to be making some extremely substantial empirical claims about the nature of our literary practices. And I, at least, am not convinced that the evidence will bear out these claims. Literary reviewers give every appearance that they are concerned with the author's actual intention, not just the best-warranted hypothesis thereof. For instance, when Peter Kurth asserts, "Writing is an act of the will, she [Chu Tien-Wien] says – and, in the end, will is the only trick we have left in our bags," I take him to be claiming that this is what she actually meant, not that this is the best available hypothesis (Kurth 1999, 13). That at least is what he says. If he is questioned about it, I conjecture that Kurth would predict that Chu Tien-Wien would assent to his interpretation, and that he would be willing to revise it if she said she had something else in mind (so long as the text supported it).

The hypothetical intentionalist cannot say that Kurth prefers hypothesized intentions over actual intentions on the grounds that Kurth has not consulted the author, relying only on text and context for his interpretation, since that is generally the way of identifying actual intentions. Moreover, his writing, like the writing of the vast majority of reviewers, gives no indication that he is making an assertion about the postulated author or the most plausible hypothesis about authorial intention; rather, he appears to be making a clear-cut assertion about actual authorial intent, one that he probably thinks could be verified.

Likewise, when ordinary readers discuss the meaning of novels, they too appear to be making assertions of actual authorial intent. They, like the reviewers, seem to be unaware of the implicit rules of literary communication as alleged to hold sway by the hypothetical intentionalist. But if most are not playing by such "implicit rules," perhaps there are no such rules.

The hypothetical intentionalist may respond that at best I have offered a hypothesis about the behavior of reviewers or ordinary readers. In effect, I have just moved the battle lines back a little – from a debate about authorial intention to a debate about the intentions of literary reviewers and ordinary readers. However, since the rules of ordinary conversation should apply to the pronouncements of literary reviewers and other readers, we should perhaps be willing to poll them about whether they intend to be speaking about hypothesized authors or intentions, or are aiming at and prefer actual intentions.

Of course, among academic critics there are theoretical positions, like New Criticism and poststructuralism, that eschew the pursuit of actual authorial intentions. But the New Critics and poststructuralists should offer no comfort to hypothetical intentionalists, since they are anti-intentionalists, not hypothetical intentionalists. Nor does it seem to me that our best evidence for the nature of our literary practices should be critics with robust theories of the practice. That they practice their own methods consistently does not demonstrate that they serve as models of the practice, especially since their methodologies, outside the circle of the converted, are generally regarded as revisionist.

Furthermore, even within the precincts of academic interpretation it is not clear that the hypothetical intentionalist's implicit contract reigns. Recent debates about the interpretation of the work of Willa Cather rage over the actual Willa Cather, not some postulated author, and over what she actually, albeit unconsciously, intended. One side claims that she expressed conflicted lesbian desires, solidarity with women, and rebelliousness against the Nebraskan patriarchy (O'Brian 1987; Sedgwick 1989). The other side rejects this on biographical grounds (Acocella 1995, forthcoming). Both sides show every evidence that they are talking about the real Willa Cather, not a theoretical entity. Furthermore, both sides appeal to paraphrases of Cather's private correspondence.[4]

Moreover, as this example reminds us, much criticism today, as well as much criticism from yesteryear, involves a moral and/or a political dimension. Authors are praised and blamed for the ethical import of their work. But surely if this moral criticism is serious, it must be directed at the actual author, not the postulated author, and at what she said, not what she could be taken to have said. And since much literary and artistic interpretation comes in tandem with moral evaluation, it is hard to believe that our literary practices, as a matter of fact, always value mere hypotheses about intent over determinations of actual intent, when actual intent can be confirmed.

It may be true that readers are often satisfied with well-warranted hypotheses of intention, but that is only because their default assumption is that these interpretations are successful. There is no reason to suppose that they will not revise their thinking if they learn, perhaps through the discovery of notebooks, that the best-warranted hypothesis (one that rejects recourse to things like notebooks) failed to identify the relevant authorial intention correctly.

Suppose, for example, that we learn, through the discovery of heretofore hidden personal correspondence, that Jonathan Swift really despised the Irish and that, in addition, he had a secret passion for the taste of human flesh. Suppose, as well, he reports the pleasure he has derived from tricking do-gooders into applauding his sincere proposal about eating Irish children as irony. Finally, suppose that this evidence is so compelling that it overturns all the other evidence about Swift's opinions found in his publicly available biography. Would we continue to treat his "A Modest Proposal for Preventing the Children of the Poor People of Ireland from Being a Burden to their Parents or Country, and for Making Them Beneficial to the Public" as an example of irony?

I suspect not – partly due to the fact that our imputations of irony to the essay in the first place were primarily based on our beliefs about his *actual* biography (which we would now understand in a new light) and partly due to the fact that we would not wish to commend Swift for his opposition to prejudice if it turns out that he is really, rather, an example of that very prejudice. But if this conjecture is correct, then that suggests, with respect to our actual practices of literary interpretation, that we do not always value well-warranted hypotheses about authorial intentions over actually establishable intentions.

Indeed, there may be occasions when audiences expressly desire reports of authorial intention in order to solve their interpretive quan-

---

4   Neither side quotes directly from Cather's letters, since the Cather estate forbids it. Presumably, they would be willing to cite Cather's correspondence, were it legally permissible to do so.

daries. I remember that after the film *Stand by Me* was released in 1986, a question arose among film buffs over the meaning of the last few frames of the film. According to the fiction, the film was being narrated to us by a writer composing his story of a traumatic childhood event on a personal computer. After the story was told, he turned off the machine, but without saving what he had written. This film was made at a time when knowledge about computers was not widespread among film viewers. But some film buffs were informed, and this raised an interpretive query.

Did the fictional narrator's failure to save his text mean that, having worked through his memory, he was now prepared to let it go? That is, was it that, having exorcised the trauma, the writing had served its purpose and could be aborted? Or did the scene end that way simply because the producers of the image did not know enough about the operation of personal computers to realize what they might be fictionally portraying? Here I think that concerned viewers were not interested in what *could* have been meant by the scene, but by what *was* meant. After all, they did not wish to applaud the subtlety of the scene which the exorcism interpretation might merit, if in fact the fictional narrator's gesture was just the result of a mistake. That would be as ridiculous as crediting a slip of the tongue as a *bon mot*. Certainly what film buffs wanted, but to my knowledge never got, was a sincere authorial avowal (confession?) of what was intended by the shot.

Dissolving this interpretive ambiguity can, in principle, be solved satisfactorily by the modest actual intentionalist, who is willing to weigh cautiously statements of authorial intention, but not by the hypothetical intentionalist, who brackets such information from the interpreter's purview.

At this point, the hypothetical intentionalist is likely to remind us of a complication in his theory, heretofore unmentioned, that might enable him to deal with the *Stand by Me* case. When the hypothetical intentionalist endorses a hypothesis of authorial intention, he considers not only the epistemically best hypothesis available under his interpretive protocols, but also the aesthetically best hypothesis – that is, the interpretation, where there is room for competing interpretations, that makes the work a better work (Levinson 1996, 179). Applied to *Stand by Me*, this might dispose the hypothetical intentionalist to say that the exorcism interpretation is the best interpretation, even if we know the author's actual intention was otherwise (say, through personal communication), because it makes the film a better film aesthetically.

Unfortunately, I do not see that the hypothetical intentionalist gives us any grounds for accepting his aesthetic criterion for interpretation. It is not a straightforward extension of interpretive principles of charity. If the aims of the practice of literary communication rule that makers always be given the benefit of the doubt in cases like *Stand by Me*, what exactly are those aims? I confess that they elude me. Rather, it seems to me that the art world is a place where people are praised for their control of their materials. They are not applauded when, unintentionally, their work gets out of control.

I suspect that most viewers would be loath to commend the producers of *Stand by Me* if it turned out that they just didn't know what they were doing. But if we discovered, perhaps by asking them, that they did make the relevant scene with the exorcism interpretation in mind, the modest actual intentionalist would be happy, as I imagine most viewers would be, to appreciate their expressive finesse. Yet if you find the modest actual intentionalist's recommended handling of the *Stand by Me* case intuitively acceptable, that supplies further evidence that our practices of interpretation are not adverse, in principle, to consulting authorial intentions in order to answer hermeneutic questions – even if that entails going beyond the information the hypothetical intentionalist endorses – to the point of consulting artists and authors by means of interviews or through an examination of their journals, correspondence, and the like.

The hypothetical intentionalist conjectures that our practices of literary communication are satisfied by the best-warranted hypotheses of actual authorial intention based on publicly available sources and recourse to authorial confidences derived from interviews, private correspondence, the author's unpublished journals, diaries, and so on. His primary reason for this seems to be that in addressing a public, the artist enters an implicit contract with that public, guaranteeing that they should be able to understand the work without doing research into the author's private life. It is probably good advice to authors who aspire to a general public to behave this way, but it dubiously represents an implicit contract that underwrites all literary communication. Literary communication is more unruly than the stipulated regulations the hypothetical intentionalist imputes to it.

Some authors trade in secret meanings, reserved for a specialized audience – indeed, meanings that are intended to exclude outsiders. This practice lies deep in our hermeneutical tradition. In the New Testament Gospel according to Mark (4.12), when discussing the parable of the sower, Jesus tells his apostles that his parables are designed so that outsiders will not understand them; the only ones who are intended to understand them are the apostles, those to whom Jesus goes on in the text to reveal the true meaning of the parable. Thus here we find an *ur*-practice of literary communication where the correct interpretation is explicitly not the best-warranted hypothesis of Christ's actual intention, but the authorial intention disclosed to a chosen audience by the utterer, in this case Jesus.[5]

---

[5] This view of the passage from Mark has been endorsed by Pascal and Calvin (Walker 1975) and, to a certain extent, by Frank Kermode (Kermode 1979), though Kermode uses it to advance a theory of interpretation different from modest actual intentionalism.

The use of secret meanings targeted for specially informed audiences did not stop with Jesus. Rabelais is said to have employed it in *Gargantua* (Walker 1975, 221–22), and modern poets, like Stefan George, have attempted personally to cultivate elite visionary followers for whom their poems carry secret meanings. In the case of occulted meanings, it seems obvious that authorial intention – where it is supportable by the text – should provide the bottom line for interpretation. And since the communication of such secret meanings is part of literary history, the hypothetical intentionalist's protestations about implicit rules of publicity in literary interpretation appear exaggerated.

Perhaps the hypothetical intentionalist will say that in cases like this the reader should not be concerned with the author's intended meaning of the text, but should stick to her guns with the publicly, "democratically" available meaning of the text. But such encouragement is useless; if people are really interested in a text, they will want to know its secret meaning, even if securing it involves violating the hypothetical intentionalist's "implicit contract." And this means that the hypothetical intentionalist's rules do not really reflect the practice of literary communication. The hypothetical intentionalist's characterization of the literary institution, though in ways commonsensical, is poor sociologically.

On the other hand, the hypothetical intentionalist may allege that his position allows the interpreter all the information available to the intended, appropriate audience of the text, where that audience is the one the text requires in order to be understood (Levinson 1996, 181–84). So if the intended audience for Christ's parables is the apostles, then the interpreter is entitled to all the information they have. However, this maneuver incurs paradoxical results for the hypothetical intentionalist, since the enabling information the apostles had was just the direct revelation of Christ's intentions.

Apart from the issue of secret meanings, other practices also fly in the face of hypothetical intentionalism's generalized rules of artistic communication. Some artists, like Frida Kahlo, are intensely autobiographical; penetrating their work interpretively may just be impossible, unless we look at their private life and whatever documentation we can find about it. And where people are intrigued by the work, they will be grateful to learn about the work's intended significance from sources otherwise off-limits according to the hypothetical intentionalist.[6]

The hypothetical intentionalist may ask why we should be interested in the meaning of the work for the artist. But if what a work is about is the artist's personal journey *and* we accept, as we often do, that this is a

[6]   The hypothetical intentionalist presupposes that all artworks should be "freestanding" in the sense that all one needs to interpret them is what is available publicly. However, the problem with this is that not all artworks are designed to be "freestanding" in this way, as the example of intensely autobiographical art indicates.

legitimate artistic enterprise, then we should ask in response: Why should we foreclose inquiry into the artist's private, not publicly documented life by examining his personal papers and gingerly interviewing her friends and acquaintances? Some artforms may include in their contract with the audience a willing preparedness to be informed of private authorial intentions.[7] And if that is so, then the hypothetical intentionalist cannot be right in alleging that the best-warranted hypothesis derived from publicly available materials is the one always preferred, over privately divulged intentions, by our interpretive institutions.

Of course, the private/public dichotomy presupposed by the hypothetical intentionalist is also worth questioning. The hypothetical intentionalist permits the interpreter to use published biographical information about an author when unraveling the meaning of a text, but forbids the use of private information, garnered from unpublished papers, interviews, and so on. But it seems that much of what is found in public accounts of artists at one time or another got there because scholars interviewed authors and their associates or found information among private papers and the like. Is the hypothetical intentionalist willing to employ any reliable reports about the author's life and intentions so long as they have been published? But sometimes the published material comes from private material.

On the one hand, it would seem utterly arbitrary for the hypothetical intentionalist to allow interpreters to use biographical facts about authors once they are published, while disallowing reference to the same facts before they are published. On the other hand, it would seem impracticable for the hypothetical intentionalist to rule that the interpreter can use published biographical information about authors only if it is known to be derived from public sources, rather than private ones. And, in any event, this is not how interpreters behave. Once it is published, no matter its provenance, interpreters will use the information.

Much of Stuart Gilbert's famous *James Joyce's Ulysses* is, as Gilbert himself makes clear in his preface, the result of close consultation with Joyce about his intended meanings, structures, and associations (Gilbert

---

[7]   For example, the filmmaker Stan Brakhage often makes highly autobiographical films. When he attends screenings of his own films, he often answers questions about the meaning of the films from spectators by reference to the autobiographical significance of the work. This seems an integral part of the author/audience relation with respect to these films. If the hypothetical intentionalist objects that this violates some imaginable author/audience contract, the appropriate response would appear to be that Brakhage's "confessions" represent a fulfillment of the real, as opposed to the stipulated, contract that is pertinent to Brakhage's work.

Moreover, if the hypothetical intentionalist argues that since Brakhage makes these pronouncements in public, they do not violate the strictures of hypothetical intentionalism, this would seem to open the hypothetical intentionalist to charges of arbitrariness – why are the self-same Brakhagean remarks interpretively available if he utters them during a screening at Millennium Film Workshop, but not if they are filed away among his personal correspondence in the library of Anthology Film Archives?

1962, v–ix). Does hypothetical intentionalism permit interpreters access to *James Joyce's Ulysses*, still surely an important commentary on Joyce's novel? If the hypothetical intentionalist allows the interpreter to use Gilbert's work as historical background information about *Ulysses*, then the hypothetical intentionalist's distinction between public and private appears arbitrary. But if the hypothetical intentionalist objects to the use of *James Joyce's Ulysses*, then he has failed to discover the actual norms of our practices of literary communication, since interpreters resort to Gilbert's discoveries shamelessly.

Perhaps the hypothetical intentionalist has a way of framing the private/public distinction in a way that can avoid criticisms like these. But until he says something more precise about that distinction than he has, we must remain skeptical of the hypothetical intentionalist's claim to have accurately captured the underlying rules of literary communication.

In summary, modest actual intentionalism argues that actual authorial intention is relevant to the meaning of artworks. With respect to literary utterances, the modest actual intentionalist takes meaning to be a function of the author's actual intention, where that intention is supportable by what has been written. In this regard, modest actual intentionalism maintains that artistic and literary interpretation is seamlessly linked with ordinary, everyday forms of interpretation. In both cases, we take utterance tokens to mean what the utterer intends, where that is supportable by what has been said.

Whereas modest actual intentionalism claims that the aim of literary interpretation is to recover actual authorial intentions (that are consistent with the relevant texts), hypothetical intentionalism alleges that the aim of literary interpretation is merely to establish the most plausible hypothesis about authorial intention. The modest actual intentionalist objects that this confuses warranted assertibility for the truth, whereas the shared methodologies of modest actual intentionalism and hypothetical intentionalism both indicate that we should prefer establishing actual authorial intent, when possible, rather than remaining satisfied with only the best-warranted hypothesis about said intent.[8]

In turn, the hypothetical intentionalist concedes that this would be so were literary interpretation on par with ordinary interpretation. But the hypothetical intentionalist argues that this is not the case. Because of its special interests, literary interpretation, the hypothetical intentionalist avers, prizes warranted assertibility over the truth about authorial intentions (where those part company). Lamentably, the hypothetical intentionalist does not tell us much about those special interests or about their grounds. Moreover, as I have tried to show at length, the overarching rules that the hypothetical intentionalist presumes reign over our interpretive

---

[8] That is, where the actual authorial intention and the best-warranted hypothesis about it come apart.

institutions and practices are liable to many criticisms – criticisms that, in fact, suggest that modest actual intentionalism provides us with a far better picture of our existing interpretive practices.

References

Acocella, Joan. (1995). "Cather and the Academy." *New Yorker* 71, Nov. 27, 56–66.

———. (Forthcoming). *Cather and the Politics of Criticism*. Lincoln: University of Nebraska Press.

Beardsley, Monroe. (1981). *Aesthetics*. Indianapolis, IN: Hackett.

Carroll, Noël. (1991). "Art, Intention, and Conversation." In *Intention and Interpretation*, edited by Gary Iseminger. Philadelphia: Temple University Press.

———. (1993). "Anglo-American Aesthetics and Contemporary Criticism: Intention and the Hermeneutics of Suspicion." *Journal of Aesthetics and Art Criticism*, 51, 245–52.

———. (1997). "The Intentional Fallacy: Defending Myself." *Journal of Aesthetics and Art Criticism*, 55, 305–9.

Gilbert, Stuart. (1962). *James Joyce's Ulysses*. New York: Vintage Books.

Iseminger, Gary. (1992). "An International Demonstration?" In *Intention and Interpretation*, edited by Gary Iseminger. Philadelphia: Temple University Press.

———. (1996). "Actual Intentionalism vs. Hypothetical Intentionalism." *Journal of Aesthetics and Art Criticism*, 54, 319–26.

———. (1998). "Interpretive Relevance, Contradiction and Compatibility with the Text." *Journal of Aesthetics and Art Criticism*, 56, 58–61.

Kermode, Frank. (1979). *The Genesis of Secrecy: On the Interpretation of Narrative*. Cambridge, MA: Harvard University Press.

Knapp, Stevens, and Walter Benn Michaels. (1982). "Against Theory." *Critical Inquiry*, 8, 723–42.

Kurth, Peter. (1999). "This Man Is an Island." *New York Times Book Review*, Aug. 22, 12–13.

Levinson, Jerrold. (1996). "Intention and Interpretation in Literature." In *The Pleasures of Aesthetics*. Ithaca, NY: Cornell University Press.

Livingston, Paisley. (1998). "Intentionalism in Aesthetics." *New Literary History*, 29, 831–46.

Nehamas, Alexander. (1981). "The Postulated Author: Critical Monism as a Regulative Ideal." *Critical Inquiry*, 8, 133–49.

———. (1987). "Writer, Text, Work, Author." In *Literature and the Question of Philosophy*, edited by Anthony Cascardi. Baltimore: Johns Hopkins University Press.

O'Brien, Sharon. (1987). *Willa Cather: The Emerging Voice*. New York: Oxford University Press.

Sedgwick, Eve Kosofsky. (1989). "Across Gender, Across Sexuality: Willa Cather and Others." *South Atlantic Quarterly*, 88, 53–72.

Stecker, Robert. (1987). "Apparent, Implied and Postulated Authors." *Philosophy and Literature*, 11, 258–71.

Tolhurst, William. (1979). "On What a Text Is and How It Means." *British Journal of Aesthetics*, 19, 3–14.

Walker, D. P. (1975). "Esoteric Symbolism." In *Poetry and Poetics from Ancient Greece to the Renaissance*, edited by G. M. Kirkwood, 218–32. Ithaca, NY: Cornell University Press.

Wilson, George. (1992). "Again Theory: On Speaker's Meaning, Linguistic Meaning and the Meaning of the Text." *Critical Inquiry*, 19, 164–85.

7

OBJECTS OF INTERPRETATION

PETER LAMARQUE

Preliminaries

Interpretation takes many forms and applies to many different kinds of objects. In the broadest terms, to interpret something is to make sense of it. The need to interpret arises when meaning is unclear. Interpretation is not merely understanding, for I could understand your greeting "Good morning" without needing to interpret it. I would only need to interpret it if I had reason to believe that you meant it to be something other than a greeting.

Natural events as well as human artifacts and actions can call for interpretation. To the extent that physical symptoms, pulsating stars, earth tremors, or the movements of particles can be said to mean something, and where that meaning is unclear, they are subject to interpretation. But meaning in these cases is what Grice called "natural meaning" (Grice 1989) and the relevant mode of interpretation will be causal explanation. Although we seek to understand natural phenomena, "make sense" of them, our inquiry will take a different form from that demanded by puzzling artifacts. For artifacts a different mode of interpretation, and accordingly a different kind of meaning ("non-natural"), is sought.

Notoriously, of course, the appropriate mode of interpretation might itself be unclear. In medieval times natural philosophers sought to read the "book of nature," making no distinction between the causal and the purposive. But it is not uncommon in any case to mistake, or be unclear about, the origins of a phenomenon, natural or intentional. The flash in the sky might be a distress signal or a meteorite, the pulsating stars signs of intelligent life or just nuclear reactions. *How* we interpret is always determined by *what* we interpret. The form of interpretation is governed by the object of interpretation.

These preliminary truisms indicate a number of useful premises for our discussion. The first is that interpretation can apply to, or have as its objects, natural as well as cultural phenomena, although the assumption is that the meaning sought in the different cases is itself different.[1] The second is that merely being a human artifact or action is not in itself sufficient to warrant interpretation. Interpretation arises only when meaning is unclear or not obvious, when there is a need to "make sense" of something.[2] This is one basis for a distinction between interpretation and description. Third, not all interpretation follows the same procedures. Having established that a phenomenon is natural rather than intentional, we seek to make sense of it through naturalistic explanation, but that would not be appropriate if we viewed the phenomenon to be of human (or intentionalistic) origin. However, even human phenomena admit of different modes of interpretation. We should not assume in advance that every human artifact or action is subject to the same methods of interpretation: a poem, a dream, eccentric behaviour at a party, a cryptic remark, evidence at a murder scene, a Rorschach blot, a quattrocento painting, a biblical passage, and a judgment of the Supreme Court might all be suitable objects of interpretation, but the constraints on how an interpreter might proceed cannot be assumed to be the same in the different cases. Finally, given the intimate connection between the mode of interpretation and its objects, there is the premise that interpretation cannot proceed, certainly cannot be successful, without the prior determination of the *kind of thing* being interpreted.

Mere Things and Interpretable Objects

The points just made will be expanded in what follows. It might be thought that the first, which allows interpretation of natural as well as cultural phenomena, can and should be set aside fairly quickly, as undoubtedly the philosophical interest in interpretation lies in the cultural phenomena rather than the natural sphere, just as the philosophical interest in meaning is in "non-natural" rather than "natural" meaning. But a moment's more reflection on the matter could, I believe, yield dividends later. The best way to engage the relevant issues is to broach the tricky topic of indiscernibles, which, like it or not, has come to play a prominent role in discussions of interpretation.[3]

The sorts of examples that come immediately to mind are those in which purely natural phenomena have all the appearance of being cultural phenomena (we will be looking at converse cases in a moment). Knapp and Michaels, in their discussion of literary intention, famously propose the case of "squiggles in the sand" on a beach that spell out two stanzas of

---

[1] Margolis (1993, 455) has suggested that interpretation is limited to cultural phenomena. However, as far as I can see, there is nothing in his view that precludes his acknowledging a sense of "interpret" associated with "natural meaning."

[2] The point is rightly emphasized by Barnes (1988, 26).

[3] For a survey of some of the issues, see Lamarque 1998.

a Wordsworth lyric (a similar example is offered in Walton 1990, 86–88). By the time the second stanza appeared, as Knapp and Michaels observe, an onlooker would be struggling to find an explanation:

> Are these marks mere accidents, produced by the mechanical operation of the waves on the sand . . .? Or is the sea alive and striving to express its pantheistic faith? Or has Wordsworth, since his death, become a sort of genius of the shore . . .? You might go on extending the list of explanations indefinitely, but you would find, we think, that all explanations fall into two categories. You will either be ascribing these marks to some agent capable of intentions (the living sea, the haunting Wordsworth, etc.) or you will count them as nonintentional effects of mechanical processes. . . . But in the second case – where the marks now seem to be accidents – will they still seem to be words?
>
> Clearly not. They will merely seem to *resemble* words. . . . In one case you would be amazed by the identity of the author – who would have thought that the sea can write poetry? In the other case, however, in which you accept the hypothesis of natural accident, you're amazed to discover that what you thought was poetry turns out not to be poetry at all. It isn't poetry because it isn't language; that's what it means to call it an accident. (Knapp and Michaels 1992, 54–55)

The example is instructive whether or not we concur with Knapp and Michaels's view of literary intention. It shows several things: first, that it makes an obvious and deep difference in how we respond to, and interpret, a phenomenon whether we think it a product of intention (and in general a cultural object) or just a natural occurrence;[4] second, that there are different levels at which "making sense" of something occurs, from a base level, which determines the kind of phenomenon at hand, right up to a higher level, indisputably that of interpretation, where, on the assumption that the marks on the sand are linguistic and poetic, detailed meanings are sought; third, that mere marks or physical configurations, which might be common to both a natural and cultural phenomenon, are not sufficient to determine the appropriate mode of interpretation.

A fourth lesson is perhaps the most important of all, in that it emphasizes just how bizarre thought-experiments of this kind are. If we had reason to believe that there was no human intention involved, we would

---

[4]   Walton (1990), in contrast to Knapp and Michaels, seeks to play down the importance of intention in identifying genuine representations. It is enough, he argues, that natural objects should have the *function* of "serving as props in games of make-believe." He writes: "A thing may be said to have the function of serving a certain purpose, regardless of the intentions of its maker, if things of that kind *are typically or normally meant by their makers to serve that purpose*" (Walton 1990, 52; his italics). But intentions cannot, I believe, be so easily dismissed in the characterization of representations. What is likely to happen in cases of "naturally occurring stories" is that in effect the marks are intentionally *appropriated* by an observer, rather in the manner of *objet trouvé* art, and made into a representation thereby. Walton is criticized along similar lines in Levinson (1996, 295–97); see also Lamarque 1991.

be at a total loss to explain how a Wordsworth lyric could appear etched on a beach. However, the crucial philosophical lesson goes beyond mere puzzlement. It tells us that we must not set the puzzling case as the paradigm. It would be wrong to suppose that in every instance of written language a first step of interpretation must be to establish whether the written marks are natural phenomena or intentional signs. *That* question does not arise, except in the most improbable scenarios (usually dreamt up by philosophers). We should recall that interpretation is only warranted when there is uncertainty or unclarity about meaning. In standard cases, written symbols present no such unclarity, so interpretation need not, and should not, as I shall put it, go "all the way down." Interpretation begins only at the level where genuine alternative hypotheses about meaning present themselves. In the case of a normal apprehension of a Wordsworth lyric – other than as squiggles on a beach – not only do we not need to entertain the hypothesis of intentionless occurrence, but there is no occasion to question whether the language is English, nor indeed whether the lines are a stretch of lyric poetry. (Nor would a suitably informed reader doubt the authorship of Wordsworth.) In standard cases of confronting a piece of verse, interpretation only becomes an issue at the level of poetic meaning, as a task for literary critics.

The idea that there should be contextually determined levels at which interpretation begins, and thus that it is wrong to assume that interpretation in all cases must go all the way down to a bedrock of physical marks, sounds, or movements, might seem obvious enough – except that it has been denied in influential circles and its implications not addressed in important debates. Richard Rorty, for example, appeals to a reductive base of "marks and noises" in the task of ascribing coherence to a text:

> The coherence of [a] . . . text is . . . no more than the fact that somebody has found something interesting to say about a group of marks or noises – some way of describing those marks and noises which relates them to some of the other things we are interested in talking about. (For example, we may describe a given set of marks as words of the English language, as very hard to read, as a Joyce manuscript, as worth a million dollars, as an early version of *Ulysses*, and so on.) This coherence is neither internal nor external to anything: it is just a function of what has been said so far about those marks. (Rorty 1992, 97–99)

Rorty's discussion is part of an argument that seeks to blur two distinctions: that between interpretation and use and that between "finding an object" and "making it." Rorty attaches priority to the second item in each case and relates them in supposing that by *using*, for example, marks and noises we thereby *make* an object of inquiry. Objects, for Rorty, like texts par excellence, do not present themselves for our attention with their natures already determined, but allow themselves to acquire natures only relative to the malleable uses to which they are put.[5]

The extreme reductionism of Rorty's position is deeply at odds with the view developed in this chapter. However, we can acknowledge a vestigial truth in it, drawing on Rorty's intuition that the line between the predetermined nature of such objects and the properties imputed to them within interpretive practices is indeed not hard and fast. It requires a great deal of stage setting, though, which will need to be presented carefully, to establish the compatibility of that intuition with the apparently contrasting earlier point about the different starting levels of interpretation.

Meanwhile, we should not leave the topic of indiscernibles, even only temporarily, without a reference to Arthur Danto, whose invaluable insight has been to show that two ostensibly indiscernible objects (structures, sounds, marks) might have radically different art-related properties, indeed, one being a work of art, the other a "mere real thing" (the *locus classicus* in Danto 1981). Significantly, for Danto, what makes the difference between a work of art and its non-art counterpart is an interpretation: "Indiscernible objects become quite different and distinct works of art by dint of distinct and different interpretations, so I shall think of interpretations as functions which transform material objects into works of art" (Danto 1986, 39). One of Danto's best-known examples illustrates this well: the nine apparently indistinguishable canvases consisting of unbroken red, which, because of different origins, grounded in different interpretations, are identified as distinct works (the Israelites Crossing the Red Sea, Kierkegaard's Mood, Red Table Cloth, etc). (Danto 1981, 1 ff.). However, there is a subtle shift here in the notion of "interpretation," for what makes the red canvases different works are not interpretations offered by art appreciators – third parties – but interpretations originating in the artists themselves. Appreciators are called upon not to interpret "mere real things," that is, red canvases, but canvases-with-titles, objects that have already been "interpreted," in a different sense, by the artists.

It might seem that Danto is committed to a view not unlike Rorty's, which locates the starting point of interpretation at a basic physical level. But that is an illusion based on a blurring of the two notions of interpretation. Danto himself appears to caution against a Rorty-type view: "Not every artwork ... is a transform[ation] through an interpretation of an *objet trouvé*, and with most works of art it takes some trouble to imagine counterparts to them ... which are not works of art." "Still," he goes on, "it is always possible, for any artwork you choose, to imagine something indiscernible from it but caused in a way which renders a transformative interpretation inapplicable" (Danto 1986, 39). This latter claim recalls Knapp and Michaels's point about the Wordsworthian squiggles, in

[5] For detailed discussion of Rorty's views on this matter, see Lamarque 1996a and 1996b, Chap. 12.

supposing that we can imagine contexts, however bizarre, in which configurations indistinguishable from, say, Rembrandt's *Night Watch* do not even count as a painting. To that I would reply, yes, perhaps we can, with a suitably ingenious background story, but that fact plays no part in our efforts to interpret the *Night Watch*, when we have no call to entertain deviant causal origins. Nor does it play any part in Rembrandt's own creative process or in an explanation of that process. From the point of view of both an appreciator's and the artist's interpretation, the thought-experiment is idle. We will come back to Danto.

Works, Kinds, and Categories

With this preliminary scene setting in mind we can consolidate some of the previous remarks and point toward more substantive theses about interpretation. A central thesis, arising out of what has gone before, is this: In standard cases, at least in the sphere of art, interpretation begins at the level of *works*. This thesis will be refined and developed as we proceed, with particular attention to the notion of a "work." When we turn attention to a poem, play, or novel, we do not begin a process of interpretation by asking about marks or noises or what language is being used or whether this is a human artifact or a quirk of nature. Interpretation gets under way, indeed, is made possible, in the light of prior knowledge about what kind of thing, broadly conceived, the object of interpretation is. The enabling assumption is that the work under investigation belongs in a recognizable generic category.[6] There are, of course, nonstandard cases, and I will return to them.

A similar point can be made about any of the arts. In musical interpretation, again in standard cases, we do not begin with bare sounds but with musical works bearing familiar features – structure, harmony, instrumentation, key, musical genre – recognition of which is a starting point, not a terminus of interpretation. In painting or sculpture, we do not need to hypothesize whether the paint arrived on the canvas or the marble found its configuration through purely natural processes or through human intention. Once again in standard cases we assume, prior to interpretation, that these are works (paintings and sculptures) produced intentionally, conforming to broadly defined conventions in a human practice, which will reward a search for further meaning.

It is not just works of art that come to interpreters in recognizable categories. The cases listed earlier, such as the evidence at a murder scene, the Rorschach blot, the biblical passage, the Supreme Court ruling, become objects of interpretation *under those descriptions*. Interpretation in these cases does not begin further back; in fact, it can only proceed in a constructive way once the point of the interpretation is understood.

---

[6] For the idea of a "category" of art, I rely on Walton 1970.

Of course, not all cases are "standard" in the way described, but we must not take the nonstandard as the norm for a theory of interpretation. We have looked at some nonstandard cases already, like the fantastic scenario of natural occurrences having the appearance of well-formed sentences in a language. But perhaps the more interesting nonstandard cases are those involving a choice, not between the natural and the intentional, but between different categories of the intentional.

Let us begin with linguistic examples. Suppose we come across sets of symbols that we know to be linguistic – products of intentional activity, possessing a meaning, part of a sign system – but have no idea what they mean. Not only do we not know the specific meaning, but we have no idea of the *kind* of linguistic act that gave rise to them, so we have no generic category (mere doodle, communicative message, poem, letter, prayer) into which to locate the signs and thereby focus our interpretation. But these rare cases do not pose a challenge to the view advanced. Interpretation is needed – it is like Quinean radical interpretation – and it does indeed have to start further back. However, we have at least *some* categories to constrain us: "human," "linguistic," "intentional." What is notable is how different such "radical" cases are from linguistic (far less literary) interpretation normally understood and how difficult, if not impossible, it would be to proceed in these conditions.

Suppose, in another example, we do know the language but nothing of the context in which the linguistic signs were produced. We have a mere text or set of sentences. Although competence in the language would allow us to assign a meaning to the sentences, merely understanding the sentences by virtue of understanding the language does not yet count as *interpretation* (here I agree with Currie 1991, 339). To interpret the sentences we need to grasp their point. But how could we do that in the extraordinary circumstance of knowing nothing about the context in which they were produced? After all, even in the case of enigmatic sentences found on a scrap of paper in a bottle adrift on the ocean, a reasonable surmise would be that this is an attempt at communication, a *message*, and as not all texts are messages, that already puts a constraint on how to make sense of it (see Lamarque 1996b, 171). Can interpretation proceed with genuinely contextless texts? Perhaps, in a sense, it can, or at least an attempt at interpretation can be made. What seems clear is that simply *using* the texts, in Rortyan fashion, as we see fit, will make no contribution to the interpretive effort. The focus for interpretation would be toward reconstructing the context in order to establish the kind of text it is, the function it seeks to fulfill.

As this focus is different from that of standard interpretation, it might be helpful to make explicit a distinction between the former as *generic interpretation* and the latter, the standard kind, as *meaning-determining interpretation*. Normally, generic categorisation is taken for granted – we know that the object of our interpretive efforts is a metaphor, a poem, a political speech, a philosophical argument – and the search for meaning is guided by that starting point. Where we do not have this knowledge, our options for meaning-determination are severely restricted. But consider how rare it is to be confronted with a bare set of sentences apparently without context or purpose. Far from being a paradigm of interpretation, as might be imagined by reductive poststructuralists, these nonstandard cases of free-floating texts render interpretation all but impossible.

Generic interpretation, or something like it, as we saw in discussing Danto's examples, is normally carried out by artists, not appreciators. It is the artist who determines the kind of object created. Only occasionally does an appreciator need to interpret at a more basic level as a preliminary to determining meaning. When a new category of art or style or genre is created – conceptual art, cubism, performance art, twelve-tone music – and when that category is not fully assimilated into the critical idiom, a first step in interpretation might be the search for an appropriate generic categorisation (which, in fact, might not be available until a later time; see Levinson 1996, 265). But once the conventions of an artistic genre are established, their recognition ceases to be a step in interpretation but becomes a background condition for interpretation. In some exceptional circumstances, such as with Paleolithic or other ancient artifacts (cave paintings, Stonehenge) the principal interpretive issue is forced to remain at the generic level, and will do so until it is resolved what *kind* of works these are.

It might be objected that the distinction between generic and meaning-determining interpretation is not sharp and that finding the correct category for a work will always be a central part of the interpretive process. There is no clear distinction, so the objection runs, between generic and more fine-grained categorisation, in the sense that there is no difference in kind between classifying a work as a poem, a speech, or a philosophical treatise, and classifying it as, say, satirical, electioneering, or literary-cum-philosophical. The latter, like the former, are still categorisations, but they are clearly part of meaning-determination and could be further refined as interpretation proceeds. I concede some of the force of this objection but reply that a precise definition of the generic is not needed for my purposes. The key point I hope to establish is simply this: A prerequisite for successful interpretation is knowing the *kind* of object under interpretation even though in some nonstandard cases another mode of interpretation (which I have called the generic) is involved in determining what that kind is.

Interpretive Practices

Behind this point, and, I believe, further substantiating it, is the thought that generic differences (between kinds of objects) relate to differences in practices and that conventions of interpretation, like the objects of interpretation themselves, are practice-dependent. The idea here is the familiar one that procedures for interpretation vary – albeit under a general heading "making sense of something" – according to the expectations associated with the object of inquiry. Literary interpretation is a different practice from philosophical interpretation, which in turn is different from the interpretation of dreams under psychoanalysis or the interpretation of conversation according to Gricean conversational implicature or the interpretation of evidence at a murder scene.

Jerrold Levinson has pointed to two broad modes of interpretation, which he calls the determinative (or DM = "does mean") mode and the exploratory (or CM = "could mean") mode:

> I suggest that behind DM interpreting, in any sphere, lies a spirit that might be qualified as scientific, practical, and knowledge-seeking. Part and parcel of this spirit is a desire for understanding, explanation, discovery, or communication. . . . Behind CM interpreting, by contrast, lies a spirit that might be qualified as ludic, liberational, freedom-seeking. Central to this spirit is a desire for cognitive play, much like that which Kant located at the core of the aesthetic, without a concern for cognitive payoff of a concrete sort, a fascination with possibilities of understanding, explanation, discovery or communication, but no care for their actuality. (Levinson 1999, 6)

He goes on to show how DM and CM interpreting will each be more or less appropriate depending on what is being interpreted. In his own examples, a clue in a crossword puzzle, an X-ray or radiograph, a puzzling situation in real life, and a joke more naturally invite DM interpreting, while Rorschach tests, ambiguous figures, and moves in chess invite the CM mode.[7] Levinson rightly points out that CM inquiry is often a useful preliminary to final DM deliverances. The distinction is helpful in sorting broad classes of interpretive practices, but it is possible, as noted, to identify more specific procedures within each class, say, the philosophical, the literary, the historical, the legal.

It is the specific practices of interpretation that lead to another key thesis, closely connected to the first: Modes of interpretation and objects of interpretation are, in standard cases, deeply interlinked, such that the practices that make the objects possible (in a sense to be explained) also define the conventions of interpretation that apply to them. This interlinking means that the interpretive processes within a practice do not merely identify properties within objects but go some way toward constituting those properties. Thus, in the case of art, an object's possessing aesthetic properties, be they expressive, evaluative, or even representational, is made possible only by virtue of the existence of a practice that determines

---

[7]   In fact, I am inclined to think that Levinson is wrong about the ambiguous figures, for those that are deliberately designed as such – the duck/rabbit, the old woman/young woman – have determinate alternatives, which should be recognized if the figures are to be correctly understood. We will be returning later to such figures and their interpretation.

a mode of appreciating such objects.[8] Without conventions underlying what *counts as*, say, expressiveness in music or thematic content in literature, there would be no such properties. These conventions both constitute the properties and dictate the correct mode of their apprehension (through, for example, interpretation).

To marshal further support for this thesis, in conjunction with the first, we need to look more closely at the types of "objects" involved in interpretive practices, especially the notion of a "work." As both theses imply that it is works, not texts, that are the (standard) objects of interpretation, this distinction should be addressed first.

Text and Work

A text, as I understand it, is an ordered set of sentence-types individuated at least partly by semantic and syntactic properties (see Currie 1991, 325). Two texts are identical if they have the same semantic and syntactic properties, are in the same language, and consist of the same word-types and sentence-types ordered in the same way.

A literary work, on the other hand, although it is, in Margolis's terms, "embodied" in a text (see, for example, Margolis 1980, 39 f.), is not identical with a text, nor does it possess the same identity conditions. The same text might embody two distinct works, in the manner of Pierre Menard's *Quixote* (Borges 1970), or embody no work at all. Literary works are cultural objects, dependent on a practice governed by social conventions concerning the production and reception of texts. As they owe their nature and existence to the practice, should the practice cease (the conventions be lost) literary works themselves would go out of existence, even though the texts remain. Literary works are, like all works of art, Intentional[9] objects, not just in the sense of having content or meaning but in the sense of being, broadly conceived, "objects of thought." Correspondingly, they possess Intentional properties, like expressive or representational properties, which can be discerned only by those sufficiently well-informed about the cultural practice in which the works are embedded. I am inclined also to follow Levinson in supposing that literary works, again like other artworks, are essentially bound to their origins, so that a literary work, in his terms, is a *text-as-indicated-in-a-context* (Levinson 1996, 195) or, more specifically, a *structure-as-indicated-by-X-at-t* (Levinson 1990, 98). This means that it is a necessary condition of a work being the work it is that it was created by a person at a time in a particular artistic context.

---

[8]   The relativity of modes of appreciation to practices or institutions is a theme in Olsen 1987, to which I am much indebted.

[9]   I follow Margolis (for example, Margolis 1999, 55) in capitalizing the first letter of "Intentionality" in order to mark a term of art, which I use in essentially the same way as Margolis.

Confusions over terminology bedevil discussions of interpretation, so let me emphasize that the use of the terms "text" and "work" as just defined is not universally adopted. A similar, but not identical, distinction between "text" and "work" was popularized by Roland Barthes in an essay from the 1960s (Barthes 1979), although his determination to give priority to text over work (a position followed by Rorty) is the opposite of the stance taken here. Also, for Barthes a work is "concrete," "occupying a portion of book-space (in a library, for example)," whereas a Text is "a methodological field" (Barthes 1979, 74; Barthes capitalizes the first letter of "Text"); in contrast, in my own usage, both works and texts are abstract entities. What occupies space on a shelf might be an instance or copy of a work but cannot be the work itself, for to destroy that copy would not be to destroy the work. Barthes's "Text" is more like my own "text," yet perhaps more indeterminate, for a Text is an instance of *écriture* (writing in general) and it is hard to see what semantic constraints operate on it, there being virtually no limits on what a Barthian Text can mean, nor what its identity conditions are.

Joseph Margolis on occasion uses the term "text" much as I use "work," although he does not restrict texts to linguistic items and expands the term to encompass any referent of an interpretation (Margolis 1993, 456), sometimes using the expression "text or artwork" (Margolis 1993, 459) as if these were interchangeable. Crucially, though, and centrally to his theory, he holds that "the individuation and identity of artworks are hardly the same as the individuation and identity of the natural or linguistic entities upon which they depend (and which they incorporate)" (Margolis 1999, 89). So something like the distinction between text and work, as I draw it, is implied by Margolis, indeed is pivotal to his view, even if his terminology is different.

The text/work distinction is an instance of a broader distinction running across all the arts and indeed other cultural objects, between that which possesses only physical (or "natural") properties and that which is "practice-dependent," cultural, and Intentional. In the nonliterary arts the distinction arises between, say, sounds (or sound-types) and musical works, canvas-plus-pigment and paintings, pieces of marble and sculptures. The notion is well entrenched in aesthetics. Examples outside aesthetics might include the distinction between bits of printed paper and banknotes, a leather sphere and a soccer ball, a flesh and blood human being and a monarch. In each pair we might say that the latter is "embodied" in the former but is not identical with it, that the latter but not the former depends on cultural factors or human practices, that in different worlds the former could retain its identity in the absence of the latter.

Not all cultural entities call for interpretation (banknotes, sports equipment, and monarchs at best yield to a straightforward DM mode of interpreting, in Levinson's terms), but many such entities, artworks in particular, are the very paradigm objects of interpretation. As Intentional objects they possess meaning; as artworks they can also be expressive, representational, and bearers of other aesthetic properties. But what exactly is the relation between an interpretation and a cultural object of this kind? Does an interpretation bring to light a meaning (or some other aesthetic property) that is already part of the nature of the object, or does it in some way help constitute that nature? The question is one of the most vexed and difficult in discussions of objects of interpretation and merits careful examination.

Imputationalism

Both Margolis and Michael Krausz have defended versions of "imputationalism," the view, in Krausz's words, that "an interpretation may constitute or impute features of its object-of-interpretation" (Krausz 1993, 67). This view is contrasted with "nonimputationalism," according to which "the character of the object-of-interpretation is understood to be fully autonomous or independent of interpretation as such" (67). Krausz contrasts "radical" with "moderate" imputationalism. While the former holds that "any particular interpretation on a given occasion may fully constitute its object-of-interpretation," the latter allows that "a given object-of-interpretation may be constituted within webs of interpretation" (94). The radical version postulates a one-to-one relation between interpretations and objects-of-interpretation and thus implies what Krausz calls "singularism," the thesis that "for any object-of-interpretation, there is one and only one ideally admissible interpretation of it" (42). Singularism, it should be noted, does not imply radical imputationalism or even the moderate kind, as it does not require that objects-of-interpretation be constituted through interpretation. Krausz himself favors moderate imputationalism and also "multiplism," the thesis that "for some object-of-interpretation, there is more than one ideally admissible interpretation of it" (42), while again recognizing that "multiplism does not require imputational interpretation" (93).

One issue that immediately arises is whether, with the resources he allows himself, Krausz can avoid radical imputationalism (Stecker [1997b, 1997c] alleges he cannot) and in consequence singularism. The very term "object-of-interpretation," coined by Krausz,[10] seems question-begging in favor of imputationalism, for the hyphens appear to link "object" and "interpretation" conceptually: no interpretation, no object-of-interpretation. But if there is this conceptual link, then what is to stop different interpretations from generating different objects-of-interpretation?

Krausz runs through a number of examples to illustrate how interpretive imputation works. One of these is the case of the ambiguous line

---

[10] Krausz's aim (1993, 39, n. 2) in coining this "term of art" is "to signal that no particular ontological construal of that which is interpreted is thereby implied. It remains ontologically neutral."

drawing that can be seen either as a vase or as two facing heads. Interpretation in this case, for Krausz, amounts to assigning salience to different features of the drawing, thus yielding the vase or the faces. He writes: "the interpretation – face or vase – prompts one to impute salience to certain features of the presented configuration, which in turn confirms the propriety of interpreting the configuration as a face or vase" (Krausz 1993, 68). He goes on: "Whether we accept one interpretation over another is not so much a matter of the fit between an interpretation and an autonomous or practice-independent object-of-interpretation, but is rather a matter of the fit between an interpretation and the object-of-interpretation *construed in the light of the interpretation in question*" (68; Krausz's italics). So now we must ask: How many objects-of-interpretation are there in the example? No doubt Krausz would want to reply "one," in line with his moderate imputationalism, but isn't the answer "two" forced upon him? "Interpretations and their objects-of-interpretation," he tells us, "are taken as packages" (Krausz 1993, 69). Yet there seem to be two packages here, so are there not correspondingly two objects-of-interpretation, namely, something like "the figure-seen-as-a-vase" and "the figure-seen-as-faces"? Further evidence that these two items are distinct is that they might well possess different aesthetic properties: The former could be graceful, curvaceous, elegant, the latter aggressive, confrontational, menacing.

All our intuitions, though, suggest that there is only one object here, the figure, and two interpretations. But has Krausz the resources in his theory to allow this? I think not. Certainly he talks, in one of the passages quoted above, of the "presented configuration," and it might seem that that is the single object needed. However, the configuration, consisting of the mere lines on the page, is not an "object-of-interpretation" in Krausz's sense, for it is not an "intentional object, so construed within a pertinent practice" (Krausz 1993, 120), nor "partly a function of . . . [an] interpretation" (Krausz 1993, 68). Indeed, the line drawing seems to be just the kind of autonomous and practice-independent entity that is contrasted with an object-of-interpretation. In our terms, it is the equivalent of a "text," not a "work."

Another example of Krausz's fares no better than the vase-face drawing in saving him from a commitment to radical imputationalism. He discusses different interpretations of Van Gogh's *The Potato Eaters* (formalist, psychological, Marxist-feminist), under which different features are made salient. In each case the "interpretation imputes an object-of-interpretation" (Krausz 1993, 73). A tension emerges, however, in the very account Krausz gives of how many objects-of-interpretation are involved:

> Despite the differences in their imputing interpretations, the resulting objects-of-interpretation . . . are sufficiently similar for the three interpretations to

compete. Of course, were one to pluralize the object-of-interpretation – that is, argue that each interpretation is really about another object-of-interpretation, whatever their relation to the physical canvas – the interpretations could not compete. But it seems perfectly natural to say that the formalist and the psychological interpretations do address an object-of-interpretation sufficiently common for the interpretations to compete. (Krausz 1993, 74)

The first sentence clearly implies that there is more than one object-of-interpretation in the Van Gogh example; apart from the fact that the plural is used, the objects-of-interpretation could not be described as "similar" unless they were distinct. The second sentence spells out the consequences of supposing there is more than one object-of-interpretation. The third sentence suggests that these consequences are undesirable and proposes that we postulate a single object-of-interpretation after all. Just to confuse matters further, the implication in that sentence is that this single object-of-interpretation is not identical to any of the earlier three but is a *fourth* one sharing common features (though presumably not all features) with the others. The result is a dramatic case of multiplying objects-of-interpretation beyond necessity. We should also note, as in the earlier example, that Krausz is not able to fall back on the "physical canvas" (mentioned in the passage) as the unifying object-of-interpretation for, like the line drawing, it is not an object-of-interpretation at all, in Krausz's terms.

The problem for Krausz is that he is trying to get by with too few resources, allowing himself nothing more than bare physical objects (configurations, canvases), on the one hand, and objects-of-interpretation, tightly tied to particular interpretations, on the other. What I suggest is needed is a threefold distinction between physical object, work (or cultural artifact), and interpretation.[11]

A Threefold Distinction

More specifically, we need to acknowledge three elements in the interpretive process. The first element involves the physical properties of the item being interpreted: the configuration of the lines in the drawing; the paint and canvas in the Van Gogh; the tones, pitches, and tempo prescribed by musical notation; the sets of sentences comprising a text; the paper, ink, and design of the banknote. Krausz recognizes this element. When he writes that "[i]mputational interpretation involves selecting features of the presented materials with which to fashion an object-of-interpretation" (Krausz 1993, 94), the "presented materials" are presumably those that belong at this level.

The second element is what I have called a *work*, as defined earlier, or

---

[11] Thom (1997, 183) also offers a threefold distinction, between "interpretation," "object-as-represented," and "further object," which is similar to, but not identical with, the one proposed.

more generally, a cultural artifact. We noted that the distinction between text and work has analogues outside art, as in that between the printed paper and the banknote that it embodies, so we should not think of "work" as restricted to works of art. Works, I have been urging, are the proper objects of interpretation (in cultural, not natural, applications). Some of their identity conditions have emerged already: They are Intentional objects, linked essentially to their origins; they are not numerically identical to their material embodiment (the latter could exist without the former); and their continued existence depends on the existence of the practices within which they acquire their identity. But are they "objects-of-interpretation" in Krausz's sense? In other words, do they owe their existence and nature to an interpretation or "web of interpretations"?

The matter is complex, but I am inclined to reply in the negative. Certainly works are objects of interpretation (without the hyphens), in the sense that they are the kinds of entities that conventionally invite (and, in the case of works of art, reward) interpretation. Also, as Intentional objects, they are "objects of thought," not natural kinds, and their continued existence as the kind of entities they are is dependent on the responses of people who reflect on them. But, crucially, they come into being through an act of *creation* (by an artist, say), not essentially through an act of *interpretation*. Being an Intentional object might imply, in Margolis's terms, being "intrinsically interpretable" (Margolis 1999, 98) but it does not imply being created through interpretation. Here we can recall again the discussion of Danto. Some works are created, in effect, by having an interpretation imposed, by an artist, on an object. This is the "transformative interpretation" of which Danto speaks. The paradigm case is the *objet trouvé* transformed into a work of art. But not all works come into being that way. Admittedly, most artists will have a conception of the work they seek to realize, and that conception is something like an interpretation. But there is an intuitive difference between realizing a conception and supplying an interpretation, certainly in an age when interpretation is viewed as the prerogative of the critic. The artist does have a role in what I earlier called "generic interpretation," the locating of an object in a *category*, as a *kind* of thing. Although subsequent appreciators might appropriate a work into a category not envisaged by the artist, the original intended category will usually retain a normative authority. Also, artists often become interpreters of their own work, in a more substantive "meaning-determining" way, but that activity is separate from the creation of the work, and arguably an artist's own meaning-determining interpretations have no more authority than, and are subject to the same justificatory criteria as, those of other appreciators.

Perhaps we can conclude this, taking a cautious line: The coming into being of a work is not dependent on an interpretation other than that which might inform an artist's act of creation. It is a further question whether the continued existence of a work depends on subsequent interpretation. Because works (like all cultural artifacts) are grounded in practices, their survival depends on that of the practices themselves and, thus, minimally the works must continue to "secure uptake" within an appropriate community of practitioners and be *recognized*, or recognizable, as the works they are. It is not obvious, though, that this requires *interpretation* in any robust sense.

Our third element covers interpretation in precisely that robust sense that seems to underlie the notion of an object-of-interpretation. At this level we move from objects of interpretation (without the hyphens) to Krauszian objects-of-interpretation, but we no longer have the concerns about multiplying objects-of-interpretation that seemed to complicate Krausz's theory. We can readily accept that interpretations are productive of entities, their own intentional objects, and we might think of objects-of-interpretation (in Krausz's sense) as more like products-of-interpretation. Thus, the vase-interpretation produces an intentional object, *the-figure-seen-as-a-vase*, which is distinct from another intentional object, *the-figure-seen-as-two-faces*. Other objects-of-interpretation might include performances of musical works; or productions of plays, say, Olivier's *Hamlet* or Branagh's *Hamlet*; or readings of poems, like (in Krausz's example, 1993, 77 ff.) F. W. Bateson's and Cleanth Brooks's readings of Wordsworth's Lucy poem; or interpretations of paintings, such as the various approaches to *The Potato Eaters*. Productions or readings or pictorial interpretations, as objects-of-interpretation, have a life of their own. They can be referred to, individuated, compared, evaluated, and have their properties described; they are genuine, if Intentional, individuals. They are distinct from the works to which they refer. Interestingly, they too can become objects of interpretation, as well as objects-of-interpretation, subject to discussion and open to misunderstanding.

Returning to the face/vase line drawing, what is the *work* in that case, as distinct from the object-of-interpretation? The answer is the *vase/face ambiguous representation* (designed to fall into that category). It is not identical with the lines on the page, nor is it identical with *the-figure-seen-as-a-vase* or *the-figure-seen-as-two-faces*. If we ask how these two objects-of-interpretation relate to the *work*, we can say they both stand for legitimate aspects of the work, in line with conventions governing representations of this kind. An interpretation that generates as an object-of-interpretation *the-figure-seen-as-an-elephant* will be dismissed as fanciful, only tenuously, at best, related to the work, and not sanctioned by the rules of the game.

Working with a threefold distinction between object, work, and object-of-interpretation puts "imputationalism" in a new light. For now, on the account given, it seems that imputationalism – the view that "an interpretation may constitute or impute features of its object-of-interpretation" – turns out to be not just true but tautological, even in the "radical" version, which postulates a one-to-one pairing of interpretations and objects-of-interpretation. And if we substitute "work" for "object-of-interpretation" in the thesis of "nonimputationalism," that "the character of the object-of-interpretation is understood to be fully autonomous or independent of interpretation as such," then it seems that in a slightly qualified form (as in the earlier remarks about an artist's creation), this thesis is true of works.

Krausz might respond in a number of ways to what no doubt he would view as an unduly precipitous dismissal of imputationalism. Thus, he might insist that he has not done away with my central notion of a *work*, lodged between text and object-of-interpretation, for it is already implicit in his notion of the "unicity" of objects-of-interpretation (Krausz 1993, 120 ff.).[12] This "unicity," or "commonality," he explains, "is a function of consensual agreement by pertinent practitioners" (Krausz 1993, 121). He goes on: "When interpretations impute different properties, they must impute a sufficiently large number of properties in common to warrant the agreement that they are addressing a sufficiently common object-of-interpretation" (121). An obvious thought, then, would be to identify the *work* with this set of common (meaning-based) properties. However, both Krausz and Margolis (1999, 91) deny that the common properties themselves must remain constant through the "career" of an artwork. This leaves them with seemingly insuperable difficulties in identifying an object-of-interpretation which, as it were, rises above the class of all other objects-of-interpretation and stands out as the (intentional) object *that is being interpreted*. In other words, they do not seem to have the resources to acknowledge what I have called the *work*.

Margolis suggests that we might look to "the relative constancy of . . . [the artwork's] physical properties" and "the norms of interpretive practice" (Margolis 1999, 91) to provide a reasonably stable *denotatum*, but insists that the question of how we "referentially fix," or individuate, artworks is separate from the question of whether they have fixed natures (which he denies) (Margolis 1993, 465). Krausz suggests that "objects-of-interpretation are co-created by text and interpreter" (Krausz 1997, 416). Curiously, neither alludes to the artist or the creative act that brings the artifact into being. Yet surely that is the foundation for the identity of works. A work is of necessity that (admittedly Intentional) entity brought into being by the intentional act (or set of acts) of a person, at a time, in a context (cf. Stecker 1997a, 244).

Levinson takes a similar robust view and thinks that it does away with the Krauszian problems about constructed objects-of-interpretation:

> There is no difficulty whatsoever with saying that there is just one poem . . . , though there are perhaps numerous interpretations or readings of it – so long as we recognize that the poem is not, of course, the brute text that it comprises

---

[12] I believe the term "unicity" originated with Margolis, who describes it as "the sense of the integral career of an artwork or cultural entity . . . in virtue of which we are able to assign a relatively stable number and nature to such *denotata*, though their natures change" (Margolis 1999, 90–91).

but rather the text poetically projected in a specific context anchored to a particular person, time, and place. That anchoring, together with the text's complete orthography, is enough to fix a literary work's identity for all critical intents and purposes, and so there is no need to bring meanings, conceptual complexes, or interpretive guises into it. (Levinson 1996, 197)

This, I believe, is broadly correct, but I don't think it is enough to dismiss an interesting core of truth (beyond the merely trivial truth mentioned above) in imputationalism. That is what I will now try to bring to light using the resources on offer.

Although Krausz struggles with unicity in finding something equivalent to a work, he might well agree with Margolis that it is one thing to "referentially fix" an artwork, another to determine its nature. Indeed, Levinson continues the passage just quoted: "A poem as I suggest we ontologically construe it will, to be sure, *generate* meanings and conceptual structures under interpretation . . .; but the poem is not to be *identified*, even partially, with such meanings, concepts, thoughts, or views" (197). But the question inevitably arises: What meaning-based properties "generated" by a work genuinely belong to it and which are "imputed" to it by an interpreter? The force of imputationalism is to insist that there is no clear distinction between what "belongs" to a work and what is "imputed" to it, for it is precisely the imputed properties that comprise the changing nature of the work over time. Whatever other doubts there might be about imputationalism, skepticism about a distinction of this kind is what makes, I believe, some version of imputationalism worth holding on to. Showing why takes us back to the close interlinking between interpretation and objects of interpretation within practices, which was one of the theses outlined earlier.

Properties "In" and "Imputed To" an Object of Interpretation

A good place to start is with views that see a clear line between "in" and "imputed to." Robert Stecker, for example, sees a dilemma in the imputationalist's position:

The problem is to understand how making a claim about an object, even an object-of-interpretation, can give it a property claimed for it. . . . If the claim is true, the object already has the property. If it is false, the object does not have the property. If it is neither true nor false, then what difference can be made by saying that the object has the property, or even by telling a plausible story according to which the object has the property? Before an interpretation is offered, an object may well be indeterminate with respect to a property, but if it is, then such saying or storytelling will not make it determinate, though it may get people to think of the object as determinate. (Stecker 1997b, 50)

Krausz's response to Stecker is this: "The non-radical imputationalist proposal does not urge that the text first does not have a given property and then gets it. Rather, it urges that, upon appropriate imputation, a more determinate object-of-interpretation arises" (Krausz 1997, 417). But the response is unsatisfactory in a number of respects. First, it makes reference to "the text," which, in both Krausz's and our own view, is no more than a set of sentences. But a text on its own, independent of context and use, has no properties of the kind identified through interpretation, although it might have semantic and syntactic properties. Second, Krausz's claim that a "more determinate object-of-interpretation arises" opens him to the charge of "pluralizing" (his own term) – in other words, generating a new and distinct object, thereby contradicting the thesis of moderate imputationalism, which requires that the nature of *one and the same object* (the "unicitous" object) is determined by imputed interpretations. If Stecker's dilemma is to be met, the solution must lie in the peculiar nature of the objects under interpretation, along with the properties attributed to them, and the form that interpretation takes.

The first move (emphasized in Margolis's [1999, 100] somewhat sketchy reply to Stecker) is to note again the Intentional nature of works. With nonintentional objects, such as ordinary medium-sized physical objects, the line between the properties they possess inherently and those that are "imposed on" them is *reasonably* clear, even if the former are not always known or fully understood.[13] But Intentional objects are *essentially* relational, in the sense that they depend for their existence on human thought processes and practices. *How they are taken* is not just incidental but determinative of their natures. Interestingly, Stecker concedes what he calls a "trivial" version of constructivism (imputationalism): "When we give a new interpretation of a work, we are thinking of it in a new way and, in virtue of this, the work acquires the property of being thought of in this new way" (Stecker 1997b, 44). He dismisses this version as too slight to appeal to full-blooded constructivists and thus "trivial," I take it, partly because it is all too easy to acquire relational properties of this kind and partly because such properties can have little to do with the *nature* of the thing that acquires them.[14] However, in the context of Intentional objects it would be wrong to dismiss all such relational properties either as trivial or as extraneous to the nature of the

---

[13]   Of course, the whole debate in metaphysics between realism and anti-realism shows that even this claim is far from controversial. But any weakening of the distinction between "inherent in" and "imposed on" in other contexts is only going to aid an argument that seeks to weaken the distinction in the cultural sphere.

[14]   Geach (1969) famously described the changes that acquiring such relational properties brings about as "mere Cambridge changes," in contrast to genuine changes. The allusion is to such philosophers as Russell and McTaggart, who held that an object changes just to the extent that a predicate truly applied to it at one time does not apply at another time.

objects, for Intentional properties, which characterize Intentional objects, are themselves relational. Aesthetic properties, for example, including expressive, evaluative, and representational properties, are also relational, resting on the responses of qualified perceivers (Lamarque, forthcoming). Of course, merely being thought about or perceived by a person is not sufficient to bring about a meaningful change in a work. But attributing aesthetic properties to a work or, to take Krausz's paradigm of interpretation, assigning salience to features of it, might do so, if the attribution or assigning is constrained, again in Krausz's terms, by the "consensual agreement by pertinent practitioners."

Stecker might reply to this that the relational properties of works that matter (par excellence their aesthetic properties) will be those that the work has, as it were, at the outset, and to the extent that interpretation characterizes these, it *discovers* rather than *imputes* them. This at least is the line taken by Levinson:

> It is not *artworks* that, in the crucial sense, change over time, it is rather *us*. We think more, experience more, create more – as a result are able to find more in artworks than we could previously. But these works are what they are, and remain, from the art-content point of view, what they always were. It is not their content that changes over time, but only our access to the full extent of that content, in virtue of our and the world's subsequent evolution. The latent and unnoticed must not be confused with the newly acquired and superadded; later history may *bring out* what *was* in earlier art, but it does not progressively *bring about* that there is *now* more in it. (Levinson 1990, 180–81)

While I am sympathetic to Levinson's attempt to defend a fairly substantial notion of a work (and work-content) independent of subsequent interpretation, I think he is hard put to confine all relevant interpretive properties within the work at the moment of its initial realization, and I do not think that he establishes an unbridgeable line between "inherent in" and "imputed to." He admits, for example, that what he calls "future-oriented artistic attributes," such as "influentiality . . . , seminality, importance, pivotalness, revolutionariness, fecundity" (Levinson 1990, 208), are difficult to accommodate to his view. He toys with the idea that instead of *making* the influentiality, future events rather *disclose* what is already present in a work. But it seems highly implausible (if not metaphysically suspect) to suppose that a relation with future contingencies can be part of a work's very nature at the time of its inception. His alternative is to exclude future-oriented attributes from his general thesis, separating out these attributes from what he calls *art-character*, the latter "compris[ing] *all* of what an artwork means or conveys" (Levinson 1990, 211). The concession, though small, is significant for the imputationalist, for here is a class of familiar properties of works – influence, fecundity, and so on – that are central to the art critical enterprise and are acknowledged by the staunchest anti-imputationalist to be acquired by works in the course of their "careers," as products of interpretation.

There are other examples as well. Levinson makes a strong case for showing that later works in an artist's *œuvre* may "augment or affect the *meaning* of earlier ones" (Levinson 1996, 245; his italics). Admittedly, the explanation he offers for this stretches credulity, namely, that an artist's *œuvre* can count as a single work, "a single artistic act" (245). Given that an artist's output might span fifty or more years, possibly including radical personal and cultural changes, the postulation of a single act could only be a theoretician's fiction. Nor could Levinson comfortably assert the theory of just some but not all *œuvres*, for it is hard to see how there could be any nonarbitrary or non-question-begging criteria for demarcating the two classes. Nevertheless, proffered explanation apart, the idea itself seems to be plausible, and its implications are congenial to the imputationalist cause in allowing us to accept that an object-of-interpretation (an early work) can change its nature in the light of later interpretation, that it is "incomplete" and seemingly "indeterminate" in its original form.

Another artistic property that causes difficulty for Levinson is that of style, particularly in the case of works that pioneer a new style or genre category that "arguably does not fully exist until other works are subsequently created that serve to stake out the boundaries of the category involved" (Levinson 1996, 265). He gives the examples of *film noir*, twelve-tone music, sculptural assemblage, and mannerist painting. Until the arrival of later works, which develop or consolidate the style, it is not just that we do not *know* what style the pioneering work belongs in but that the style simply does not exist at the time the work is created. This was the kind of case considered earlier to show that interpretation sometimes cannot take the generic or categorial level for granted. Levinson offers a number of ways around the problem, but one of them takes us back to Krausz and the idea of making an object-of-interpretation more determinate:

> One might grant that art content can become more *determinate* over time, through gradual emergence in concrete fashion of a work's historically correct categories of interpretation, while insisting on a real difference between that kind of focusing and wholesale alteration in art content. (265; Levinson's italics)

The final clause is a gesture to distance the view from imputationalism, but the use of "wholesale" suggests a nervousness on that score. Can imputationalism be defended in terms of the indeterminacy of works or their added determinacy over time through interpretation? Prima facie this does not look especially promising for the imputationalist. For one thing, it suggests a linear view of the development of a work, as if it consisted in the gradual accumulation of more determinate features; yet it seems to be compatible with imputationalism that a work should lose features as well as gain them. There is also Stecker's objection to the effect that if a work is inherently indeterminate in certain specifics (for example, the number of Lady Macbeth's children), then no amount of subsequent interpretation is going to change that fact, unless presumably the interpretation shows that what initially seemed to be an indeterminacy was in fact no such thing. Stecker's point, though, faces the obvious charge of begging the question.

Works and Indeterminacy

The idea of indeterminacy is worth pursuing, I suggest, for it takes us right back to our earlier discussion about the relation of interpretation and particular kinds of objects. Not all cultural objects have indeterminacy. Margolis is not right to suppose that indeterminacy is an inevitable concomitant of Intentionality.[15] Having the value of five cents is an Intentional property, but it is perfectly determinate that a nickel possesses that property. In fact, we can say that it is an *intrinsic* property of the *nickel* (not the piece of metal) that it has the value five cents. Similarly, within a game of soccer, kicking the ball between the goal posts during play without incurring a penalty is an action that has the determinate Intentional property of scoring a goal. Determinacies of a similar kind are to be found in all cultural objects, including art. That *The Potato Eaters* depicts human beings sitting around a table is a determinate, Intentional, fact about that work. Of course, it is true that the mere physical object embodying the nickel, just like the mere action of kicking the ball or the canvas per se, does not *independently of a complex Intentional structure* have the cited Intentional property. It is only given a rule-governed practice that the Intentional properties are made possible. But that does not impugn their determinacy. Indeed, it might be one reason why we are not called upon to *interpret* a nickel or a soccer goal or the ostensible subject of a painting.

But is the value of the nickel "in" the coin or "imputed to" it? The answer seems to be *both*, once we acknowledge the special status of the Intentional object. Having the value of five cents becomes an *intrinsic* quality of the "work" (the coin) in virtue of having the value *imputed to* it within the practice or "institution." This is a clear-cut case in which the very conventions of the practice dictate what it is to have a particular quality and also how we are to identify that quality (recognizing salient features of the metal's design and appearance).

---

[15] He makes this supposition when he claims that "Intentional attributes are not determinate . . . when compared with what is usually taken to be the determinate nature of physical or non-Intentional attributes" (Margolis 1999, 58) or that "Intentional properties are determinable . . . but not antecedently determinate" (Margolis 1999, 73).

What about properties of works of art that are subject to interpretation, which do seem to have indeterminacies, and so the question of what is "in" and "imputed to" them becomes more pressing? Consider the example of Dostoevsky's *Crime and Punishment*, for which a long-standing critical crux has been trying to make sense of the conflicting motives behind Raskolnikov's crime. Numerous psychological and political interpretations have been offered, and it is sometimes even suggested that the novel fails for not presenting a unified character. Here is one, not untypical, reading:

> The whole point of the book lies precisely in the process by which Raskolnikov moves from one explanation of the crime to another, and in so doing discovers the truth about the nature of the deed he has committed. . . . Why, for example, does Dostoevsky begin his narrative just a day before the actual commission of the crime, and convey Raskolnikov's *conscious* motivation in a series of flashbacks? One reason, of course, is to obtain the brilliant effect of dramatic irony at the close of Part I. For the entire process of reasoning that leads to Raskolnikov's theory of the altruistic Utilitarian crime is only explained in detail in the tavern-scene, where Raskolnikov hears his very own theory discussed by another student and a young officer; and this scene is the last important one before the crime is committed. . . . Temporarily, the tavern-scene and the murder itself are at the very opposite ends of a single time-sequence; but they are telescoped together deftly by Dostoevsky's narrative technique. . . . The purpose of [the] juxtaposition and telescoping of the time-sequence is obviously to undermine Raskolnikov's *conscious* motivation for the reader. The hypnotic hysteria in which he kills the old pawnbroker could not reveal more clearly, in an objective, dramatic fashion, that Raskolnikov's crime is not being committed according to his altruistic, Utilitarian theory. . . . Each step, then, in the *backward* process of revealing Raskolnikov's conscious, altruistic motive . . . is accompanied by another episode moving *forward* in time that undercuts it. (Frank 1975, 567–69)

A number of observations can be made about this passage. First, it is paradigmatically a *literary* interpretation, proceeding on the assumption that the work is literary (and fictional), not, for example, a work of biography or empirical psychology. The ways that thematic developments are connected to individual episodes and narrative techniques are features unique to the practice of literary reading. Imagine how anomalous such remarks would be applied to a police report of a murder. Second, the reading assigns salience, to use Krausz's term, to narrative elements – time-sequencing, flashbacks, juxtapositioning of scenes – to help establish interpretive points. The elements are there already, but the salience assignments come with the interpretation. Third, the property attributed (in this passage by implication) to Raskolnikov as a coherent, unified character, albeit with tension in his motivation, is a property (broadly, an aesthetic property) that again emerges only *through an interpretation* or *under a description*. It makes no sense to say that the *text* possesses that property, any more than it makes sense to say that the text is aesthetically coherent. This is the vestigial truth behind Rorty's position.

Are the saliences described in the passage "in" the work, from its very inception, or "imputed to" it in an interpretation? Again, as with the case of the nickel – although here with the added background of indeterminacy – the answer is *both*. Every element in a work, given the kind of work it is, has potential saliency, but the aesthetic function of elements like the time-sequences and flashbacks is determinable only relative to an interpretation. Margolis is right that at this level the insistence on bivalent truth-values – either truth or falsity of interpretive statements – is gratuitous. Instead, we look at consequences: What follows from assigning salience in *this* way, of making *these* connections? Does a more or a less coherent work emerge? Does a particular assignment of salience draw together more elements or does it make some unaccountable? These questions themselves are already grounded in a conception of a literary work. The search for thematic unity, coherence of characterization, connectedness of episode, symbolic or figurative meaning, narrative functions fulfilling aesthetic ends, is at the heart of the practice of literary interpretation. It is not a merely contingent fact that works of literature should reward such a search, for literary works are defined within a practice that dictates the expectation of this reward. We must conclude, then, that so close is the linking of work and mode of interpretation that there is an inevitable blurring of what is "in" a work, or part of its inherent nature, and what is "imputed to" it through interpretation. That is the insight of imputationalism.

A Sketch of Two Models for the "Incompleteness" of Works

Let me end by sketching two further models for explaining the indeterminacy of works: that of fictional characters, whose properties are incomplete, and that of metaphors, whose meanings are open-ended. The models are not incompatible.

There are several parallels between the ontological status of fictional characters and that of literary works. Both, arguably, are abstract entities, created artifacts, cultural objects, dependent on originating texts, sustained in existence by Intentional acts and attitudes, and subject to interpretation (for an illuminating account of these and other parallels, see Thomasson 1999, 139 ff.). They are also both "incomplete," if only in the formal sense that there are some predicates that can justifiably neither be asserted nor denied of them. There are many "facts" about fictional characters (including the hoary example of whether there is a mole on Sherlock Holmes's back) that remain permanently indeterminate, there being no principles of inference that warrant acceptance or rejection.[16] On the other hand, there are many psychological or motivational properties, which, although indeterminate in the sense that they are not explicitly ascribed to a character in the narrative, nevertheless appear warranted *relative to an interpretation*, or under a perspective that itself might fall within consensually defensible bounds (Lamarque 1996a, 64); Raskolnikov's motives, as described in the quoted passage, might be one example of such a property.

Often when fictional works are dramatized for stage or film, decisions have to be made about details, physical as well as psychological, that are indeterminate in the original narrative work. The same is true for pictorial renderings. What we have then in the case of fictional characters are objects-of-interpretation (in the sense of products-of-interpretation) comparable to those associated with interpreted works (like Branagh's *Hamlet*). The question arises whether such an object-of-interpretation retains the identity of the character or creates a new character. On reflection, it turns out that character-identity is no more determinate in this regard than work-identity. The necessity of origins holds for both, but on the matter of *content* it seems reasonable to suppose there is some degree of tolerance in property-ascription. Thus, in the case of fictional characters, we can say (1) that some more or less stable *core* of characteristics must be shared by representations of the *same character* (Lamarque 1996a, 49), but (2) that there is room for alternative supplementations of the character in drawings or other works that add new properties (under suitable constraints of consistency, coherence, and the like) without jeopardizing the basic identity. In the case of minor unspecified indeterminacies, particularly trivial details (like the presence of moles, the number of hairs on the head, and so on), it will often *make no difference* what form the supplementation takes – imaginatively, pictorially, conceptually – as long as it coheres with the core properties.

If this is a plausible story – albeit very roughly sketched – for the identity of fictional characters, and if characters share important ontological features with works, then the parallel offers further support to the imputationalist case about properties imputed to works. One other factor can be introduced, which also might throw light on the kind of indeterminacy involved, namely, that character-identity is often thought of, or treated as *interest-relative* (Lamarque and Olsen 1994, 132). In other words, rather than thinking there are absolute criteria for sameness of character, perhaps we need to take into account the interests behind our talk of characters. From the point of view of literary history, for example, fairly loose criteria might be acceptable, whereby the Faust-character or the Christ-

---

[16] Currie labels as "narrative interpretation" the investigation of what is "true in" a story and recognizes that "one kind of interpretive disagreement is about whether some aspect of the story is indeterminate or not" (Currie 1993, 415, n. 5).

character can be seen to be cropping up in different guises across time and even cultures. But a careful student of Goethe, for example, might insist on the uniqueness of Faust in Goethe's treatment and its deep divergence from that of, say, Christopher Marlowe. So from the perspective of literary history, the Goethe and Marlowe characters are the same; from that of work analysis they are different. Again there might be a fruitful analogy between characters and works with regard to such interest-relative identity, and this analogy again might be congenial to the imputationalists.

The other model is that of metaphor, where the indeterminacy is not that of incompleteness or "missing facts" but of meaning. There are accounts of the semantics of metaphor that hold that any meanings discoverable in a metaphor must already be present within the literal meanings of the component terms, making the process of interpretation something akin to disambiguation.[17] Such a view, which might parallel extreme "realist" theories of cultural objects, is open to many objections (Lamarque and Olsen 1994, 354–55). But a more familiar dispute among theorists of metaphor is between those who ascribe some special metaphorical meaning or content to a metaphor, a product of interaction, transference, comparison, or other mechanisms, and those, usually followers of Donald Davidson, who reject the idea of metaphorical meaning altogether. In favor of the former it can be said that they acknowledge the structured and rule-governed nature of metaphor and seek to show in systematic ways how metaphorical meaning is generated and can be recovered; the anti-content school acknowledges the more unruly aspects of metaphor, its appeal to the imagination, its nonreliance on propositional content, its causal powers. Perhaps there are echoes of Levinson's DM and CM interpreting in these positions.

But the real lessons from metaphor that I believe bear on literary (or artistic) interpretation lie in a conception of metaphor that brings together the rule-governed and the imaginative aspects. Rather than thinking of metaphor as a kind of assertion, or vehicle of truth, or propositional content, it is more illuminating to think of it as an act of a certain kind, embedded in a practice. The act is not assertion but exhortation, an encouragement to pursue comparisons conceptually, propositionally, or imagistically. There might be context-specific aims in any given metaphorical utterance – to convey a thought, to say something true, to advance an argument – but the core of a metaphor has the force more of an invitation to *do* something than to *believe* something.

Clearly much more needs to be said to flesh out the theory (see Lamarque and Olsen 1994, Chap. 14), but whether or not the theory is sustainable with respect to metaphor, it yields an instructive model for

---

[17]   Perhaps the clearest account of such a view is in Cohen 1979.

literature and art. The idea that literary (and artistic) works also invite a kind of imaginative exploration, at least in relation to those aspects that are indeterminate and thus subject to interpretation, takes us away from the paradigm of semantic content. Artistic works, unlike certain other cultural objects (coins, judicial rulings), are precisely the kind of objects that invite an imaginative and exploratory response, the seeking of new saliences, the forging of connections. That is part of their practice-dependent nature, just as it is with metaphor. This is not to say that every imaginative response is warranted by the work – some will perhaps create their own objects-of-interpretation with a separate identity. But it shows that what is *in* the work, as part of its nature, given to it by the very practice that makes it a work, is an invitation to *impute* things to it. If interpretation is making sense of something, then we should not lose sight of the creative connotation of "making."

References

Barnes, Annette. (1988). *On Interpretation*. Oxford: Basil Blackwell.

Barthes, Roland. (1979). "From Work to Text." In *Textual Strategies: Perspectives in Post-Structuralist Criticism*, translated and edited by Josué V. Harari. Ithaca, NY: Cornell University Press.

Borges, Jorge Luis. (1970). "Pierre Menard, Author of the *Quixote*." In *Labyrinths*. Harmondsworth, England: Penguin.

Cohen, L. J. (1979). "The Semantics of Metaphor." In *Metaphor and Thought*, edited by A. Ortony. Cambridge: Cambridge University Press.

Currie, Gregory. (1991). "Work and Text." *Mind*, 100 (July): 325–40.

——. (1993). "Interpretation and Objectivity." *Mind*, 102 (July): 415–28.

Danto, Arthur C. (1981). *The Transfiguration of the Commonplace*. Cambridge: Harvard University Press.

——. (1986). *The Philosophical Disenfranchisement of Art*. New York: Columbia University Press.

Frank, Joseph. (1975). "The World of Raskolnikov." In *Crime and Punishment*, written by Feodor Dostoevsky and edited by George Gibian. New York: W. W. Norton.

Geach, Peter. (1969). *God and the Soul*. New York: Schocken Books.

Grice, H. P. (1989). *Studies in the Way of Words*. Cambridge: Harvard University Press.

Knapp, Steven, and Walter Benn Michaels. (1992). "The Impossibility of Intentionless Meaning." In *Intention and Interpretation*, edited by Gary Iseminger. Philadelphia: Temple University Press. First published as "Against Theory," in *Against Theory: Literary Studies and the New Pragmatism*, edited by W. J. T. Mitchell (Chicago: University of Chicago Press, 1985).

Krausz, Michael. (1993). *Rightness and Reasons: Interpretation in Cultural Practices*. Ithaca, NY: Cornell University Press.

——. (1997). "Rightness and Reasons: A Reply to Stecker." *Journal of Aesthetics and Art Criticism*, 55 (4), 415–18.

Lamarque, Peter. (1991). Review of *Mimesis as Make-Believe*, by Kendall Walton. *Journal of Aesthetics and Art Criticism*, 49, 161–66.

——. (1996a). *Fictional Points of View*. Ithaca, NY: Cornell University Press.

——. (1996b). "Marks and Noises and Interpretations." *Semiotica*, 108 (1/2), 163–75.

——. (1998). "Aesthetic Value, Experience, and Indiscernibles." *Nordisk Estetisk Tidskrift*, 17, 61–78.

——. (Forthcoming). "Aesthetic Essentialism." In *Aesthetic Concepts: Essays after Sibley*, edited by Jerrold Levinson and Emily Brady. Oxford: Oxford University Press.

Lamarque, Peter, and Stein Haugom Olsen. (1994). *Truth, Fiction, and Literature: A Philosophical Perspective*. Oxford: Clarendon Press.

Levinson, Jerrold. (1990). *Music, Art, & Metaphysics: Essays in Philosophical Aesthetics*. Ithaca, NY: Cornell University Press.

——. (1996). *The Pleasures of Aesthetics: Philosophical Essays*. Ithaca, NY: Cornell University Press.

——. (1999). "Two Notions of Interpretation." In *Interpretation and Its Boundaries*, edited by Arto Haapala and Ossi Naukkarinen, 2–21. Helsinki: Helsinki University Press.

Margolis, Joseph. (1980). *Art and Philosophy: Conceptual Issues in Aesthetics*. Atlantic Highlands, NJ: Humanities Press.

——. (1993). "Reinterpreting Interpretation." In *Contemporary Philosophy of Art: Readings in Analytic Aesthetics*, edited by John W. Bender and H. Gene Blocker, 454–70. Englewood Cliffs, NJ: Prentice Hall. First published in *Journal of Aesthetics and Art Criticism*, 47 (1989).

——. (1999). *What, After All, Is a Work of Art?* University Park: Pennsylvania State University Press.

Olsen, Stein Haugom. (1987). *The End of Literary Theory*. Cambridge: Cambridge University Press.

Rorty, Richard. (1992). "The Pragmatist's Progress." In *Interpretation and Overinterpretation*, written by Umberto Eco and edited by Stefan Collini. Cambridge: Cambridge University Press.

Stecker, Robert. (1997a). *Artworks: Definition, Meaning, Value*. University Park: Pennsylvania State University Press.

——. (1997b). "The Constructivist's Dilemma." *Journal of Aesthetics and Art Criticism*, 55 (1), 43–52.

——. (1997c). "The Wrong Reasons: A Response to Michael Krausz." *Journal of Aesthetics and Art Criticism*, 55 (4).

Thom, Paul. (1997). Review of *Rightness and Reasons* by M. Krausz, *Interpretation Radical but Not Unruly: The New Puzzle of the Arts and*

History by J. Margolis, and "The Constructivist's Dilemma" by R. Stecker. *Literature and Aesthetics*, 7 (October).

Thomasson, Amie L. (1999). *Fiction and Metaphysics*. Cambridge: Cambridge University Press.

Walton, Kendall L. (1970). "Categories of Art." *Philosophical Review*, 79, 334–67.

———. (1990). *Mimesis as Make-Believe*. Cambridge: Harvard University Press.

8

INTERPRETATION AND ITS "METAPHYSICAL" ENTANGLEMENTS

MICHAEL KRAUSZ

Joseph Margolis identifies me as one of many "who offer theories of interpretation [and who] . . . confidently affirm (without success) that they
avoid all metaphysical entanglements" (1997b, 87). But that's not quite
right. I affirm a rather more narrow thesis, namely, that ideals of interpretation are detachable from the ontology of objects of interpretation
(including realism, constructivism, and constructive realism). For convenience, I refer to the latter sorts of theories as ontological. The claim of
detachability still allows that there are wider "metaphysical" concerns that
are ineliminable in a more ramified theory of interpretation, and that such
concerns include the intentionality of cultural achievements, which
Margolis so centrally features. I do not embrace the view that *all* metaphysical entanglements can be avoided. Indeed, any moorings that secure
the objectivity of interpretation are bound to implicate metaphysics in a
broad sense.

The separation between interpretation and its objects is broadly metaphysical to begin with. And such separation is necessary for the very
formulation of singularism and multiplism. So it cannot be the case that
the general discussion about interpretation can be pursued completely
independently of such metaphysical entanglements. But while it is one
thing to say that some metaphysical entanglements are inevitable, it is
another thing to say that ontology as here understood bears specifically on
the narrower issue of singularism versus multiplism. My principal and
narrow claim concerns the logical detachability of ideals of interpretation
from the ontology of its objects. In this chapter I shall offer a sample of
ontologies by way of abductive support for this claim.

I

Here is an *initial* argument for the logical detachability of ideals of
interpretation from the ontology of its objects. First, I define ideals of

interpretation (ideality) in terms of the distinction between singularism and multiplism, where, roughly, singularism is the view that for any object of interpretation there is one and only one ideally admissible interpretation of it, and multiplism is the view that for such an object of interpretation there may be more than one ideally admissible interpretation of it. Note that *both* singularism and multiplism distinguish between ideally admissible and inadmissible interpretations. Second, I map the ontological field in terms of the distinction between realism and constructivism (constructive realism will come later), where, roughly, realism holds that that which is interpreted is fully constituted independently of interpretive practices, and constructivism holds that at least some of its defining properties are dependent upon such practices. So understood, realism and constructivism are taken to be exclusive and exhaustive. Third, I allow that the compound positions generated by these two pairs of distinctions are each coherently adoptable. The positions are singularist/realist, singularist/constructivist, multiplist/realist, and multiplist/constructivist. Given these conditions, it follows that the issue of singularism versus multiplism (ideality) and the issue of realism versus constructivism (ontology) are detachable. If "ideality" is understood in terms of the first distinction, and "ontology" in terms of the second distinction, the argument for the claim that ideality is logically detachable from ontology stands as valid (Krausz 1993).

Now, even if the ontological field were not mapped in terms of an exclusive and exhaustive distinction between realism and constructivism, where, for example, constructive realism were added to our inventory of ontologies, the thesis might still stand if any such further coherently adoptable ontologies were also neutral with respect to the contest between singularism and multiplism.

II

We will later consider whether constructive realism entails singularism or multiplism. But first let us now consider why realism and constructivism do not entail singularism or multiplism.

I offer a sketch of the dialectic between realism and constructivism. Realism distinguishes between an *object as such* and an *object as represented*. An object as such would be an object whose properties are independent of any representation of it. Constructivism holds that the distinction between an object as such and an object as represented is a distinction without a difference. For constructivism, not all properties of an object are independent of a representation of it. All would-be objects as such are tantamount to objects as represented. On the constructivist view it would be better to drop all talk of objects as such. If objects as represented are taken to talk about the same things, they do so depending upon the agreement or disagreement between objects as represented. Objects as such cannot be fixed independently of their representations. The constructivist holds that agreement of symbol systems does not mandate realism. One should resist the thought that agreement between symbol systems betrays an approximation to a "most basic" object as such.

The realist might suggest that one could identify the object as such by ostention, that is, by pointing. But, as Wittgenstein famously showed, one needs a supplementing story to identify which of the possible things pointed to is the thing one is being shown. For example, were one to point to a gray stone wall, it would be an open question whether one would be pointing to the stones in it, or to a particular stone, or to the wall's grayness, or to the color contrasts between the different gray stones, or to the overall design formed by the mortar around the stones, and so on. Only by adding or assuming a narrative does one get individuation. These sorts of considerations give rise to the constructivist alternative.

Constructivism holds that objects as such are never "given." They are always "taken" in a certain way, taken in terms of some representation in some symbol system. The intelligibility of any putative object as such will depend upon its being nested in some symbol system. It's construction all the way down – might as well let the object as such drop out of the account. Or, as Nelson Goodman says, "We do better to focus on versions rather than worlds" (1982, 21). And whichever symbol system one assumes is, as Goodman says, a matter of "simplicity, convenience, suitability to context, efficacy for a purpose, and accessibility by those we must communicate with" (1989, 84).

Notice that the agreement between symbol systems provides the conceptual space in which particular things may be said to be "real" in contrast with the illusory, but not in contrast with the unconstructed. In this sense the real would not be understood to implicate a symbol-system-independent order. Accordingly, one should not confuse the assertion that particular things are real with the *theory* of realism. The constructivist holds that the assertion of particular real existents cannot be made uniquely by realists. Realism should not hijack real particulars.

In short, for the constructivist, any attempt to drive a conceptual wedge between objects as such and objects as represented will fail, for any described object as such will be a represented object. It is nested in a symbol system of some kind or other. This is inescapable. Any attempt to say what a version is a version of will issue in yet another version! It is best to let go of the temptation to speak of symbol-system-independent objects as such. I call this the constructivist's reductio (of realism).

In contrast, the realist might observe that all that the so-called constructivist's reductio shows is that what is *said* is inevitably nested in some symbol system. That does not show that there is nothing that is not nested in some symbol system. The realist might affirm that there are objects in the world that nobody has thought of, despite the fact that this very assertion is presently made in some symbol system. Despite our conceiving of them in the present thought experiment, the realist could hold, there are specific rocks in the Himalayan Mountains that may yet come to be discovered. And their being *there* is a matter quite separate from anyone's conceiving of them, or from their representations' being nested in some symbol system deploying the concept "rocks." Even if, as Goodman says, there are shared terms or kindred concepts and mutual translatability between representations or world-versions, that is not enough. The rocks (or something, however described) are *there*, just as the Himalayan Mountains (or something, however described) are *there*, independent of any representations of them.

III

Perhaps there is room for some reconciliation between the constructivist and the realist. Consider a kind of constructive realism which combines features of realism and constructivism. So far I have characterized the constructivist and realist positions in terms of first-order objects. But suppose now that the realist and the constructivist were to agree that *at the first order* there *is* a difference in kind between certain sorts of objects, say, between sticks and stones, on the one hand, and cultural objects, on the other hand. They might agree that some first-order objects are representation-independent and that others are not. Yet they might still disagree *at the second order* about what licenses them to make this agreed-upon first-order distinction. A second-order realist could say that these different kinds of things are parceled in accord with a real difference. The difference is found, not made. On the other hand, a second-order constructivist might say that the differences between first-order objects are themselves constructed. First-order parceling is a matter of constructing differences for certain purposes and interests. The differences are made rather than found. What might have appeared at the first order as a difference in real versus constructed kinds was itself a difference between different constructed kinds. The second-order constructivist would subtend real-looking kinds under a second-order constructivism. What appeared at the first order to be representation-independent would upon inspection turn out to be representation-dependent after all!

The challenge facing second-order realism is to make itself immune from the constructivist's reductio, for the constructivist may counter that, say, even the physical properties of sticks and stones are intelligible only in terms of the periodic table of elements or some cognate symbol system. Further, second-order realism must make coherent the thought that the distinction between representation-independence and representation-dependence is itself representation-independent. In contrast, the challenge facing second-order constructivism is that it must account for what appear to be first-order representation-independent objects all in constructivist terms, all the while keeping those objects' apparent resilience and apparent invariance as explanatory data. The difference between representation-independence and representation-dependence cannot be a difference between constructed and nonconstructed. It must be a difference between types of constructed things. The second-order constructivist is committed to saying that, finally, all first-order objects are representation-dependent, that finally they are constructed.

Perhaps one could bring the second-order realist and the second-order constructivist still closer together. First, they might be brought to agree that there is a difference in kind between certain sorts of first-order objects, however that difference is accounted for. And, second, they may be brought to agree that *what they both refer to as the real is constructed.* This would not be as significant a concession for the second-order realist as it might first appear if he or she may still posit *something* beyond the symbol system – if, that is, he or she might still legitimately ask such questions as From where does the real object come? and What presystematic "materials" are there for the construction of real things? The concession would allow that the "real" is subtended under the constructivist rubric, *so long as the real is not exhaustive of what may be presystematically countenanced.* The concession would disallow that that which is presystematic is the real. The real would turn out to be a characterization internal to a symbol system.

Were the second-order realist to agree to this concession, we might collect our second-order realist and second-order constructivist under a rubric which we may dub as "constructive realist." They would both agree to the constructive realist's motto, namely, *the real is constructed and the constructed is real.* Now the remaining difference between the second-order realist and the second-order constructivist would be understood in terms of the distinction between *internal* and *external* constructive realism. The internal constructive realist would say that there can be no appeal to anything – real or otherwise – that precedes the symbol system. The external constructive realist would say that although it cannot be countenanced as *real*, some presystematic "material" needs to be appealed to in order to account for the construction of the real. Understood in these terms, Margolis is an internal constructive realist, and Rom Harré, Paul Thom, and Hilary Putnam are external constructive realists. I shall briefly consider the views of each of these philosophers with an eye toward our overriding question of the detachability of ontology from ideality.

IV

First, let us consider Margolis's ontology. He holds that any coherent realism must be constructivist and that any coherent constructivism must be realist. Every viable constructivism cannot but be realist, and every viable realism cannot but be constructivist.

> Constructivism is *not* (or need not be) an abandonment of realism. Rather, I believe, there can be no viable realisms that are not also constructivisms; no other strategy . . . can escape incoherence and unacceptable paradox. This is as true of the natural world as it is of the cultural. (1997b, 79)

According to Margolis, no principled distinction between realism and constructivism can be sustained. It is not just that the two ontologies in our first mapping of the ontological field are not exhaustive. It is not just that constructive realism should be *added to* realism and constructivism as coherently adoptable views. Rather, constructive realism unseats both realism and constructivism.

Margolis argues that if one allows that natural languages, for example, are real and that they are not independent of interpretive activities, then realism and constructivism cannot be granted exclusivity.

> It does not make sense to claim that natural languages are *real* in any way that is said to be entirely independent of the discursive and interpretive activities of a society of apt speakers. Natural languages are real "in spite of" any such dependence. . . . But if languages are real if spoken (or written) by apt speakers, then, plainly, *any* realism that claimed unconditionally that whatever *is* real *is* "fully constituted, autonomous and independent of any interpretive activity" must mean at least that language and artworks are not real at all! (1997b, 80)

Yet keep in mind that a constructivist (like Goodman) can allow that that which is constituted is real if by that one understands that the real is contrasted with the imaginary or the like. (Recall: "Realism should not hijack real particulars.") At the same time, the constructivist demurs from building anything more robust into his or her claim than that some distinction between real and nonreal might apply. But for Margolis the constructivist's idea of the real is not robust enough, and the realist's idea goes too far. Yet for Margolis whatever is taken as the real cannot escape the fact that any claim of the real must be subtended under the matrix of "historied" human practices. Margolis emphasizes the point when he says

> It's perfectly all right to treat the physical world as independent of human inquiry and interpretation; but it is *not* possible to make sense of doing so without conceding that it – and every would-be determinate truth *about that world* – is epistemically constructed in accord with our cognitive abilities. (1997b, 83)

So for Margolis, any claim of the real is *subtended under a second-order constructivism*. Even the concession that the physical world is "independent of human inquiry and interpretation" is itself "epistemically constructed in accord with our cognitive abilities." Margolis emphasizes the cultural artifactuality of the physical world and of knowledge generally when he says:

> Although we conjecture (reasonably, of course) that the physical world is older than the advent of human culture, the conjecture itself occurs only within the space of the human: knowledge is a cultural artifact; also, the determinate structures we impute to the physical world (what we take realism to signify) are . . . logically inseparable from the emergent powers of the human world. In short, our theories of the physical world are endogenously horizoned by the cognitive history of human science. (1993, 181)

Margolis also says:

> We open our eyes and see a world we cannot ignore; still, what we see is due to what we are; and what we are we are as a result of our continuous self-formation and transformation within a larger history and the larger processes of nature. So the "resistance" of the encountered world is not at all incompatible with its being "constituted." (1994, 91)

Margolis places his thought that our theories of both the physical and the cultural worlds are "horizoned by the cognitive history of human science" in his larger thesis of fluxism. His fluxism is global, according to which all human activity (including the activity of theorizing about objects of parceled disciplines) is historical and therefore cultural. Margolis commits himself to this double doctrine: (1) the world does not have a constant and changeless structure and (2) knowledge of that changing order, including logic, mathematics, science, morality, interpretation of the arts, or any other similar discipline, is possible. Consequently, there are no invariant or exceptionless, changeless, timeless, universal principles for a thing to properly be a thing of its kind. And for him, the use of the same predicate does not commit one to an invariant order. One can use the same predicate in a world that is not invariant. The notions of sameness and difference are embedded in the interests and uses to which creatures put their intelligence. Correspondingly, principles, rules, genres, laws, and the like, are abstractions from within some form of life, practice, *Lebenswelt*, *Lebensform*, or the like. When such forms of life change, the abstractions which arose from earlier enabling cases will have become otiose in the face of new enabling cases and subsequent abstractions. Generally, then, what we impute as the real structure of the physical world itself is a function of the historical inquiry of human persons. Margolis's pan-fluxism applies not only to cultural entities but to the objects of the physical world as well. For all these entities, identity and reidentity are subject to determinability in accord with their pertinent histories.

Following upon his thought that "the determinate structures we impute to the physical world . . . are . . . logically inseparable from the emergent powers of the human world" (1993, 181), Margolis restricts determinability to the *nature* of Intentional entities. More fully, Margolis distinguishes an object's nature from its number when he says:

> Artworks . . . are *not fully determinate but are, characteristically, interpretively determinable* in Intentional ways. . . . in spite of having such a nature, they are reasonably *determinate in number*, individuable, and reidentifiable. (1997a, 17)

While the numerical identity of an artwork is "reasonably" fixed, it is its nature that is taken to be variously determinable. The nature of artworks, for example, can be made more determinate by culturally informed activity. As a result, one can then *discover* those works as having the properties imputed to them. Imputation is a process whereby, in virtue of interpretive activity, the nature of that which is interpreted changes. Aesthetic designs can be imputed and so they become part of the work's nature without making numerically different artworks.

> There is no reason why, granting that criticism proceeds in an orderly way, practices cannot be sustained in which aesthetic designs are rigorously *imputed* to particular works when they cannot be determinately *found* in them. Also, if they may be imputed rather than found, there is no reason why incompatible designs cannot be jointly defended. (1980, 160, emphasis added)

Margolis's thesis of determinability or imputability applies to the nature of numerically fixed artworks. It is not meant to imply the multiplication of numerically distinct artworks. Consequently, the fact that an artwork might answer to incongruent interpretations does not mandate multiplying or pluralizing (as I say) the work into correspondingly separate and distinct works. Margolis underscores the point that the numerical identity of a cultural entity is determinate when he says:

> Although the interpretation of a history or artwork or sentence cannot . . . alter the identity of any *denotatum*, the interpretation of Intentionally qualified entities *can* indeed alter the "nature" of what may be thereafter interpreted. . . . All we require is a careful distinction between the predicative oddities of artworks and their denotative fixity. (1997b, 84)

So how then should one treat the numerical identity of the object whose nature is determinable? Margolis answers:

> I recommend . . . that we treat "entity" in a very lax way: allowing, as an "entity," anything that we are prepared to say exists as an individuated *denotatum*, about which predicative claims can be made and validated. (1997b, 83)

Clearly, Margolis needs to hold fixed the numerical identity of a pertinent object in the face of the determinability of its nature, since otherwise changes in the object's nature would result in changes in its numerical identity. In that case, no incongruent interpretations of the *same* entity would obtain. And that, in turn, would undermine Margolis's whole relativistic project. The stakes are high. If the entity does not remain numerically one and the same thing over time, then, "it" cannot answer to multiple (indeed incongruent) interpretations.

But can Margolis's thesis of the flux sustain the distinction between nature and number? Why should a change in an object's nature *not* result in a change in its numerical identity? It is plausible to draw the distinction between nature and number, but doing so is at odds with Margolis's own pan-fluxism.

Be that as it may, let us return to our overarching concern about the detachability of ideality from ontology. Margolis ties interpretability to *multiple* interpretability. He says that the interpretability of a cultural object's nature "invites" incongruent judgments. And such judgments are "unavoidable."

> There is a run of phenomena – events and particulars – that "have natures" that intrinsically include complex *intentional* properties, such that those natures or features are vague or indeterminate enough to *invite* incongruent judgments regarding what they are, or such that their natures and properties are so alterable by interpretation alone that incongruent judgments *cannot be avoided* in specifying them. (1991, 19–20, emphasis added)

Notice that from the remark that Intentional objects are interpretable it does not follow that they answer to more than one ideally admissible interpretation. The singularist could actually embrace the thesis of determinability. Whatever "invitations" or "unavoidabilities" might be claimed of interpretability, why not just say that *one cannot say* whether an indeterminate object answers to one or more interpretations, rather than say that it answers to more than one interpretation? Or, why not say that with sufficiently thick descriptions of the surrounding context there could be only one way to impute and so interpret the object of interpretation? Again, what blocks a singularist from embracing Margolis's thesis of determinability?

While Margolis affirms both the thesis of determinability and multiple determinability (I also call the latter the thesis of alternativity), they are detachable claims. The thesis of determinability alone does not entail multiple determinability or multiplism. Again, a singularist might well embrace Margolis's thesis of determinability, adding that there is one way to determine an Intentional object's nature. I conclude that determinability as to nature is logically neutral with respect to singularism or multiplism.

V

Consider a second constructive realism. Rom Harré is an external constructive realist. He holds that there is a "world stuff" (or "glub" as he also sometimes calls it) independent of interpretive activity (hence realism). But the actual ascribable properties are afforded in the context of experiential or experimental "setups." That is, the ascribability of particular properties to the world is interpretation-dependent (hence constructivism).

Harré draws upon suggestions from physicist Niels Bohr and psychologist J. J. Gibson in holding that the world is indefinitely complex and capable of displaying a huge variety of aspects of itself, depending on the way that it is approached and experimented with. None of the actual properties in which the world reveals itself are identical with the properties of the world as it is independently of the situations and setups in which various and different aspects of its character are manifested. All we ever experience are effects of certain powers and dispositions of "apparatus-world" or "people-world" combinations. All we can properly ascribe to the world are powers to produce this or that effect in us or in our apparatus. Consequently, all we say about the world must take a conditional form, namely, *if* certain conditions are fulfilled, *then* the world will (or could) manifest itself in this or that way. The track in a cloud chamber, for example, is a manifestation of electronhood that is available to human beings only in the context of that cloud chamber. It is the complex of world and cloud chamber that has a disposition to display itself as electron-tracks. What of the electrons that we picture as causing the tracks? They, too, are but "affordances" of the total setup. (Harré borrows the term from Gibson.) It follows that the way in which the world is manifested to human beings depends upon which instrument is being used to bring forth that disposition. For Harré, it makes no sense to ask what is the complete and determinate nature of an object independent of "apparatus-world" or "people-world" complexes.

> We cannot infer that because our apparatus in interaction with the world affords electrons, it has revealed something that would have existed had the apparatus not been switched on. Yet we do want to say that, in some way or other, what we do in physics with an apparatus tells us something about the world – but what does it tell us? Clearly, if the Bohrian view is in general correct, then it cannot be telling us what the dispositions of the world are. . . . There is a refinement of the concept of a disposition that comes from psychology of perception developed by J. J. Gibson . . . , namely, the "affordance." An affordance is a disposition the display of which occurs in circumstances created by or relevant to human interests. For example a pair of scissors affords cutting or the ice on a lake in the winter affords walking. The human element in the spelling out of affordances can never be eliminated. Applying this idea in physics we have the claim that the world affords electrons just in combination with a particular kind of apparatus. Ice affords walking so long as I do not have my pet elephant with me. What the causal powers of the world afford experimenters will depend on the apparatus employed. . . . The world has the power to afford electron

phenomena when in indissoluble union with instances of a certain class of apparatus. But we cannot strip away the contribution of the apparatus and ascribe pure powers to the world. (1997, 25)

Harré says further:

> Electrons exist *as such*, that is as spatio-temporally individuatable entities, only in the context of the apparatus/world complex. *They* are brought into being in the apparatus. If we set up and activate another kind of apparatus, we will bring wave-like phenomena into existence. . . . The phenomena are afforded by an apparatus/world complex only if the world has the power to generate such beings when intimately interconnected with the relevant apparatus. The world affords electrons in just this kind of apparatus, the world affords waves in just that kind of apparatus, and so on. (1997, 26)

And finally:

> This allows us to say there are properties of the world that are such that their empirical content is always given by their mode of manifestation. (1997, 27)

To the construction-independent world-stuff, Harré ascribes a minimal property, namely, that in union with pertinent setups the world-stuff has the power to afford empirical manifestations in one form or another. This minimal claim qualified Harré as a kind of realist, an *external* constructive realist in that the world-stuff is taken to be representation-independent and lacking in empirical content. Yet phenomena are constructed in the union of the world with pertinent apparatus. This constructive element qualifies Harré as a *constructive* realist. Accordingly, Harré describes the emergence of *empirical content* in this way:

> Bohr saw that the performing of an experiment created an "internal" relation between the material apparatus as used by the experimenter and the material stuff with which it interacted. The relation is "internal" in that the apparatus, when in use, brings into being a state of affairs which, though it is the manifestation of a real disposition or tendency or natural power of the world stuff, is not just a manifestation of those dispositions. The form that manifestation takes is shaped by the apparatus and the way it is used. The indissoluble totality of the apparatus-world manifestation is what Bohr meant by phenomenon. It makes no sense to ask "What would an electron be like if there were no electron-displaying apparatus?" since the world disposition in question is only displayed *as an electron* in that kind of set-up. There is nothing subjectivist or relativist about this idea. "Electrons" are relational properties of some well-defined types of apparatus-world ensembles. . . .
> We shall say . . . that a certain kind of apparatus-world ensemble *affords* the relevant category of entities, properties, processes, and so on to some instrument or observer or manipulator. (Aronson, Harré, and Way 1995, 179–81)

Let us collect Harré's salient claims. For him physics tells us something about the world. Yet we cannot strip away the contribution of the apparatus and ascribe pure powers to the world. The *entity* we call an electron is an aspect of electronic *phenomena*. The phenomenon of the electron qua electron is brought into being by a certain kind of apparatus bringing out something from the world. The entity is not a parcel of the world but a feature of a particular apparatus-world complex. The world *affords* electrons just in combination with a particular kind of apparatus. What the causal powers of the world afford will depend on the apparatus employed. The world has the power to afford electron phenomena when in indissoluble union with pertinent apparatus. The apparatus in interaction with the world affords electrons. But we cannot infer that it has revealed something that would have existed had the apparatus not been switched on. As Harré says, "an affordance is a disposition the display of which occurs in circumstances created by or relevant to human interests," and this human element can never be eliminated. Thus, Harré's philosophy of physics does not desert realism.

We can think of Harré as offering a four-tiered structure: (1) world-stuff which, in indissoluble union with apparatus, constitutes a "phenomenon" and affords (2) an object as such which has empirical content and may be represented as (3) objects-as-represented which may answer to various (4) interpretations.

Notice that Harré's world-stuff can do no criterial or methodological work, only the philosophical work of making sense of the apparatus-world complexes that afford phenomena. He can say nothing about the world-stuff except (paradoxically) that it has the disposition to be manifested in certain ways.

Harré's constructive realism seeks to satisfy the concern that without something *there* (the world-stuff) to which to ascribe properties, it remains mysterious what interpretations might be about. Yet the paradox is that, preceding apparatus-world complexes, properties as such cannot be ascribed at all. Yet Harré ascribes the property of affordance to the world-stuff.

How does all this bear on singularism versus multiplism? Being noncriterial, the world-stuff is not denumerable. It is not countable. One cannot say that it, singularly, is that which interpretations are about. Even if one were to say that interpretations are *indirectly* about the world-stuff, its singularity could not be assumed – not because, again, it might be multiple, but rather because it is not countable at all. Countability could obtain at the level of phenomena, but not at the level of the world-stuff. It is only at the level of apparatus-world that an object as such can be constituted as countable. The world-stuff cannot be differentiated as to number. So the question as to whether the world-stuff is one or more cannot arise. While the world-stuff is meant to ground apparatus-world complexes, it is not countable. Thus, as regards interpretations of the world-stuff, neither singularism or multiplism can be affirmed. And unless the object of interpretation is grounded as singular, multiplism could not obtain. We can go further. Even pluralism presupposes that pertinent "objects" of interpretation are countable, that a given object of interpretation answers to a given interpretation, and that a separate object of interpretation answers to another interpretation. So without a singular object of interpretation not only does multiplism not obtain, but pluralism also does not obtain. If the world-stuff is not countable, then with respect to it singularism and multiplism are *undecidable*.

Further, in conjunction with his ontological claim of phenomena in apparatus-world complexes, Harré adds the rider of alternativity, namely, that there are a multiplicity of setups. But this joint claim of ontology and alternativity still does not entail multiplism, for, as I suggested, it is undecidable whether the interpretations address the same object. The claim that phenomena reside in apparatus-world complexes does not by itself entail multiplism. For a singularist might agree that phenomena reside in apparatus-world complexes and still assert that there is one and only one admissible apparatus which should be coupled with the world-stuff. Harré's claim that phenomena obtain in apparatus-world complexes is *logically distinct* from the rider of alternativity. And the rider of alternativity itself mandates neither singularism nor multiplism, since alternativity is compatible with there being one *or* more than one object of interpretation to which the interpretations address themselves. Thus, Harré's ontology of constructive realism remains neutral with respect to singularism and multiplism.

VI

Consider a third constructive realism. Paul Thom introduces a three-tiered structure which seeks to articulate the relation between (1) an interpretation, (2) an object-as-represented, and what he calls (3) a further object. And the further object plays a critical role in Thom's view of reference and predication. It precedes interpretive activity. It is representation-independent. Further, Thom holds that it is an object-as-represented that may be differently imputed. And while the object-as-represented is not one and the same thing when differently imputed, in an *indirect* way the interpretations in question still address the same thing, namely, the further object which affords and is represented by the objects-as-represented.

The important point is that interpretation displays a three-tier structure. For present purposes I am calling the three levels "interpretation," "object-as-represented" and "further object." The labels are not vital; the number of levels is. (1997, 183)

Thom applies his scheme to the face-vase configuration.

> In discussing a line-drawing which can be seen either as two facing heads or as
> a vase, Krausz states "the object-of-interpretation is understood in terms of its
> imputed properties." . . . Now it is true that different aspects of the drawing
> become salient in the two interpretations, and that if there are different saliences
> there are different intentional objects. Further it is true that "the interpretation –
> face or vase – prompts one to impute salience to certain features of the
> presented configuration, which in turn confirms the propriety of interpreting
> the configuration as a face or a vase." But if we take this to mean that there are
> two objects-of-interpretation, then we need to remember that behind these
> distinct objects-of-interpretation there is a single further object. This, we might
> say (following Margolis), has been identified in the two interpretations.
> Further, we could say that the two interpretations represent the further object
> differently, provided that our concept of representation did not rule out selec-
> tivity. The imputed properties (leading to the interpretation "face" or "vase")
> are, we can agree, part of the object-of-interpretation; but they are no part of
> this *single further object* [emphasis added; I shall comment presently on this
> phrase] of both interpretations, namely the configuration of lines in the figure.
> (The same points can be made with reference to Krausz's other examples –
> Van Gogh's *The Potato Eaters*, Wordsworth's Lucy poems, self-interpretation
> and interpretation of other cultures.) (1997, 182–83)

In other words, according to Thom, different aspects of the configuration are imputed as salient by the two interpretations. If there are different
saliences, there are different objects-as-represented. The interpretation
prompts one to impute salience to certain features of the presented
configuration, which in turn confirms the propriety of interpreting the
configuration as it is. Different imputations result in different objects-as-
represented. Yet behind these distinct objects-as-represented, there is a
further object, the configuration. And that has been identified in the two
interpretations. The imputed properties are part of the object-as-represented, but they are no part of this further object.
    Thom goes on to say:

> Krausz himself recognizes that what he calls the object-of-interpretation (what
> I call the object-as-represented) is "not spun out of nothing" but rather, "impu-
> tational interpretation involves selecting features of the presented materials
> with which to fashion an object-of-interpretation." . . . These "presented mate-
> rials" are what I have been calling the further object of interpretation. (1997,
> 183)

It is the properties of the object-as-represented and not those of the
further object that are imputed by interpretation. In the present case, the
configuration is the further object, which is seen as a pair of faces or as
a vase. These are the objects-as-represented. And it is in light of the
pertinent interpretations that saliences are imputed and warrant the

objects-as-represented in the way they are. In this sense there is a symbi-
otic or hermeneutic relation between objects-as-represented and interpretations.

But Robert Stecker reads the "object-of-interpretation" as the "further
object." So he raises the vexing question how interpretation could change
that object's nature or number. More fully, Stecker says:

> The problem is to understand how making a claim about an *object*, even an
> object-of-interpretation, can give it a property claimed for it. . . . If the claim is
> true, the object *already* has the property. If it is false, the object does not have
> the property. If it is nether true nor false, then what difference can be made by
> saying the object has the property or even telling a plausible story according to
> which the object has the property? Before an interpretation is offered, an object
> may well be indeterminate with respect to a property, but if it is, then such
> saying or story telling will not make *it* determinate, though it may get people
> to think of the object as determinate. (1997, 50, emphasis added)

It appears that Stecker collapses the object-as-represented into the
further object, and thus generates a paradox from the mistaken thought
that it is the properties of the further object that are taken to be imputed.
Accordingly, this is how Thom answers Stecker.

> Stecker poses the question of how interpretation can involve both construction
> and predication – how an interpretation can complete an object-of-interpreta-
> tion by making a claim about it. As Stecker puts it (p. 50), "The problem is to
> understand how making a claim about an object, even an object-of-interpreta-
> tion, can give it a property claimed for it." Our three-tier structure for inter-
> pretation provides one answer to this puzzle: the interpretation makes a claim
> not about the further object but about the object-as-represented, while the latter
> may go beyond the former. Interpretation does indeed involve both construc-
> tion and predication, but at different levels: the object-as-represented is a
> construction from the further object. . . .
>
>   In each case, by processes of selection, suppression, highlighting and
> contextualization a representation of the painting is constructed, and this repre-
> sentation is then claimed to fall under a specific interpreting concept. This way
> of thinking allows interpretation to have both constructive and predicative
> elements, and thus perhaps provides a solution to Stecker's puzzle. At the same
> time, it allows for a type of constructive interpretation not mentioned by
> Stecker – namely where the concept, applied by the interpreter to the object-
> as-represented, has itself been constructed precisely for this purpose. (1997,
> 184–85)

Thom clarifies his point when he says:

> A predicative relation holds *in the first instance* between the interpretation and
> the object-as-represented, but . . . it transfers to the further object to the extent
> that that object is appropriately represented by the object-as-represented. If the

representation is appropriate to the type of interpretation being attempted, then the transfer works, otherwise not. (1998)

So understood, Thom's thought is that, indirectly, the further object answers to the interpretations of the objects-as-represented, in virtue of the fact that the further object is the "material" out of which the object-as-represented is constructed. Accordingly, where multiplism obtains, it does so indirectly between the interpretations of the further object via the object-as-represented. Multiplism does not obtain directly between the interpretations and the object-as-represented. Where objects-as-represented are imputed, different objects-as-represented obtain. That is, pluralism rather than multiplism obtains between interpretation and object-as-represented.

It is worth noting that Thom's idiom of "object as represented" resembles Margolis's idiom of "intentional *denotatum*" as expressed, for example, in Margolis's response to Stecker:

> Interpretation imputes a determinate sense to what (interpretively) is constituted as an Intentional *denotatum* – determinate as a *denotatum* and, as such, determinable in nature. The distinction is critical and is ignored by those (Stecker, for one) who neglect the complexity of Intentionality or who see no fundamental difference between Intentional and non-Intentional properties. But, of course, that is precisely what is at issue. (1999, 100)

Thom summarizes his thesis in the penultimate page of his forthcoming book, *Making Sense*.

> Our three-tier structure – object, object-as-represented, and interpretation – allows us simultaneously to maintain the Principle of Pluralism [or multiplism] and that of the Hermeneutic Circle, given a modified version of the Hermeneutic Circle which states that if the interpretation is different then the object-*as-represented* is different. One and the same object can have several interpretations, even if one and the same object-as-represented can't, provided that one and the same object can be represented in several ways. So Pluralism is compatible with the modified Hermeneutic Circle. To this extent, the three-tier structure provides us with a way of preserving both our principles.
>
> By contrast, if we stick to a two-tier structure consisting just of the object and its interpretation then we couldn't maintain *both* the Hermeneutic Circle and Pluralism. We can't maintain pluralism along with DIDO [Different Interpretation Different Object], since DIDO tells us that if there are several interpretations then there are several objects.

As already remarked, according to Thom, an interpretation and an object-as-represented are symbiotically related. That which is represented as salient is a function of the favored interpretation, and the favored interpretation is affirmed by the object-as-represented, constructed in light of the favored interpretation. For example, in the case of the face-vase configuration, the object-as-represented is the configuration seen as a face or a vase. And it is seen as one or the other in light of a face-interpretation or a vase-interpretation. An interpretation may impute certain properties to an object-as-represented and thereby change the properties of the object-as-represented. This leaves open the nature of the further object. At the same time, the interpretation of one object-as-represented may be jointly defended with another interpretation of another object-as-represented. Under these conditions no direct conflict between interpretations would obtain because the interpretations would not be addressing the same object-as-represented. Yet indirectly interpretations might conflict because the objects-as-represented have been afforded by a common further object.

Thom wishes to preserve both a modified hermeneutic circle and the principle of pluralism (again, "multiplism" in my usage). Since, on his account, the hermeneutic circle entails that different interpretations mandate different objects-as-represented, multiplism with respect to objects-as-represented cannot be sustained. Multiplism requires that that which is variously interpreted be about the same thing. Yet Thom does *indirectly* ground multiplism – in the sameness of that which is *indirectly* interpreted, namely, in the further object.

The question arises how Thom can establish that the further object is singular or, for that matter, even countable? (Recall the emphasized phrase "single further object," in Thom's passage quoted above.) The sameness of that which is indirectly interpreted may not be grounded or known to be grounded in a single further object. Yet the further object must be singular if it is to perform the job of "grounding" the objects-as-represented. If the further object is not singular, then Thom's pluralism (again, my multiplism) could not be generated. But Thom provides no grounds for individuating further objects. He simply assumes that it is one and only one further object which affords and is represented by objects-as-represented. If more than one further object were in place, or if there is no way of counting the further object, then the job that Thom assigns to the further object could not be performed. Put otherwise, Thom's principle of pluralism (or my multiplism) cannot be sustained if one were to disallow the countability and the singularity of the further object.

Thom means his further object to be read in a realist way. Yet it is made intelligible at the level of the object-as-represented. In this way, his three-tiered structure combines elements of both realism and constructivism. As already indicated, his three-tiered structure results in a pluralism as between interpretation and object-as-represented. But the further object is left without conditions of individuation, such that whether the further object actually answers to singularism or multiplism remains undecidable. Put otherwise, Thom allows for the alternativity of assigning salience and thus the multiplicity of objects-as-represented. But as in the views of others considered here, such alternatively entails neither singularism nor multiplism with respect to the further object.

VII

Finally, consider a fourth constructive realism. Putnam's so-called internal realism qualifies in my terms as a constructive realism. In her lucid book *Realism versus Realism*, Chhanda Gupta follows Putnam in defending his view and she outlines it in an especially perspicuous way. I offer an extended quote from Gupta which contrasts transcendental realism and immanent realism, internal realism being a particular version of immanent realism. Keep in mind our question: Does internal realism entail either singularism or multiplism? Gupta says

> Old-style realism takes a transcendent metaphysical stance, focusing on reality, on what there is in itself independently of what we know or say about it.
>
> Opposed to this are "realisms" that take an *immanent* stance insisting on the need of linking the question: "what is there?" with the question: "what do we conceive, know and say about it?"
>
> A few points may be noted to make the contrast between these two views leap to vision. They also highlight the main strands of the type of realism I have tried to defend following Putnam's lead.
>
> 1. Things exist independently and must be described too in terms that have nothing to do with us, according to transcendental realists. Things have features intrinsically, non-relationally, and not as objects of anyone's belief, thought, experience and knowledge. This is the requirement of absoluteness.
> 1'. Things and their features do exist independently and are not our own making, the internal realists maintain like all realists. These are not projections and reifications of our own conceptual and cognitive nature, and are in this sense nonepistemic. But internal realism maintains additionally that such realities can be intelligibly talked about only when construed as thinkable, knowable and and describable. No meaningful discourse is possible about anything, including its most fundamental features, unless it is an object, at least a putative object of some belief, conception or knowledge. To stress the relativity of things and their features to thought in this way, however, is not to deny that things exist whether or not we know or say anything about them. Relativity here means that things which we may or may not know, are not transcendent, that is, they are not trans-conceptual, trans-cognitive and transphenomenal.
>
> 2. Things and their features according to transcendental realists are *radically nonepistemic* in the sense of being entirely independent of *all* beliefs and conceptions. This is another way of saying that all our beliefs and conceptions may remain just as they are and yet reality and truth about reality may be entirely different from what we believe and conceive.
> 2'. Things and their features according to internal realists on the contrary are

nonepistemic simpliciter, not radically nonepistemic. They are so in the sense that they are not our own making. The features are real, not projected on to something which does not have them. Nevertheless they *are* what we conceive and believe them to be (in numerous cases).

3. Transcendent realism perpetuates the reality/appearance divide.
3′. Internal realism rejects the dichotomy. The way things appear *is* the way they really are.

4. Transcendental realists regard the world in itself and things that have intrinsic features by themselves as real. This tempts one to label appearances as unreal. There is no knowing, according to them, whether what appears is really what a thing is by itself. This suits the skeptic's game plan.
4′. Internal realists believe that things really do have the features, even the most fundamental features, which our best available theories conceive and believe them to have. But how can this claim to truth staked on behalf of our best available theories be defended? The very claim that the way things appear is the way they are is suspect. Not all appearances are real. (1995, ix-xi)

Notice that the transcendental realist's requirement of absoluteness holds that "things have features intrinsically, non-relationally, and not as objects of anyone's belief, thought, experience and knowledge." Several remarks are pertinent here. First, intrinsicality, nonrelationality, and independence of beliefs, thoughts, experience, and knowledge, entail neither singularism nor multiplism. That is, even if the pertinent features fulfilled the requirement of absoluteness (the absolute independence of the epistemic conditions mentioned), they might answer to one or more ideally admissible interpretations. And from the absolute independence of epistemic activity, it does not follow that one or more than one interpretation could be admitted. All that the requirement of absoluteness mandates is epistemic independence.

Second, while Gupta mentions independence of beliefs, thoughts, experience, and knowledge – which could be construed in individualist terms – these epistemic conditions apply as well to social conditions, such as practices, norms, and the like. Consequently, when she denies the possibility of "projections" in various forms of realism, she disallows the sort of route taken by Margolis, for example, who stresses social intentionality.

Third, let us stress that transcendental realism endorses the thought that things "must be *described* [my emphasis] . . . in terms that have nothing to do with us." This (fair) way of characterizing the transcendental realist position makes it suspect, for description as such has everything to do with us.

Consider now Gupta's characterization of Putnam's contrasting and favored internal realist position (1′). In contrast to the constructivist, the internal realist holds that "things and their features do exist independently and are not our own making." This condition of independence qualifies internal realism as a realism. Things and their features, as she says, are "not projections and reifications of our own conceptual and cognitive nature, and are in this sense nonepistemic." Notice how Gupta contrasts transcendental realism with internal realism. The latter concerns what "can be intelligibly talked about," namely, that which is "construed as thinkable, knowable and describable." Put otherwise, what distinguishes internal realism from transcendental realism is the range of meaningful discourse. Accordingly, "No meaningful discourse is possible about anything . . . unless it is an object, at least a putative object of some belief, conception or knowledge." The internal realist assumes the object-discourse duality. This leaves it open "that things exist whether or not we know or say anything about them." That is how it is that things which we may or may not know "are not trans-conceptual, trans-cognitive and trans-phenomenal."

Let us proceed to consider Gupta's (2) and (2'). Again, she characterizes transcendental realism as holding that "things and their features . . . are *radically nonepistemic* in the sense of being entirely independent of *all* beliefs and conceptions." On Gupta's account of transcendental realism, things and their features are entirely independent of all beliefs and conceptions. Gupta explicates the point by saying that "reality and truth about reality may be entirely different from what we believe and conceive." She suggests that, in contrast, internal realists are not radically nonepistemic. Yet things and their features, on her account, "*are* what we conceive and believe them to be (in numerous cases)." Our challenge is to understand how this might be so. We get a clue in (3'), where Gupta affirms that for the internal realist "the way things appear *is* the way they really are." And according to (4'), "things really do have the features . . . which our best available theories conceive and believe them to have." How is this possible? It is so because, going back to (1'), an object must be thought to be an "object of some belief, conception or knowledge." That is, the very condition of intelligibility is *built into* the notion of an *object* (or reality, or any cognate thereof). So the reality and objectivity of things are internal to the notion of a real object – hence, *internal* realism. So understood, the very idea of the transcendental realist, who holds that reality might be radically different from how we conceive it to be, is incoherent.

So far I have been following Gupta's excellent explication of internal realism. But the general point is well illustrated by the famous example Putnam himself provides:

> *Given* a version, the question "How many objects are there?" has an answer, namely "three" in the case of the first version ("Carnap's world") and "seven" (or "eight") in the case of the second version ("The Polish Logician's World").

Once we make clear how we are using "object" (or "exist"), the question "How many objects exist?" has an answer that is not at all a matter of "convention." That is why I say that this sort of example does not support *radical* cultural relativism. Our concepts may be culturally relative, but it does not follow that the truth or falsity of everything we say using these concepts is simply "decided" by the culture. But the idea that there is an Archimedean point, or a use of "exist" inherent in the world itself, from which the question "How many objects *really* exist?" makes sense, is an illusion. (1987, 20)

In sum, internal realism makes a dual claim, namely, (1) a real thing and its features are independent of anyone's belief, thought, experience, and knowledge, that is, it is not of anyone's making. At the same time, (2) the condition of intelligibility is built into the notion of an object (or reality) such that it is "thinkable, knowable and describable." Accordingly, while no particular properties or features of a thing are projectable on to that thing (that is, no object "takes on" properties in virtue of imputation upon it), it remains that objects and their features are "thinkable, knowable and describable." The first condition is the condition of independence, and the second condition is the condition of intelligibility.

For our purposes the critical point is that both of these conditions of internal realism may be conceded by both the singularist and the multiplist. The conditions of independence and intelligibility are each compatible with the claim that there is one and only one ideally admissible interpretation of an object, or with the claim that there may be more than one ideally admissible interpretation.

VIII

I have suggested that the applicability of the ideals of singularism and multiplism depends upon what one allows by way of the identity of that which is interpreted. The mere agreement that practitioners are addressing the same thing might not be sufficient. For, in the absence of an articulated account of sameness in change, they could well be mistaken. And I have suggested that alternativity does not entail multiplism. Yet even if one were to grant that the entailment does not go through, that in itself would not unseat the claim of multiplism. One might hold that there is no reason why one should expect that such an entailment relation should obtain in the first place, that the demand for entailment is too strong, that only informality in such things can be reasonably expected. But then, given that multiplism is not entailed by alternativity, the question arises as to what sort of informal justification would be convincing for the instantiation of multiplism.

My limited aim has not been to settle upon the superiority of any of the inventoried ontologies, be they realist, constructivist, or constructive realist. With an added inventory of ontologies, including those of Margolis,

Harré, Thom, and Putnam, my aim has been to provide abductive support for the claim that such ontologies mandate neither singularism nor multiplism. The contest between singularism and multiplism remains detachable from the mentioned ontologies. That is not to deny that there is an important place for metaphysical considerations such as intentionality in providing grounds for the objectivity of interpretations. But if metaphysical entanglements are inevitable, let us be clear where they lie.

References

Aronson, Jerrold L., Rom Harré, and Eileen Cornell Way, eds. (1995). *Realism Rescued*. Chicago: Open Court.

Goodman, Nelson. (1982). "The Fabrication of Facts." In *Relativism: Cognitive and Moral*, edited by Jack Meiland and Michael Krausz. Notre Dame, IN: Notre Dame University Press.

———. (1989). "Just the Facts, Ma'am." In *Relativism: Interpretation and Confrontation*, edited by Michael Krausz. Notre Dame, IN: Notre Dame University Press.

Gupta, Chhanda. (1995). *Realism versus Realism*. Calcutta: Allied Publishers.

Harré, Rom. (1997). "Is There a Basic Ontology for the Physical Sciences?" *Dialectica*, 51, 16–34.

Krausz, Michael. (1993). *Rightness and Reasons: Interpretation in Cultural Practices*. Ithaca, NY: Cornell University Press.

Margolis, Joseph. (1980). "Robust Relativism." In *Art and Philosophy: Conceptual Issues in Aesthetics*. Atlantic Highlands, NJ: Humanities Press.

———. (1991). *The Truth about Relativism*. Oxford: Basil Blackwell.

———. (1993). *The Flux of History and the Flux of Science*. Berkeley: University of California Press.

———. (1994). *Interpretation Radical but Not Unruly: The New Puzzle of the Arts and History*. Berkeley: University of California Press.

———. (1997a). "Relativism and Cultural Relativity." *JTLA* [Journal of the Faculty of Letters, University of Tokyo, Aesthetics], 22, 1–17.

———. (1997b). "Reconciling Relativism and Cultural Realism." *JTLA* [Journal of the Faculty of Letters, University of Tokyo, Aesthetics], 22, 79–93.

———. (1999). *What, After All, Is a Work of Art?* University Park: Pennsylvania State University Press.

Putnam, Hilary. (1987). *The Many Faces of Realism*. La Salle, IL: Open Court.

Stecker, Robert. (1997). "The Constructivist's Dilemma." *Journal of Aesthetics and Art Criticism*, 55 (1), 43–51.

Thom, Paul. (1997). Review of *Rightness and Reasons*, by Michael Krausz, *Interpretation Radical but Not Unruly*, by Joseph Margolis, and "The Constructivist's Dilemma," by Robert Stecker. *Literature and Aesthetics: The Journal of the Sydney Society of Literature and Aesthetics*, October, 181–85.

———. (1998). Personal communication to Michael Krausz, October 20, 1998.

———. (Forthcoming). *Making Sense*. Lanham, MD: Rowman and Littlefield.

9

REPRESENTATION AS THE REPRESENTATION
OF EXPERIENCE

F. R. ANKERSMIT

Introduction

In the last few decades the notion of representation has acquired a prominent role in contemporary intellectual debate.

The explanation is a certain imbalance in twentieth-century investigations of the relationship between language and reality. These investigations – as best exemplified by analytical philosophy as it developed in the
postwar period – focused mainly on notions such as reference, meaning,
truth, sense data, and the epistemological problems surrounding these
notions. Useful as these investigations have undoubtedly been, they ordinarily took their point of departure in the simplest utterances – "the cat is
on the mat" being the paradigmatic example – because of the assumption,
at first sight not unreasonable, that the kind of problem occasioned by the
specimens of a more complex use of language could be adequately dealt
with only after a satisfactory solution had been found for those simpler
epistemological technicalities.

However, contrary to expectations, these epistemological problems
turned out not to permit solutions that were acceptable to all participants
in the discussion. And the result was that philosophical debate got stuck in
the debate on these elementary uses of language, while the problems occasioned by the more complex uses of language were never addressed.
Because of that, hermeneuticists, literary theorists, semioticians, historical
theorists, theorists of poetry, rhetoric, or the pictorial representation of
reality, and so on, were all left very much to their own devices when
attempting to deal, as well as they could, with the question of how the relationship between complex chunks of language and reality should be
defined for their respective disciplines.

Two observations are in order here. In the first place, the theorists of
these more complicated uses of language all tended to use th term "representation" for referring purposes. But, second, though the term "representation" was almost universally adopted, everybody tended to see his own

discipline as presenting us with the paradigmatic examples of representation. For obvious reasons this has seriously hampered the debate on representation. If an interdisciplinary discussion of representation took place at all, this discussion rarely was more than a *dialogue des sourds*. And though postmodernism must be praised for its effort to develop an interdisciplinary discussion, its well-attested lack of interest in and respect for philosophical rigor made things worse rather than better.

Hence, though the notion of representation was frequently used and much discussed in recent decades, a thorough and well-considered analysis was never given by any theorist: the term functioned rather like a coin that was passed from hand to hand without anyone ever closely scrutinizing it. Therefore, in trying to bring some light to the darkness in which the notion of representation is still hidden, this essay will not begin with a historical survey of the debate on representation up till now. For this strategy could only result in a prolongation of the present impasse. Instead, I propose to begin again with the idea of a true singular statement. However, my effort will not be to explain representation in terms of that idea, but to explain just where representation goes beyond the singular statement and all that one could say about the relationship between it and the world. Put differently, my point of departure will be the conviction that an important step toward a correct understanding of the notion of representation will have been made as soon as one realizes that the relationship between a representation and what it represents is essentially different from the relationship between a true statement and what it is true of.

The Singular Statement, the Text, and Representation

As the etymology of the word suggests, a representation makes present what is absent. And it might certainly seem that a true singular statement should, if only because of this, be considered to be the paradigmatic case of representation. For in asserting true statements, we ordinarily use language to compensate for an absent reality. For example, you may say "the cat is on the mat" to somebody who is for some reason or other not in a position to observe this part of reality for himself – perhaps because he is in another room, or because he is asking you about the cat over the telephone. And then the true statement will be as good as reality itself for this person and will rightly seem to him to be a "representation" of reality in the proper sense of the word.

This trivial and unpretentious observation may already deepen our insight into representation and suggest how representation differs from a true statement. I said just now that the true statement about S may, in a way, be as good as S itself for us, if we are unable for some reason or other to see S ourselves. But this phrase "for some reason or other" should make us think. For this qualification is less innocent than it may seem at first sight. Its very casualness suggests that this contingent inability to see S for

ourselves can always be remedied "in one way or another." More specifically, the phrase suggests that subjects of knowledge are in principle interchangeable: "for some reason or other" you happen to be elsewhere and
that's why I am telling you about the cat. But if you were sitting where I
am sitting now, you could have seen for yourself that the cat is on the mat.
This seems to be an essential condition of the statement's being true. For
truth is no private matter – hence the perennial attraction exercised by the
notion of the transcendental ego or intersubjective cognition as soon as the
notion of truth is under discussion.

However, suppose a student asks you about a book he had not read and
you tell him what you know about it. Surely, nothing seems wrong, at first
sight, with this phrase "telling somebody what you know about a book."
But it will then not be easy to indicate "where" the student should place
himself in order to see for himself the truths you mentioned (as in saying
"the cat is on the mat"). Reading the book is obviously not the right
answer to this "where" problem, since people interpret books differently.
I am sure that any other answers one might be tempted to try would be
even less plausible. Hence, in this case at least, there is a problem with the
interchangeability principle. We should perhaps agree with Gadamer's
view that there is no room for this "interchangeability of knowing
subjects" – so essential to the notion of truth – in the context of reading
and interpreting books. Gadamer is undoubtedly correct in inferring from
this that hermeneutic interpretation can never be reduced to truth. What
you tell the student about the book, your "representation," surely
"compensates" for the student's ignorance to a certain extent, but never in
the way that a true statement may plausibly be said to do so.

Things may get worse. A book is at least something that you can take
into your hand; you can read it, and everybody who does so will see in it
exactly the same chapters, sentences, words, and letters as any other
reader. Even Derrida could not deny this – though Derrida, being Derrida,
would undoubtedly devise some sophistry attempting to do so. But think
now of the kinds of things that historians represent in their writings, for
example, the French Revolution. What are, so to speak, the "chapters,"
"sentences," "words," and "letters" of the French Revolution that will look
exactly alike to all its students? Obviously this is a question impossible to
answer – not because we happen to lack the means to do so (though we
may indeed have an idea of what *would be* a good answer to such a question), but simply because it is a nonsensical question. Here nothing could
be said to be given, objectively or intersubjectively.

Hence, not only will we agree with Gadamer that all readers will come
up with a different reading of books offering representations of the French
Revolution; it will also be impossible to affirm unequivocally what the
French Revolution *is*, that is, of *what* is represented in these books. The
French Revolution is not something like the state of affairs of the cat's
lying on the mat or like a text (seen as a complex of words, sentences,

chapters, etc.) – not simply because of its immense complexity, but, even more, because the French Revolution is part of the past and therefore unobservable. This is far from being a contingent fact about historical representation. For Arthur Danto was undoubtedly right in claiming that historical representations essentially compensate for the past's absence (Danto 1968, 95). Since we have no access to the past as we have to present states of affairs about our cat (or even texts viewed as long rows of letters, words, sentences, etc.), historians write their histories of the past to compensate for this absent past. It will now begin to dawn on us that *both* from the perspective of the subject *and* from that of the object the relationship between the representation and what it represents is essentially unlike that between a true statement and what the statement is true of.

Let me offer a more pointed formulation. We must realize that the relationship between a true singular statement and reality can be investigated epistemologically, although this does not hold for representation. Epistemology investigates the relationship between reality, meaning, reference, and truth and presents us with a philosophical matrix within which such notions are usually analyzed. It is hardly necessary to explore these matters here: to have a bearing upon representation it should be sufficient to point out that we can be certain a priori that representation, as such, can *never* be adapted to the parameters of epistemological debate. For representation admits of a certain liberty regarding the relationship between language (the representation) and reality (the represented) that would be utterly unthinkable even in the most liberal of epistemologies. A circle may "represent" a city on a map, the letter *o*, the sun, the earth, a human face, and so on (Ankersmit 1994, Chapter 4), and what it actually represents is to a large extent dependent on context and tradition or even simple convention. It hardly needs to be said that such a degree of freedom would make nonsense of the whole enterprise of epistemology.

One might conceive of an extreme conventionalist epistemology, such as that advocated by Hegel in his *Phenomenology*, and argue that epistemology must itself be historicized. In the writings of authors such as Kripke or Davidson, we may find attempts to develop such an epistemology. We may be sure, then, that such a historicist and conventionalist epistemology will be able to deal with conventions such as circles representing the sun, or a city on the map, by giving a justification (probably causal) of these conventions. And then we would have made the world safe for epistemology, by disposing of the threat posed by representation. However, this strategy would reduce epistemology to toothless irrelevance. For what could possibly be the use of an epistemology justifying all our incompatible and purely contingent conventions? Our reaction would probably be that under such circumstances, we would be better served by a *history* (and thus a *representation*) of the different ways in which words and things have been tied together in the past than with such a conventionalist epistemology. In other words, the only epistemology that can be reconciled with representation is an epistemology that presupposes (historical) representation instead of conferring such standing to any would-be bearer.

It is decisive that epistemology (whether historicized or not) is, by its very nature, incapable of dealing adequately with representation. For if we admit a represented and its representation, *both* will give rise to exactly the *same* epistemological problems. For example, the categories of the understanding in Kantian epistemology do not and could not distinguish between a representation and what is represented without properly fulfilling the tasks assigned to them within the framework of Kantian epistemology. The Kantian categories of the understanding do not care whether they are applied to a landscape or to a picture of that landscape – if all is well in epistemology, they will be just as effective in *both* cases. Epistemology does not enable us to articulate philosophically what differentiates the represented from its representation, just as, for example, the purely physical properties of two books are useless if we want to articulate their difference in content. In other words, by its very nature epistemology is indifferent to the problems of representation and therefore is of no help in solving the problems of representation. Furthermore, as soon as epistemology succeeds in distinguishing categorically between the represented and its representation, something will seem amiss, since its *sui generis* work transcends that distinction. Hence, the fact that a true singular statement is epistemology's favourite research object automatically prevents the statement from serving as a paradigm of representation.

And, indeed, all attempts in the last few decades to achieve an epistemological reduction of the representation of reality to the problems of true statements have utterly failed. The following may explain the failure: logically, a historical representation is a *proposal* – that is, a proposal to see part of the past from a certain (metaphorical) point of view. Put differently, the historian's representation is a proposal for the *organization* of knowledge (i.e., the knowledge expressed by the singular statements that constitute the representation) and therefore is not knowledge itself.[1] Similarly, the alphabetical organization of the telephone directory does not reflect some order existing among the people listed in the directory (nor even among their telephone numbers). The alphabetical organization is, instead,

---

[1] Our age, with its overwhelming mass of information, has every reason to be interested in how knowledge is organized by the historian. But that is what historical writing has always been about. The notion of metaphor can help us to understand how this organization of knowledge is achieved in and by the historian's text: for example, the metaphor "the earth is a spaceship" organizes knowledge of our earth into a coherent whole not only by furthering our understanding of the earth's ecosystem, but also by suggesting how best to deal with it (Ankersmit 1983, Chapter 7; 1994, Chapter 2). One might say that metaphor defines, organizes, and structures a *context*. The significance of context, thus understood, is nicely brought out by Saffo: "It is not content, but context that will matter most a decade from now. . . . In a world of hyperabundant content, point of view [as always defined by metaphor] will become the scarcest of resources" (Saffo 1994, 74, 75).

a device for making knowledge (about their telephone numbers) accessible. And so it is with historical representation: it gives us an organization of knowledge about the past – making the past as accessible as possible – though other historians may disagree and argue that another organizational representation will be better.

I hasten to add this note. The fact that representations are proposals about how to organize our knowledge (of the past) certainly does not imply (as is often argued by structuralist and poststructuralist theorists of history) that we cannot rationally assess the merits and the demerits of competing representations. Fortunately reason has more strings to its bow than merely showing us how to discover truth. We must realize that although we cannot possibly characterize a proposal (even the wisest or the most stupid) as either "true" or "untrue" – because it would be a category mistake – that hardly prevents us from being able to say (un)reasonable and (un)tenable things about them. The proposal to light the fire if we feel too warm is not a "false" but a "stupid" proposal. Someone might object that we could rephrase our proposal into a set of epistemologically analyzable statements (e.g., "lighting a fire will increase temperature" or "if one feels too warm, temperature must be lowered"), but that would be of no help to the epistemologist. For the representation suggested by the historian is a proposal regarding what (is thought to be) the best representation of the past; and the notion of the best representation, in its turn, necessarily (if my account is correct) implies making a proposal that would affect any rephrasing of the notion of representation in terms that the epistemologist might ask us to consider. We would otherwise lack any criterion bearing on how to reformulate the proposal in the idiom to which the epistemologist would like to restrict himself. Similarly, it is possible to paraphrase statements about feelings, like being in love, as statements about hormones and their effects – but the notion of being in love is of course the indispensable basis for advancing pertinent statements about physiology. Without the first we could never tell which statements of the second sort would yield a correct paraphrase.

To conclude: it is not a true singular statement but the *set* of such statements that constitutes a historical narrative and that constitutes the paradigmatic representation. It is, therefore, to the notion of such a set of statements that we shall soon turn.

Narrative and the Work of Art as Representations

An obvious candidate for representation is, of course, the work of art. Hence, a comparison between historical narrative and work of art may deepen our insight into the nature of representation. Flint Schier has successfully argued for a crucial logical difference between a true singular statement and the representation of reality afforded by a work of art (Schier 1986, 115ff.). Suppose we compare a picture (or even only a photograph) of Marlon Brando in which Brando looks surly with the state-ment "Brando is surly." In the case of the statement, we distinguish clearly and unambiguously between the subject-term and the predicate-term and, hence, between what the statement refers to and the property being attrib-uted to it. No such distinction is possible in the case of the picture or photograph: we cannot divide the picture into two parts, of which the former corresponds to Brando and the other, to the surliness attributed to him. Referring and attribution always go together in the picture (Ankersmit 1995).

Much the same holds true of the historian's representation of the past. The historical text consists of individual true statements, while their total-ity is the representation proposed by the historian; hence, from the level of the true statement to the narrative, we move from the epistemological level to that of representation. Elsewhere I have argued that this shift in level from epistemology to aesthetics becomes possible thanks to the presence in historical narrative of a logical entity whose existence and function have not been noted before. This entity, which I call the "narrative substance," can be defined as follows. All the individual true statements in a narrative that determine its character must be considered to be the parts of the narra-tive substance that is proposed in the historical representation in question. On the basis of this definition we can formulate statements such as "N_1 is F," "N_1 is G," and so on, where 'N_1' is the name of the narrative substance presented in the historical text, F and G are predicates in p, q, and so on, and p, q, and so on, are the true statements contained in the text.

In the first place, the notion of the narrative substance thus defined will enable us to clarify and to explain a number of properties of (historical) representation, of the nature of historical debate, and the (nonepistemo-logical) criteria by which to decide the acceptability of individual histori-cal representations of the past (Ankersmit 1983, Chapters 5, 8). In the second place, this may contribute to a better understanding of the asym-metry between individual statement and (narrative) representation. For statements like "N_1 is F" and "N_1 is G" are all analytically true, since they can analytically be derived from the notion N_1. And that means that we cannot distinguish in the case of these statements between a subject that is referred to and the properties that are attributed to it – the predicate is already contained within the notion of the subject and, therefore, finds itself, so to speak, on both sides of the copula. As already argued, the meaning of the true singular statement in a historical narrative is therefore twofold: the statement asserts that something is the case in reality (p) *and*, at the *same time*, the statement contributes to the definition of a certain representation of the past ("N_1 is F"). And we can *never* isolate these two functions of the statement from each other, just as we cannot say of an individual brushstroke in a portrait that the brushstroke refers to the sitter *or* attributes a certain property to him or her.

There is a difference between the historical text and the painting, however: we could not say of the individual brushstroke what we can say of the narrative's individual statements, namely, that they can be either true or false.[2] But apart from this, there is a close symmetry between the historical and the artistic representation of reality; they cannot both be reduced to the matrix of epistemology, and thus they require a new and open investigation of the relation between the representation and the represented.

Historical Representation

If, as we observed a moment ago, the relationship between the represented and its representation is, in the case of the painting, still obscured by the problems occasioned by the individual brushstroke, it becomes clear that historical representation is ideally suited to aiding us in investigating the relationship between the representation and what it represents – hence, to investigating the notion of representation as well. The problem of historical representation exceeds the interests of historical writing and of historical theory, in that the analysis of historical representation helps us penetrate the secrets of representation and of what lies beyond the framework of epistemology.

Where, in historical writing, do we actually find the representation and the represented? Perhaps an introduction and synopsis by the historian would help the reader of a historical text identify those statements that constitute its narrative substance, but, often, that is doubtful. More often than not, it will not be clear whether a statement actually serves this function or merely serves the cognitive purposes of the historian. The double aims of all historical writing – to tell the truth about the past *and* to achieve a *specific* narrative representation of the past – inhere indissolubly in the text as it is presented to the reader. With the exceptions just mentioned, the reader has no adequate clue about how strictly or unambiguously the two levels of meaning may be distinguished from each other.

However, this does indicate what means the reader *does have* at his disposal. For if the historian wishes to present a specific representation,

---

[2] This places us in the dilemma of either conceiving of the individual brushstroke as a representation, consisting of components that can be said to be either true or false (as in the case of the statement), or of conceiving of the brushstroke as being already such a component. But whatever way we would decide, the question would arise what could be meant by the notion of the truth of falsity of these components. However, Goodman's exemplification might prove helpful here: if the component correctly exemplifies the corresponding part(s) of the represented, the component could be said to be a "true" rendering of it. Obviously, the application of Goodmanian exemplification to the components of the work of art does not imply that under the aegis of exemplification the notion of truth can be introduced in aesthetics in order to sustain the notion of the truth of the painting as a whole. We need only recall here that the truth of the individual statements of a historical representation has no implications for its quality. And so it is in painting.

something can be said in a negative way, that is, by contrasting *this* representation with *other* representations of (roughly) the same part of the past. For example, suppose that in a representation of the Enlightenment – say, Foucault's – statements can be found about how the ideology of the Enlightenment effected a certain regimentation of the human individual, whereas such statements are rare or absent in more conventional representations (focused, say, on the liberation of humanity from its *selbstverschuldeten Unmündigkeit*). We should then be able to identify, at least partly, those sets of statements that determine the nature of the narrative substance separately proposed in the two accounts. In any case, without such contrasts, we cannot hope to succeed in determining the substance of narrative representations. Narrative representations are recognizable only by their contrasts with other representations.

Four consequences follow. First, we must associate representation with "negativity" rather than with "positivity." For the specific image of the past that is offered acquires its contours only in the (implicit) *denial*, and not in the *confirmation*, conveyed by other representations. Here you find the essentially "dialectical" character of representation – the very site, in fact, where the logic of representation agreed with the *Negativität* so much valued by the young Hegel. Indeed, Hegelian dialectics achieves its march through history thanks only to denial and negation; historical insight into the past comes into being in a similar way. Second, we can now grasp the notion of "intertextuality" so much emphasized by the deconstructivists. Representation is "intertextual" in the sense that it is relational; the conditions for its existence are not entirely intrinsic to itself but depend on the existence of other representations. From that perspective, one might as well say that the text, or representation, is what it is *not* and that the generation of representational meaning is the result of a process of "dissemination" via other texts. Third, it will be clear by now that competing texts are part of a *Wirkungsgeschichte* having its origin in a specific historical problem and that clarity with regard to a historical representation can be achieved only by viewing it in the context of such a *Wirkungsgeschichte*. This is how Hegelian dialectics, Derridian deconstruction, and Gadamerian *Wirkungsgeschichte* are connected in representation.

Nevertheless, within the framework of this essay, a fourth conclusion is of even greater importance. Although Hegel's dialectic promises the ultimate triumph of Absolute Mind, no such guarantee can be given for historical representation. Representation requires debate, as deconstruction suggests; and representations cannot be created ex nihilo, according to the Gadamerian *Wirkungsgeschichte*. And yet, debate and tradition cannot ensure the optimal representation of the past. On the contrary, if the statement can be tested for its truth and falsity by observation (and I wish to distinguish clearly here between observation and experience), the logic of representation suggests that the actual development of representations is determined most decisively by interpretive traditions (and all kinds of circumstantial factors influencing such traditions), not by the intrinsic nature of what is represented. Hence, representational meaning has a tendency to withdraw within "the prisonhouse of language" – the "prisonhouse" of representations – to use Jameson's expression.

This finding is not only generally agreed on, but also regretted, which is perhaps why people speak of a "representation crisis" in contemporary modernism/postmodernism disputes. Current theories of representation, from Hegel to Gadamer to Derrida, confirm that a direct contact with the represented is impossible; contact is always mediated by other representations and by a representational history. In this sense, the representations may be said to repress the represented.

We begin to see here the point of the priority of representations over the represented – observed by such theorists as Gombrich and Danto and by such postmodernist authors as Baudrillard.[3] Already in "The Decay of Lying," Oscar Wilde had pursued the paradox that life imitates art, that an acquaintance with Balzac's novels might well reduce our friends to mere shadows of Balzac's characters. Great art is not a copy of the world; it is, rather, the world that imitates art. The truth is that we ordinarily know the represented only through its representation. Here, we may agree with Baudrillard when he describes the representation as a "simulacrum," a "hyperreality" that is more "real" than represented reality itself. This priority of the representation over the represented is already evident from the fact that such relatively weak and aimless factors as tradition and convention are ordinarily more powerful in determining the nature of representation than the represented itself. (Think of the history of art.) Hence, we need not restrict ourselves to art, nor even to how the media represent the events of our contemporary world – in the newspapers and on television – in order to appreciate the powers of representation: representation forms a great deal of our quotidian reality. In this sense, aesthetics is an integral part of our daily life. Without representation we would have no represented – and that would mean the loss of a great part of our world and our grasp of it. (This is no postmodernist version of idealism.) Similarly, although we would not say that merely using the name "United States of America" created a certain part of the globe's surface, we may still say, reasonably, that a representation gives us access to something that was not "there" before we had the relevant representation. Thus, the United States did not exist in a certain sense before people used the name to designate it, even though using the name certainly did not create rivers or fields or mountains. Idealism is a crude philosophical notion distinctly unsuited to the realist import of representations.

In a sense, then, without representation we would lack what is represented

---

[3] Needless to say, the priority of the representation over the represented is an entirely different matter from my claims discussed at the beginning of this essay regarding the irreducibility of representation to epistemology.

(in a sense contrary to that in which physical states of affairs obtain, even in the absence of statements describing them). If it were objected, for example, that in the case of a portrait the represented surely precedes its representation, it may be remarked that if we were presented with different paintings of the same sitter, his so-called objective features are certainly not, as such, decisive in determining "the best representation." It is not photographic accuracy that makes us prefer Titian's portrait of Charles V to the one painted by Van Orley. It would be wrong-headed to regret the priority of the representation over the represented as if there might be some lamentable imperfection or incurable defect of representation – hence, proof of its sad incapacity to satisfy the demanding standards of true statements. That representations do not satisfy such standards is precisely why we have representations: they contribute something more than does a true statement, something that conveys a sense of order in daily, not scientific, reality, that makes it possible for us to live life and deal with our world. A "true representation" of reality would be just as useless to us as the facsimile of a text handed to us after we had asked how best to interpret it.

The Representation Crisis and Historical Experience

Still, though it is only representation that makes our world a livable world, "our" world is enclosed within itself by tradition, by language, by our representational habits and conventions. And this raises the question of whether we might ever break through the magic circle of representation and the traditions governing it. That an affirmative answer must be given was already suggested at the end of the previous section. For it is certainly difficult to indicate exactly what guides and constrains our traditions of artistic representation. Surely Goodman and Gombrich are right to criticize Ruskin's "myth of the innocent eye"; surely the way the world appears to us and all artistic representations of the world are mediated by tradition. But that does not prevent the specific history of art from being richer and more variegated than other histories; the constraints of context and tradition may be stronger in the history of representation than elsewhere. But it is precisely this that makes artists eager to escape from their constraints. Where tradition is strongest, the will to break with it may be strong as well.

Once again, historical writing affords the best departure for investigating the chances of escaping "the prisonhouse of representation." Although artistic representation has, from ancient times, favored the precept *docere, placere, et movere*, art has tended to emphasize *placere et movere* (though there is indeed a tradition spanning Vasari and Goodman that features the cognitive aspects of art). By contrast, historical writing has viewed as its primary (if not its only) task the presentation of the past *wie es eigentlich gewesen*. The disciplinary goal of historical writing has always been mainly cognitive. Hence, if we associate the cognitive dimension of historical writing with the urge to escape from the "subjectivity" of tradition and context, historical representation will, perhaps better than artistic representation, bring us to the strange no-man's-land between the domain of the true and the domain of the beautiful that is so rarely visited by philosophers.

If, then, we ask ourselves how historians sometimes succeed in breaking out of "the prisonhouse of representation," we should be well advised to consider what has been called either "historical sensation" or "historical experience." Many historians and poets since Herder and Goethe have recorded how, in a moment of supreme historical grace, they underwent a direct and immediate contact with the past.[4] The most important features of "historical experience" have been summed up by Huizinga (Huizinga 1950a, 564ff.; 1950b, 71ff.). According to Huizinga, historical experience is typically effected by relatively trivial objects or events, such as an antique print, an old song, or entering a building that has not changed for centuries. The explanation is, first of all, that, say, a painting by Titian or Raphael is, for us, so much the paradigm of the development of the history of art that we find ourselves unable to view it as the immediate expression of a certain historical reality. Second, historical experience is "an ebriety of the moment," as Huizinga puts it; it is something the historian undergoes rather than constructs or conveys at will. And, third, in historical experience, the historian has the conviction of being in a direct and completely authentic contact with the past. In this connection, Huizinga tellingly links historical experience to the sense of touch rather than to sight or hearing. The eye and the ear are our most "educated" senses: what they present to the mind is always part of a complex history of seeing and hearing and hence is in need of decoding. The sense of touch, however, adapts itself to the most direct and immediate contact with reality. The sense of touch does not require a medium in the way visual and auditory perceptions do. By the way, this is also why the Aristotle of *De anima* and *De sensu* elevated the sense of touch over the other senses and why we may find in his conception additional insight into the nature of historical experience.

Two questions need still to be answered. First, can the claim be justified that historical experience really transcends a representational tradition (or *Wirkungsgeschichte*)? And, second, if so, how can the content of historical experience find its way to a representation of the past?[5] If we start with the first question, we may observe that almost all of twentieth-century philosophy opposes the idea of the possibility of a direct and

---

[4] For a more detailed "phenomenology" of historical experience, see Ankersmit 1993 and the last chapter of Ankersmit 1994.
[5] I shall not deal with this question here. For an attempt to answer it, see Ankersmit 1997.

immediate contact with reality that historical experience suggests. We have all become Kantians in one way or another: we all dismiss out of hand a contact with reality that is *not* mediated by language, narrative, scientific theories, Kantian categories of the understanding, or so forth.

It is not my intention to attack this nearly universal consensus. Indeed, all experience, even historical experience, is irrevocably contextual. Surely, when Huizinga had his historical experience of the late Middle Ages during his visit to the van Eyck exhibition in the summer of 1902, from which his *The Waning of the Middle Ages* originated, he could only have acquired his special susceptibility to those paintings through what he already knew of the period. Even so – and this is crucial – it does not follow that we should also accept the contemporary dogma of the context-bound character of the *content* of experience. My thesis is precisely that although it is undeniable that the *occurrence* of a historical experience is context bound, the same need not be true of the *content* of the experience occasioned.

A metaphor may clarify my intentions. Suppose one looks down from an airplane to the ground beneath. Often clouds will prevent us from seeing the ground, but when there is an opening in the clouds, we will have an unobstructed view. This is how it is with historical experience. Most often the clouds of tradition and context prevent us from seeing the past itself, but that does not preclude the possibility of a direct view of the past in the momentary passing of these "contextualist" clouds. We are surely justified in arguing that it is the clouds that determine whether this may happen or not – and in that sense historical experience is indeed context bound. However, though the clouds may determine the fact *that* we see the ground (or the past) at all, they cannot determine *what* we will actually see under favorable circumstances. This unwarranted shift from the "that" to the "what" is the non sequitur that we may discern in many contemporary arguments in favor of the context-bound character of all experience. Furthermore, the metaphor suggests that what historical experience offers the historian will not have the character of a deeper penetration of or extrapolation from knowledge (of the past) already possessed (i.e., what is given by context), but a sudden awareness of an "openness" in the contextual clouds themselves – an awareness that, in a sense, requires and is determined by the nature of those contextual clouds. Thanks to this, something of the past that was hitherto obscured by context and tradition becomes visible for the first time. It is at such moments that the historian succeeds in breaking out of "the prisonhouse of language and of representation" and that a fresh contact is made with the past that makes possible new avenues of historical research not dictated by prevailing context and tradition. Speaking more generally, insofar as the development of historical writing is determined not by a logic of its own (Ankersmit 1994, Chapter 5), but by what the past itself is actually like, historical experience realizes this direct and immediate contact.

The metaphor of the airplane suggests a further determination of the conditions of the possibility of historical experience. We can see the ground from the airplane only when the airplane (and we ourselves) are located above an opening in the clouds. Similarly, the past can be experienced only when there is a certain congruity between the relevant part of the past and the subject of experience. Hence, all preoccupation with these contextualist and traditionalist clouds (favored in Gadamer and Derrida) is at odds with the desire to escape from the representation crisis. More specifically, we may anticipate that that preoccupation necessarily leads to an attack on experience itself. Both Derrida and Gadamer themselves were well aware of this: Derrida's statement "il n'y a pas de hors-texte" eliminates experience together with its potential object. If there is nothing outside the text, there is nothing to be experienced "out there." Gadamer is even more explicit: "Wir wissen, was für die Bewältigung jeder Erfahrung ihre sprachliche Erfassung leistet. Es ist, also ihre drohende und erschlagende Unmittelbarkeit in die Ferne gerückt, in Proportionen gebracht, mitteilbar und damit gebannt würde" (Gadamer 1960, 429). Language as the embodiment of context and tradition, as "das Haus des Seins das, verstanden werden kann," destroys, as Gadamer himself explicitly recognizes, the structure of experience and places itself between us and the world in the way that the Kantian categories of the understanding did for the first time two hundred years ago.

However, this momentary overcoming of context, tradition, language, narrative, and so on, is possible only if the harmony between the historical subject and the relevant part of the past is actually realized. This can be clarified with the help of Dewey's theory of aesthetic experience, developed in his *Art as Experience* (Dewey 1987, 287 ff.). We should note, in this connection, that historical experience can be seen as a variant of aesthetic experience. For not only is historical experience most often effected by works of art from the past; but, more important, the submission of our perceptual apparatus to the object of experience is the defining feature of both historical and aesthetic experience. Turning, then, to Dewey's account of aesthetic experience, we find that Dewey distinguishes between two extremes in our experience of reality. In one, we can undergo reality passively in the way a stone rolls down a hill without "being aware" of what happens to it. The other extreme presents itself when we react to reality with what Dewey calls a "mechanical efficiency," that is, when the impulses sent out from reality to us are merely "read" as the symbols or signs of the existence of certain states of affairs in reality. In the latter case, reality disappears, so to speak, behind the "screen" of symbol or sign. In the former, the *subject* of experience is reduced to irrelevance; in the other, the *object*, the reality, becomes an irrelevance, a mere *occasio* (to use Malebranche's terminology) of subjective processes. Dewey emphasizes (in a way closely similar to the Aristotelian notion of *mesótes*) that aesthetic experience comes into being only when the right balance has been struck between the extremes. (One is reminded that communication between equals is far more complex, far richer, than that between master and slave.) Both aesthetic experience and historical experience come into being only when neither reality nor subject is the absolute master in the relationship.

If this requirement between subjects and objects of experience is not met, if either the subject or the object is too strong a partner, we shall find a loss in the authenticity of experience itself. We can now fathom what motivates contemporary resistance to the very idea of a direct experience of reality. Indeed, when experience is exclusively related to its simplest components, to the most elementary perceptions, to "sense data," as Western epistemology has been in the habit of claiming since Descartes's method of resolving disputes, it need not surprise us that experience completely collapses beneath the heavy load of tradition and context that hardens into fixed theory and prejudice. Indeed, the "indivisible atoms" of elementary *Protokollsätze*, "sense data," immediately lose their inner structure (if they have such a structure) when they have to be reduced to already existing categories, theories, narratives, languages, and so on. However, if the content of experience has the character of a "surface" or a "volume" rather than of a "point," it will be able to resist successfully the powers of language, tradition, and so on.

Hence, the direct contact with the past afforded by historical experience is possible thanks only to the *complexity* of the content of experience itself. Paradoxically, the direct experience of reality is possible solely on the occasion of a complex contact (that seems initially to favor context and tradition), whereas, in truth, a mere "pointlike" experience yields unproblematically to the pressures of context and tradition. The modernist's reduced and simple analytic posits are not the natural enemies of context and tradition but, in fact, its best friends. This explains another feature of historical experience. The two requirements we have arrived at – the complexity of experience and the Deweyan and Aristotelian equality of subject and object – imply that what reality offers the subject should, in a certain sense, have its counterpart in the subject. There must be an appropriate "harmony," just as the person looking down from the airplane has to do so at precisely that moment when the clouds have momentarily lifted. This is why historical experience is always so personal and even tied to a specific moment in a person's existence, why it cannot be repeated at will, and, more important, why it shares a strong element of self-awareness with the experience of the sublime, as defined by Kant.[6]

---

[6] For a further explanation of this self-awareness and for a correction of Kant's argument to the effect that this self-awareness involved in the experience of the sublime is a recognition of our moral destination, see Vall 1994.

Once Again, Statement and Representation

Let us return for a moment to the singular statement and representation. I want to argue that, in accord with our foregoing discussion, the singular statement – that traditional paradigm of knowledge, the prime object of epistemological investigation in Western philosophy – does not deserve the name, since it is essentially "imperfect," or unable to be analyzed completely as it stands, in the sense that it always needs further "perfection" through connection with either a lawlike statement or a narrative representation. The lawlike statement perfects the singular statement because it expresses a certain relationship between predicates and, in this way, eliminates the indeterminacy that always exists in the relationship between the subject-term and the object-term of a true statement. For we may make as many true statements about the subject of a statement as we like, but there is no analogue in a lawlike statement. Representation, in turn, perfects the true singular statement because, as we have seen, it binds all statements contained in the representation by a relationship of analyticity. This places the epistemologist's enterprise in a peculiar light. For if singular statements are by no means the perfect expressions of knowledge one used to prize, would that not imply that most of the epistemologist's efforts have always been misguided? For if a singular statement has its perfection only in relation to some lawlike statement or representation, it follows that the statement can be fruitfully investigated only after its relation to a lawlike statement and/or a representation has been adequately defined. In sum, epistemology has the bad luck of fastening on a hybrid piece of language that it took to be the key to all the secrets surrounding the relationship between language and reality. For a true singular statement is, in fact, a complicated mix of the "purer" uses of language that we find in lawlike statements and narratives. Contrary to appearances, these two uses of language are more elementary than what we find at the level of a true singular statement.

It may be objected that if a representation consists of statements (as I have been arguing), such statements are presupposed by representation and not the reverse. However, our notion of the (types of) things that we discern in reality and to which the subjects of statements typically refer is itself the result of a typification process of representations (Ankersmit 1983, 155–69). To mention an example: suppose a specific narrative substance regarding the Enlightenment were accepted by everybody, not just historians. Then the notion of "Enlightenment," which, as a representation, initially served only to *organize* our knowledge of that period, would change into the name for a certain *object*. From then on, sentences like "the Enlightenment is G" are no longer analytical statements, as is always the case in representations, but statements with the same general logical structure as "this house is white." In this way *representation* can turn into a *description* of (that is, supplies categories of) objects, and narrative proposals can become the names of things (Ankersmit 1994,

88ff.). If someone were to object that this account still has singular statements at its deepest level – hence, that representation presupposes true
statements – I should answer in the following way. First, we should
conceive of daily reality (and the objects contained in it) as a *hierarchy*.
That is to say, if we have statements regarding things, for example, like
historical individuals, books, paintings, and so on, these statements can be
used within representations, and if these representations get codified by
context or tradition, new sets of things come into being in conformity with
the process described in the previous section. But at the deepest level we
will *not* find *statements*, only *experience*; for, both logically and tempo-
rally, experience precedes statements. In the most primary contact with
reality, reality is still not codified in the way that daily reality always is,
but then of course true statements will not be able to be formulated. As
understood here, experience denies (or perhaps defies) convention and
tradition and the way these determine the categories of things that are met
with in reality, while, at the same time, it possesses a complexity that
could be construed in accord with the notions of objects and their properties as structured in the statements of a later phase. In the beginning was
not the object (as modernist philosophers like the Strawson of *Individuals*
believe), or the word or language (as postmodernists and hermeneuticists
believe). In the beginning was *experience*.

If we recall that convention, tradition, and context (not epistemological
criteria) determine the relationship between representation and the represented, it follows that the (categories of) objects that we discern in reality
are not the result of some quasi-divine decision but the result of convention and tradition. As we know, the Foucault of *Les mots et les choses*
provides some striking examples of the culturally determined and even
arbitrary way in which we cut up the universe into (categories of) individual things. Accordingly, the following picture obtains: first, we have the
reality that is investigated by the sciences (and that corresponds to lawlike
statements), and, second, we have our daily reality, which is the result of
a culturally determined codification process of our representations of the
world. One cannot say that one of these two "realities" is more basic or
more fundamental than the other. It would be misguided to conceive of the
reality of the scientist as having its foundations in daily reality (as we
often claim). First, the very solidity and objectivity of daily reality, which
seem indeed to anticipate and reflect the rigidity and severity of scientific
argument, are, as we saw a moment ago, the product of tradition, context,
and convention and typically lack the solid foundations on which all scientific research is built. Second, in many ways, scientific reality is the result
not of an analysis of the nature of daily reality, but of an alienation from
it. For the codification of representations (that gives us our daily reality)
is nullified by science, by dissolving the things of that world into their
lawlike properties and by discovering deeper patterns in those properties
that do not have a counterpart in daily reality.

Here science and representation move into opposite directions: the lawlike statement leaves daily reality behind, whereas representation, in an ever expanding and changing system of semantic layers, constructs ever new codifications of daily reality upon older codifications, thus making our daily reality more and more complex. The reality of the physicist may appear to be fundamentally "unreal" to us, but it consists of, in Leibniz's apt phrase, *phenomena bene fundata*. By contrast, daily reality, in spite of being so much more "real" to us than the physicist's reality, is poorly grounded because its shaky foundations rest in vaguely recurring patterns of how we represent the world (or, more precisely, how we experience it). Here we may discern the deceitful authenticity of daily reality and the reason we should associate authenticity not with the experience of daily reality, but with the kind of aesthetic experience I mentioned earlier.

Indeed, much of this repeats itself on the level of experience. I must (to gain the point) invoke a bit of intellectual history. Ever since Dilthey, Lukasiewicz, and Mates, it has been pointed out that most of Western epistemology and metaphysics after Descartes may be viewed as a reprise of classical Stoicism. We must think here primarily of the Stoic speculation about the so-called *logoi spermatikoi* believed to inhere both in reality and in rational thought about reality – thus guaranteeing the possibility of reliable knowledge. It may be argued that most of Western philosophy since seventeenth-century rationalism has been a series of attempts to develop an epistemological and metaphysical definition of these Stoic *logoi*. Alternatively, philosophers were always looking for the *tertia comparationis* that would enable us to argue from reality to knowledge, and vice versa. Needless to say, the search made sense only on the assumption that there were indeed such things as *logoi* or *tertia* of the kind invoked.

It should not surprise us where these *tertia* were sought. Their roots might be situated in the objects of the world: they were supposed to provide patterns repeated on the level of experience and knowledge. This is how the empiricist and positivist systems actually originated. The *logoi* or *tertia* supplied the forgotten metaphysical assumptions behind such systems. Hence, the world of things cannot form the unshakable basis of knowledge the positivists and empiricists supposed: we now have every reason to agree with Hegel's criticism (in the *Phenomenology*) leveled against empiricism. Again, the world of daily reality proves to be an abstract world. All these approaches, so popular nowadays and so widespread among such different branches of contemporary philosophy as analytical philosophy, philosophy of science, and deconstruction, are obviously descendants of Kant's Copernican revolution.

We now understand why the kind of experience discussed in this essay can play no more than a subordinate role in contemporary thought. For it is obvious that these *tertia* tended to take the place of experience – as intermediaries between subjects and objects. Stoicism and its postmodernist variants succeed to the extent that they eliminate experience. Empiricist systems tended to see reality as the stronger partner in the "transmission line" from reality to knowledge, whereas rationalist systems tended to see the subject as the stronger partner. But both systems required *tertia* in arguing from one to the other. For related reasons, postmodernism is no more than a continuation of modernism, not the radical break it has always claimed to be. Because of postmodernism's sovereign disdain for reality, *tertia* tended to become useless parts of the metaphysical machine or, perhaps, wheels that invariably produced twentieth-century textualist variants of nineteenth-century idealism. All that postmodernism has contributed to contemporary thought originated in the linguistic definition of the *tertia* it proposed, but it soon turned into a profoundly counterintuitive linguistic appropriation of all reality.

A break with both modernism and postmodernism can therefore be achieved only if we are prepared to abandon the *tertia* proposed. Only then can the equilibrium that Dewey attributed to aesthetic experience be achieved. The *tertia* will always and inevitably destroy this equilibrium. This is where postmodernism, for all its alleged interest in aesthetics, has so sadly and conspicuously failed. It need not surprise us, therefore, that Stoicism never attempted to develop even a rudimentary aesthetics. Despite their own aestheticism and their aestheticist rhetorics, postmodernists have never really been aware of the nature and force of the challenge posed by aesthetics. This is why, in the end, they have remained too close to (modernist) Stoicism to be able to offer a viable alternative. For what the postmodernists insufficiently appreciated is that what interests us in the work of art, and why we claim to discover its never-ending "newness," is that it challenges each limited content that we might ascribe to the *tertia*. It is precisely the absence of the *tertia*, or, more specifically, our *awareness* of their absence, that prevents the domination of subjects over objects in the sense postmodernists advocate. For by eliminating the *tertia*, we break the link by which the subject and the object might dominate one another.

We see, therefore, what aesthetic experience and historical experience have in common, how the former contributes to a better understanding of the latter, and why (in both) the complexity of the content of experience ensures the directness and immediacy that Huizinga associated with historical experience.

Conclusion

Modernists believe that the true singular statements holds the key to the most important philosophical secrets. Postmodernists, with their interest in texts and the representation of reality mediated through texts, demonstrate what is wrong with the underlying intuition of twentieth-century philosophy of language. Hence, postmodernism is a correction and displacement of modernism.

Nevertheless, we must not forget that postmodernism uncritically accepts one of the major tenets of modernism: namely, the idea that our theories, our narratives, our language – in short, all those variants of the Kantian categories of the understanding that have been invented in our resourceful century – determine our knowledge and experience of the world. Here, the hermeneuticists, the deconstructivists, and other theorists of context and tradition can be said to have been even more radical than their modernist predecessors.

We reach a stage beyond postmodernism only if we consistently and relentlessly detranscendentalize both modernism and postmodernism. We can achieve this goal if we take aesthetics as our point of departure in reflecting on how we ourselves relate to the world, if we ruthlessly eliminate all *tertia* from our conceptual inventory, and if we recognize that the notion of experience is best suited to carrying out these new philosophical tasks. We should then have moved from modernist truth, via postmodernist representation, to post-postmodernist experience.

References

Ankersmit, F. R. (1983). *Narrative Logic: A Semantic Analysis of the Historian's Language.* The Hague: Martinus Nijhoff.
——. (1993). *De historische ervaring.* Groningen, the Netherlands: Historische Uitgeverij.
——. (1994). *History and Topology: The Rise and Fall of Metaphor.* Berkeley: University of California Press.
——. (1995). "Statements, Texts and Pictures." In *The New Philosophy of History*, edited by F. R. Ankersmit and H. Kellnerr. London: Reaktion Books.
——. (1997). "Sprache und historische Erfahrung." In *Historische Sinnbildung*, edited by J. Rüsen. Reinbek.
Danto, A. C. (1968). *Analytical Philosophy of History.* Cambridge: Cambridge University Press.
Dewey, J. (1987) *Art as Experience.* New York: Berkley Publishing Group.
Gadamer, H. G. (1960). *Wahrheit und Methode.* Tübingen, Germany: J. C. B. Mohr (Paul Siebeck).
Huizinga, J. (1950a). *Verzamelde Werken II.* Haarlem, the Netherlands: Tjeenk Willink.
——. (1950b). *Verzamelde Werken VII.* Haarlem, the Netherlands: Tjeenk Willink.
Saffo, P. (1994). "It's the Context, Stupid." *Wired* (March).

Schier, F. (1986). *Deeper into Pictures*. Cambridge: Cambridge University Press.

Vall, R. van de. (1994). *Een subliem gevoel van plaats: Een filosofische interpretatie van het werk van Barnett Newman.* Groningen, the Netherlands: Historische Uitgeverij.

10

HISTORICAL KNOWLEDGE AS PERSPECTIVAL AND RATIONAL: REMARKS ON THE ANNALES SCHOOL'S IDEA OF HISTORY

CECILIA TOHANEANU

There is an obvious parallel between foundationalism, which ignores history in working out the conditions of knowledge, and radical relativism, which contends that by virtue of its own historical character there is no way to choose among different interpretations, all of which are "equally good." Might it not be, rather, that the recent historicist attack on the very idea of rationality is as damaging as foundationalist objections against the plurality of conceptual schemes or frameworks? Can philosophy maintain the traditional distinction between the form and content of knowledge, between rationality and historicity – between *doxa* and *episteme*?

This chapter questions the very idea of a principled incompatibility between rationality and historicity, a conviction common to foundationalism (essentialism or cognitivism, for instance) and radical relativism. The idea reveals a misunderstanding of the nature of knowledge and results in either dogmatism or skepticism. Ultimately, we must go beyond philosophical schisms, dichotomies, all the familiar oppositions set in conceptual stone, if we are ever to recover the epistemic and historical – in short, the perspectival – dimension of knowledge. History should be regarded as a form of interpretive discourse that does not preclude, but on the contrary presupposes, epistemic constraints.

The present approach to historical knowledge is influenced to a large extent by the *annalistes'* approach to history and to the historian's "workshop."[1] *Annaliste* historiography supports the idea that history is a

---

[1] The Annales School, also known as *the new history* or *l'histoire-problème*, emerged in the 1930s in France. Its programmatic theses were defined by Lucien Febvre (*Combat pour l'histoire*) and Marc Bloch (*Metiér de l'historien*) and rendered into such paragon works as Braudel's *La Mediteranée*. From the 1950s until the 1970s, the Annales scholars labored to link history more closely to other human sciences, and their efforts are to be found in works of historical geography, historical demography, economic history, and, later, the history of "mentalities" (Jacques Le Goff, Henri-Irénée Marrou, Le Roy Ladurie, François Furet, Georges Duby, Paul Veyne, Michel de Certeau, and others).

construction or "invention" of the past, intimately bound to a cultural context, yet open to evaluation and comparison.

If dogmatism and skepticism are to be avoided, the relationship between the interpreter and what is interpreted must be emphasized. In a Kantian spirit, we might say that interpretation without historical records is nothing but fiction, legend, myth. Conversely, the idea of a historical record without interpretation conveys no meaning at all and hence is not a history in any recognizable sense. In short, the past is "given" neither in documents nor by their interpreter. It is, rather, an open concept or a transient conclusion implying an ongoing relation between document and interpreter.

This chapter divides naturally into two parts. The first concerns myths about the philosophy of history, which illustrate the familiar but questionable dichotomies between rationality and historicity, or between epistemology and interpretation. The second deals with the double perspectival and rational dimension of historical discourse, which requires both hermeneutic and epistemic perspectives. The first part of the chapter accounts for historical pluralism; the second justifies the idea that, all things considered, inasmuch as history is not fiction, only some interpretations can be accepted by the historical community. For it makes no sense to say, as it does of fiction, that we simply like a particular historical text, but it makes eminently good sense to say that we find a particular history coherent or plausible.

Philosophy of History and Its Myths

It is not often noticed that the myth of universal rationality is shared by traditional theories of history (as in the ontologies proposed by Vico, Herder, Hegel, and Spengler) and Hempel's neopositivist model. According to the former, there is a so-called "essence" or ultimate meaning of history, which is not available to the ordinary person, nor even to the ordinary historian. It can be determined only by someone, say, the Platonic philosopher described in the *Republic*, whose direct grasp of Reality enables him to reach the universal meaning of things – hence to formulate the laws or principles by which to account for the entire historical process. On this view, to be rational supposes a capacity to assert something definitive and general, but also unrevisable, about the nature of the historical world. In this way, *episteme*, entirely dissociated from *doxa*, signifies knowledge of historical reality (in itself, so to say) as distinct from its mere human appearances. It follows from this perspective that rationality has nothing to do, ultimately, with human beings, whose cognitive capabilities are finite, limited, and confined to appearances. Such theories of history transform the knowing subject into a sort of God able to discover universal invariants or to capture and foresee, through a network of atemporal concepts, all the forms of human becoming. In this way, the historical condition of the knowing subject is disregarded, and simple suppositions concerning the nature of the human world (causality or finality) are upgraded to the rank of *first* principles.

Despite its reputation among analytic writers, logical empiricism is no better than what it rejects, since it remains attached to the old idea of rationality as universality and merely substitutes normativism for essentialism. This is as true of Carl Hempel's nomological model of history as it is of William Dray's rational model, in spite of the latter's break with the positivist tradition. Hempel and Dray disagree about the nature of history, but they both claim that particular events do have a unique meaning. From this vantage, rationality requires a completely adequate explanation of individual human actions with the aim of recovering their meaning. For Hempelians, for whom rationality is synonymous with the nomological dimension, historical discourse is meaningful if and only if it relies on empirical laws. From the antimetaphysical positivist perspective, historical discourse can, indeed must, dispense with metaphysical suppositions in restricting itself to factual statements – or statements that are at least empirically translatable.

This and similar claims simply disregard the nature and real conditions of our coming to understand the human world. The question of how we know the historical world is posed and answered without regard to the conceptually prior question of what it is that humans actually seek to know. To put it differently, the real (human) subject is postulated in accord with the metaphysics of *things* rather than examined in its own right. Yet that is surely nothing but a *posit*.

In Hempel, human time and physical time are assumed to be the same, since one cannot claim (as Hempel does) that an event is nomologically explicable without accepting a deterministic view of history. It follows that logical positivism does not really free itself from metaphysics, as it claims, but only from the metaphysics of the human being and his world. It is on this basis that the rationality of history is defined in nomological terms. The thesis of the logical-conceptual unity of all knowledge relies therefore on a reductionist view of the real, or mind-independent, world, as well as on a reductionist but also hierarchical view of knowledge. It is scarcely surprising, therefore, that the admission of historical pluralism, or of plural *histories*, is a violation of the positivist view of rational discourse.

One finds in Dray a similar attempt to limit the infinite regress of interpretations and to establish a universal criterion for discerning historical facts. Dray's vehement objections to the very idea of the (conceptual) unity of the sciences do not prevent him, in Rickert's wake, from believing in the possibility of an autonomous theory of social-human knowledge. His theory, which correctly starts from the idea of historical *agent*, unfortunately transforms intentionality into a principle of human actions, or into a criterion for selecting historical facts. Whatever his intentions, and even if Dray rejects the "intellectualist" connotations of his concept of *rational calculation*, this very concept clearly suggests a "rationalistic" reading of history (von Wright 1971). To be sure, a causal explanation of historical facts is not, in principle, excluded. But for Dray, causal explanation is inherently incomplete, as opposed to rational explanation, which he regards as complete. This leads to the idea of a necessary, rather than a merely probable, connection between human events and their goals. In other words, any individual action should, in principle, be deducible from pertinent human reasons and projects. Thus, Dray regards intentionality as a historical principle, hence as an absolute constraint on historical discourse.

As opposed to the scientific, or nomological, concept of explanation, Dray's model may be read as an attempt to reconcile epistemology and hermeneutics. It is in fact meant to rehabilitate interpretive discourse. But here Dray errs, for he believes that interpretation can be appraised and compared essentially in terms of truth; hence, an analytical, or logical, approach to understanding is possible.

It appears that neither Dray nor Hempel is content with interpreting rationality as mere probability. Hence, both denounce historical pluralism as leading to the incoherence of history. For it would follow (from their own views) that history was a conceptual chaos; pluralism would admit a number of interpretations, and some might well be incompatible from the vantage of a bivalent logic.

We know that history can be understood in different ways, both in narrative accounts of particular events and in the study of repetitive occurrences. Metatheoretical or normative theories of rationality may, accordingly, be challenged when they appear to disregard the actual conditions of historical knowledge. Dray's and Hempel's policies mean to restrict history to what they regard as suitably explicable in, respectively, intentional or causal terms. Since the meaning of facts cannot be decided a priori, and since meaning depends on interpretive prejudices or perspectives, the very idea of putting a cap on the diversity of interpretations can be no more than an illusion.

The denunciation of the myth of "the universal conceptual framework" or of the unique meaning of facts is sometimes accompanied by a tendency to mythologize pertinent *differences* by employing them against the very idea of rationality. This practice is typical among the historicist "new wave," also known as postmodernism (if we include Jacques Derrida and Paul Feyerabend, among others), a trend described by Paul Ricoeur as a "wild" return to subjectivity. Postmodernists, above all Derrida, are mainly concerned with the supposed genesis of meanings, including the context in which they are constituted. The result is a thesis as questionable as that of the so-called "universal conceptual framework." The postmodernists claim that meanings are arbitrarily constituted, and since there is nothing "outside" or "beyond" them, the very attempt to justify interpretation is completely useless. Representationalism is replaced by textualism, which turns the world into a piece of language and turns contexts into a generative source of radical conceptual schemes. In this way, radical relativists repeat the mistakes of the logical empiricists, since they also impose a particular kind of discourse – in their case, literary discourse – as the unique conceptual model of the world. It is not surprising, therefore, that they deny the relevance of legitimate questions. For literature, which features fiction rather than facts, has nothing to do with such questions (Harrison 1991, 11).

Obviously, human knowledge is perspectival. Hence, Rorty may be right in saying that there is no important difference between electrons and poetry, since both are constantly interpreted and endlessly interpretable. If historicity is undeniable, then we are obliged to admit that any view of knowledge must include a skeptical component, which does not, however, entail a commitment to skepticism. For Derrida, historicity affords an argument for jumping to skeptical conclusions. Here, the effort to decide among possible interpretations is said to fail because of the fundamental indecidability of meanings. If the issue of decidability were approached exclusively in terms of bivalent truth, interpretation would indeed be a failure. For this reason, skeptics think of rationality as necessarily linked to the idea of a transcendental subject and, hence, to the possibility of privileged knowledge – a foundationalist prejudice, after all, as Joseph Margolis points out. On the skeptic's view, the incompatibility between historicity and rationality would be self-evident. According to the skeptical train of thought, our various forms of discourse cannot be assessed and compared once we give up the myth of the ahistorical subject. In other words, either discourse is justified in terms of truth, or truth-claims cannot be justified at all. Since, under historicist conditions, the first position is inadequate, it follows (it seems) that any discourse is viable – as good as any other.

The latter claim would be acceptable if it signified the admissibility of several kinds of discourse or ways of approaching the world, including the perspectives of the physicist and the historian. It is entirely reasonable to treat such alternatives as equally relevant and, moreover, to aim at maintaining as large a diversity of perspectives as possible. But the postmodernist's thesis is more radical and, for that reason, questionable. For the claim that within a certain discourse, say, historical language, all interpretations are equally valid is not only arbitrary but results in conceptual anarchy. This may be nothing more than a plea for irrationality. When confronted with actual historical research, the textualist model cannot answer two main questions. First, how is it that we are able to distinguish between a literary fiction and a history? Second, why are there any limits on interpretation at all or, to put it differently, why are some interpretations regarded as unreasonable?

History as Perspectival

The positivist historians (Von Ranke, Langlois, and Seignobos, among others) believe that "facts" cannot simply be drawn from the available documentary material. Almost no one now regards history as a mere totality of preexisting or preinterpreted facts. Like other objects of knowledge, the object of history is not a mind-independent "real" which already exists "out there," but rather it is "invented" or "constructed." This claim seems obvious and difficult to deny. The constructed or perspectival aspects of history derive essentially from history's dependence on a particular cultural context or *horizon*, rather than from anything resembling direct access to independent objects. The role of such a horizon – the precondition of historical knowledge at any given moment – obtains no matter whether we are dealing with present or past facts. Even if we were eye-witnesses to an event, hardly anyone thinks it would be possible to reconstruct that event as it really happened independently. Although so-called immediate history would, if admitted, be regarded as neutral, it is simply not "reachable." The constructive aspect of history derives primarily from our indirect access to the past – through documents, data, the testimony of historical agents, and the like, which, in their entirety, constitute what is called the historical record.

The defeat of objectivist illusions owes much to the *annaliste* historians. Consider Henri-Irénée Marrou's claim that history is what historians succeed in elaborating (1954, 56), which suggests that what we know about the past is inseparable from what we ourselves put into it – that is, into the would-be data. Historical documents are interpreted or constructed from the vantage of a certain conceptual framework or tradition, which is itself ultimately rooted in the problems and questions of the historian's own world. No document is historically meaningful in itself, but only within a discourse. The idea of "pure" data is epistemologically indefensible. The very notion of the historical record is linked to one or another *Weltanschauung*, which yields different meanings as a function of the historian's suppositions regarding the nature of the human and social world. Thus, the positivists' hierarchical, or elitist, view of society yields a conception of history featuring what they took to be important, namely, political, military, and diplomatic events. From this viewpoint, they thought that the historical record was restricted mainly to written data stored in archives.

The positivist tradition is vehemently criticized by the *annalistes*, whose own democratic, or populist, view of history is apparent in their idea of the historical record. Unlike the positivists, *annalistes* are concerned with documents about the life and thought of the anonymous "little men and women" of the past. This new topic, namely, the study of the "quiet zones" of human life – mentalities, languages, customs, festivals, climates – results in a very different "hunt" for very different documents. The scope of the historical record is thus enlarged to include traces of the past in folklore, literature, archaeology, artworks, the remains of buildings, and so on. Before the Annales School, this kind of evidence was viewed as irrelevant and totally disregarded. A document, therefore, is not a historical document prior to some knowing subject's intervention. To claim that it is a document *for us* emphasizes that there are in fact no universal criteria for historical documents or indeed for historical facts.

Data of all kinds, written or unwritten, are, finally, texts open to a plurality of readings and constructions. It is interpretation that turns the traces of the past into the historical record. This is all the more true in the case of unwritten data. Material objects such as inscriptions, building remains, even the ash from a hearth, cannot be documents unless they are "interrogated" and hence interpreted. As material reality, such objects have no historical relevance. They become relevant only when the historian, in studying them, construes them – and thus constructs them – as meaningful symbols or signs signifying what they are taken to disclose.

Not accidentally, then, the *annalistes* name their view of history *l'histoire-problème*. They call attention to the fact that the historian's discourse is a response to the questions of his time. There is a "solidarity" among historians living in a particular historical context, based on a shared view of fundamental problems and inquiries. This results in similar trends within the "guild," as well as in the tendency to adopt a similar style. The very existence of distinct historiographical traditions or paradigms clearly shows that history is itself historical.

The philosophical question about whether historians should study certain sorts of facts, or whether they should adopt such-and-such ways of proceeding, is not only nonsensical but discloses a basic misunderstanding of the relation between fact and value. There is no "answer." It is not surprising that the normativist epistemologies proposed by Hempel and Dray did not "solve" this issue. Their respective approaches are doomed from the start. For it cannot be shown that only regularities or, on the contrary, "irregularities" or historical exceptions are worthy of the historian's interest. No such claim can be defended. Neither the nomological principle featured by Hempel nor the rational principle proposed by Dray "constrains" historical discourse. The bare facts are not important as such; their significance is wholly and solely a function of the historian's interest. Every hierarchy, every comparative evaluation, is merely subjective. "Our world," as Paul Veyne notes, "is a world of becoming, and at every given moment there is a possibility for events of all kinds to happen. It is useless to think that some of these events would be of a peculiar nature, that they would be *historical*, or that they would constitute History. . . . We must admit that any event, any fact is history. . . . Everything that happens is equally worthy of the name of history" (1971, 32, 35).

It has already been mentioned that from the *annaliste*'s viewpoint, the repetitive and banal aspects of daily life are more interesting than so-called unique or exceptional events. The historian's aim is not to reconstitute the individuality of life, but to point out its repeatable character. Different texts describing, for example, a battle in the thirteenth century can be significant both for "narrative" and "conceptual" or "structural" history (*l'histoire-récit* and *l'histoire-problème*). But the meaning of the battle is not at all the same from these two perspectives. The former accents the details of the battle, interprets it, therefore, from a political and military perspective; the latter takes the same "fact" as a basis for a study of the behavior on the battlefield and, possibly, the thinking of the feudal knights. An *annaliste* is always disposed to use the description of such a battle as a starting point for sketching an anthropology of feudal war (Duby and Lardreau 1980, 63). It is, then, scarcely surprising that Duby's perspective on the Middle Ages is so different from traditional views. These distinctions would not hold if knowledge of the past were not mediated by the interrogating subject's values and interests. It is only thus that we can explain the existence of an indefinite number of historical interpretations as well as their limits. No reconstruction of, say, the events of Waterloo is the battle of Waterloo as it "really" happened. We can never get more than several perspectives on what is called a historical event.

Foundationalist epistemology has uselessly attempted to show the opposite. It has already been pointed out that Hempelians believe that meaningful historical explanation is possible if and only if history is purged of subjectivity by renouncing metaphysical suppositions, intuitions, metaphors, or "vague analogies" deemed responsible for its "intuitive plausibility." From that viewpoint, to be rational has nothing to do with subjectivity. It is this disregard of the real condition of the knowing subject that encourages the illusion that a logical reconstruction of historical facts is straightforwardly possible.

A historian is not an abstract entity but a *human-being-in-the-world*, who can provide only his own version of the facts. Georges Duby's avowal is relevant in this respect: "As for me," he says, "I'm ready to say that what I write is *my* history, that is, it is I who speak, and I do not at all intend to hide the subjectivity of my discourse" (Duby and Lardreau 1980, 38). He continues: "I am the prisoner of my own Self and of my environment. . . . A being who has neither the same past nor the same passions, who does not write in the same time and place, will not use the same data similarly" (194).

Discourse about the past is intimately connected with a particular situation or context. The construction of the facts inevitably starts from certain conceptual or cultural frameworks. These schemes should be deemed the preconditions of what we call historical knowledge at a given moment. Future historians can accept or revise or reject them. History, which aims to understand change, is itself subject to change through time. The differ-

ence between the Annales School and the positivists confirms the historicity of history, the relativity of the so-called basic principles of historical
knowledge.

Traditional history, which adheres to the myth of progress, is largely the
narration of exceptional events. The *annalistes'* break with this historiography signifies the utter abandonment of that myth. We can only understand the "new history" as a response to a new historical *situation*: events
such as the Holocaust and the communist horrors definitively undermine
the view of a linear, progressive movement of humanity.

Historians need to answer what can be called the anthropological challenge, which points toward the plurality of civilizations. Different societies obviously evolve not only in different ways but according to different
rhythms. What is called historical progress must be measured against
different mentalities, different customs and traditions, or what may be
called sociocultural inertia (Furet 1982, 93–95). The multiplicity of different civilizations cannot be accounted for in terms of the widespread paradigm of economic and technical progress that has dominated European
historiography in the nineteenth and twentieth centuries. We must shift our
interest from the unique history of those few nations thought to embody
progress in an exemplary way to the diverse histories of the actual human
world. For the *annalistes*, the former model is doubly compromised – by
the treatment of social and ethnic conflicts of our own world and by the
attempt to apply "our" model of linear development to the non-European
world.

The distinction of the Annales School can be defined in a few words. It
involves (1) disowning these simple equivalencies: history = national
history = public history = the history of exceptional events, that is, the
record of the actions of "great men," and (2) enlarging and revising,
accordingly, the notion of the historical record, as concerns the role and
scope of historical documents. The *annalistes* hold that anything in the
human world may be historically meaningful and may, therefore, be the
object of history. They plead in favor of historical pluralism, both epistemologically and ontologically – that is, in favor of a plurality of discourses
as well as of agents. The claim that the history of ordinary men is as legitimate as that of great men draws on the fact that since any human being
belongs to history, every human being contributes to history.

History as a Rational "Invention" of the Past

Both foundationalists and skeptics are dubious about historical knowledge. They press their shared supposition about the inherent incompatibility of rationality and historicity in opposite directions. Foundationalists
view history as irrational (or at least arational) to the extent that historians
are unable to eliminate the plurality of interpretations in favor of a single
true account. Skeptics claim the equally radical view that totally different

or conflicting points of view are equally plausible. Both verdicts ultimately draw on a willingness to convert any and all kinds of discourse, scientific or literary, into some single acceptable pattern of knowledge that would exclude whatever deviates from the appointed norm.

It seems more plausible to enlist both epistemology and hermeneutics as essential to the work of historical knowledge. Historians require both in accounting for the great spread of plural and diverging interpretations as well as in questioning and testing them in comparative terms. Historians, who debate the merits of different interpretations, do not proceed in the manner of the physicist or the artist. They do not view reconstructions of the past as either "true" or "false," or as pleasing or disagreeable. They are concerned, rather, with the reasonableness of their interpretive hypotheses.

From this perspective, the radical relativist's rejection of an epistemological approach to historical interpretation must itself be rejected. Historical epistemology features the real link between rationality and the actual historical condition of the inquiring historian (the knowing subject). It attempts to show, precisely, that and how interpretations of the past can be defended and compared under historicist constraints. History is neither a fixed and rational nor an incoherent and irrational reconstruction of the facts; it is, rather, a historical reconstruction under the conditions of real history.

The fact that historians judge their own interpretations in terms of plausibility suggests the inadequacy of a bivalent logic for historical claims. To justify the rigor of history we may have to invoke what Paul Ricoeur (1986) terms *the logic of subjective probability, or the logic of uncertainty and quality.* Similarly, Joseph Margolis points out the need for a *many-valued logic* for "interpreted domains of discourse" where we should admit weaker epistemic values such as "plausible," "apt," "reasonable," and the like. Margolis calls attention to the fact that the way in which truth-values are assigned depends jointly on language and world (1995, Chap. 4). Every form of knowledge has its own rationality. In the case of interpretive discourses, including history, rationality should be understood in terms of the plausibility of diverging views, rather than of bivalent truth. To judge the *annalistes'* interpretive models from the vantage of a bivalent logic would merely repeat the Hempelians' mistakes. Since historical models are not, and are not conceived as, a set of verifiable statements or as implying empirical consequences, they are, strictly speaking, neither true nor false. They are, rather, hypotheses about *possible* relations between the so-called long-, mid-, and short-term historical processes. Even the *annalistes'* generous use of statistics can only warrant the plausibility of their interpretations. Even the reading of the clearest, most unambiguous data, demographic, for instance, can never be counted on to be certain (Furet 1982, 81–96).

That the construction of the past is only "probable" is not a reason to regard history as irresponsibly speculative or dogmatic. A historian must consider the hypothetical and limited character of his "construction": that is, that the "order" he discovers is always *post factum*, never preestablished, not fixed in stone, no more than only a "possible" interpretation among others. Would we be justified in charging Duby, for instance, with dogmatism if, as in his introduction to the *History of Private Life* (*Histoire de la vie privée*), he warns the reader that his work is by no means a final version of the historical record, but only a research program concerned more with raising questions than with answering them definitively?

The historians' appeal to a "logic of quality" reveals, in fact, that they do not mean to invoke anything so grand as a method in the Cartesian sense. "Plausible," "probable," and the like are actually epistemic values adjusted to a many-valued logic. Moreover, the fact that these values can have several degrees running between the bivalent limits ("true" and "false") suggests that they are not at all incompatible with bivalence itself, as Margolis emphasizes (1995, 67–70).

According to Richard Rorty, historicity and method exclude one another. Rorty claims that the attempt to look for rules indicates the temptation to copy science or, in other words, to escape from history and contingency. Apparently, an interest in method already manifests an attachment to foundationalism (1991, 26–41). Rorty treats the natural sciences as basically uninterpreted, as possessing sound norms or rules (situated beyond interpretation) that ensure the success of the usual predictions. He continues to associate the natural sciences with the Cartesian idea of certainty as well as with the older Aristotelian model of intelligibility.

Rorty's rather standard view of the natural sciences is at odds with the views of many philosophers of science and working scientists who, on a phenomenological basis, reject the principle of invariance in favor of new views of time, irreversibility, potentiality, probability, and the like. Working scientists are rethinking the notion of rationality in terms of concepts such as *event* or *flux* (Prigogine and Stengers 1988; Bohm 1980). This is not to deny invariance or repeatability but to question the very idea of invariance as an absolute principle of the real, basic to all science. In addressing the problem of scientific validation, they find that they must consider the double possibility that the real is both regular and in flux.

Rorty goes beyond the familiar claim that there are no universal principles or universal rules to defend – as in Feyerabend's argument "against method." For Rorty, the very idea of method presupposes a priori rules. Since rules are only relative, it is not surprising that Rorty opts for radical relativism. The model of rationality he proposes, inspired by comparative anthropology and favoring such moral virtues as tolerance, betrays the emphasis he places on discontinuity over continuity.

The idea of the irrelevance of method, which depends on disregarding historical continuities, is questionable even with regard to the social sciences.[2] Paradoxically, the Annales School, which probably offers the most convincing demonstration to the effect that history is itself historical (or discontinuous), also confirms that discontinuity is only partial, never a complete destruction of previous views of historical knowledge, never the simple rejection of traditional historiography. It would be wrong, therefore, to view the "new history" as a "reversed" positivism, one that substitutes nothing but imagination or intuition for historical documents. In breaking with the representationalist view of historical evidence, the *annalistes* rethink the concept of a historical record; they do not simply renounce documents. The *annalistes* object to the positivist treatment of documents as absolute sources of knowing the past. They call attention to the fact that, no matter how reliable the data may appear to be, any construction or interpretation of "objects" is merely probable. The limits of history are, and remain, the limits of the knowing subject.

Nevertheless, to be aware of these limits is not to embrace skepticism or to abandon the effort to legitimate historical discourse. Skeptical as they are, even if the *annalistes* construe documentary materials as texts, as a sort of "springboard" for drawing up multiple interpretations, they oppose identifying their work as mere "art." In their opinion, knowledge of the past is not only a "theoretical" endeavor consisting in the construction of hypotheses, but a "technical" effort as well, involving historical criticism. This explains why history is not literature, even if one speaks of history as a literary genre. "Inventing" the past is not the exercise of a fanciful imagination, as in the writing of a poem. It is true that the selection and treatment of the data depend on the historian's tacit philosophy, but it does not follow that these are arbitrary or guided exclusively by intuition and imagination. History is constrained by the available evidence – apparent historical records, written documents or documents of other kinds, archaeological remains perhaps. In a word, the writing of history must balance its constructivist temptations with the need to base its "inventions" on precise data.

It would be hasty and inaccurate to treat the construction of a historical "object" and a work of art in the same way. For Duby, the concern with rigor remains central. His emphasis on the subjectivity of historical discourse does not prevent him from claiming that no construction of the past is cognitively meaningful unless it relies on documents that are

---

[2] Paul Ricoeur, for instance, insists on the importance of methodology, despite his hermeneutic approach to the social and human sciences: "The struggle against emotive self-projection, against hatred and the spirit of indictment, debars the historian forever from a subjectivity uninformed and uncorrected by methodology. Thus, the relativist or perspectivist aspects of historical consciousness, which certainly seem to be part and parcel of historical knowledge, must be raised to the level of systematic methodology" (1978, 1275).

rigorously scrutinized. He rejects the very idea of a merely imaginative history altogether lacking in methodological discipline.

The *annaliste* break with the prevailing tradition is not abrupt but rather gradual. Paul Veyne, for instance, insists on a proper understanding of the abandonment of scientism. The ontological commitment of historical discourse should not be taken as suggesting that history is fundamentally "subjective" or that the construction of the "facts" is at the complete mercy of a subject's discretion. History, Veyne claims, is an "intellectual activity," a "bookish notion," not what is fashionably called an existential engagement. He deplores the fact that objections to scientism and positivism are sometimes used as a pretext for embracing irrationalisms of every sort (1971, 53–56). Like Duby, he regards historical criticism as an indispensable means for recovering history, even a "discipline in the 'strong' sense of the word, in short as a set of rules" that history cannot escape. He makes a particular point of reminding historians of the contribution of nineteenth-century German and French historiography in this regard (Duby and Lardreau 1980, 52–56).

For the "new history," the concept of method remains quite relevant, although the rules are no longer mythologized or taken as warranting more than interpretive plausibility. The "skepticism" of the Annales School is not a commitment to objectivism or scientism, and certainly not an attempt to avoid the complications of historical time. On the contrary, it signifies an effort to avoid arbitrariness under historicist and contingent conditions.

The programmatic idea that any human fact can be the object of history may in fact be read as a sign of the relevance of prior historiography. It certainly does not intend to dismiss such historiography. After all, though the Annales School raises doubts about narration as a model of historical knowledge, it does not oppose the very idea of history as narration. In this regard, its reading of the multidimensionality of time is conclusive. Although it admits the importance of individual time (*short-term* processes),[3] it emphasizes that the human world implicates social time (*medium-term* processes) and geographical time (*long-term* processes) as well (Braudel 1969, 112, 119).

This contributes to defeating the myth that history has a unique meaning in pointing to the dual nature of the human world as both regular and irreversible. The various historical processes, which unfold in different ways and at different speeds, possess their own rationality and are neither reducible to, nor separable from, one another. The decision to consider history as either an account of particular events or a study of civilizations – that is, a choice between detail and comprehensiveness – remains of course the historian's option. Both kinds of history are entirely suitable,

---

[3] Moreover, at present, within the French School, one can discern a tendency that historians describe as a "coming back to the event."

though not perhaps of equal interest. This might well lead to confusion if it were taken to signify that all interpretations of the past are of equal value. But to recognize the relevance of various ways of writing history does not entail that any particular such discourse is reasonable or plausible. Interpretations may well differ in being more or less probable, and some may even be unreasonable.

The *annaliste* view of history may be described as follows: There is no one idea of *History*, which, since it would belong to a transcendental subject, would be a mere myth. History is what historians decide it is, which is to say, a function of their suppositions about the nature of the human world. Nevertheless, in constructing the past, historians base their histories on documents of all sorts. Data can only support the probability of an interpretation, but it cannot dispense with all supporting evidence, on pain of transforming history into fiction.

If the historian's "invention" is both ontologically and methodologically constrained, then there are no reasons to regard hermeneutic and epistemological approaches to historical knowledge as incompatible. Each is relevant and necessary, the indispensable dimensions of historical research. Recent efforts to unify the epistemic and the perspectival aspects of knowledge signify the beginning of a dialogue between the Kantian and Hegelian approaches, which were previously thought to be irreconcilable. These two great traditions may not be as opposed to one another as they were once thought to be. As Tom Rockmore points out, Hegel should not be viewed solely as an anti-Kantian, since it was his intention to complete Kant's project of legitimation – although Hegel abandoned his predecessor's *linear* strategy in favor of a *circular* one (Rockmore 1993).

References

Bohm, David. (1980). *Wholeness and the Implicate Order*. London: Routledge.

Braudel, Fernand. (1969). *Écrits sur l'histoire*. Paris: Flammarion.

Duby, Georges, and Guy Lardreau. (1980). *Dialogues*. Paris: Flammarion.

Furet, François. (1982). *L'Atelier de l'histoire*. Paris: Flammarion.

Harrison, Bernard. (1991). *Inconvenient Fictions: Literature and the Limits of Theory*. New Haven, CT: Yale University Press.

Margolis, Joseph. (1995). *Historied Thought, Constructed World: A Conceptual Primer for the Turn of the Millennium*. Berkeley: University of California Press.

Marrou, Henri-Irénée. (1954). *De la connaissance historique*. Paris: Éditions du Seuil.

Prigogine, Ilya, and Isabelle Stengers. (1988). *Entre le temps et l'éternité*. Paris: Librairie Arthème Fayard.

Ricoeur, Paul. (1978). "Man and Social Reality." In *Main Trends of*

Research in the Social and Human Sciences, vol. 2: *Legal Science/Philosophy*, edited by Jacques Havet. The Hague: Mouton Publishers/UNESCO.

——. (1986). *Du texte à l'action. Essais d'herméneutique*, vol. 2. Paris: Éditions du Seuil.

Rockmore, Tom. (1993). *Before and After Hegel*. Berkeley: University of California Press.

Rorty, Richard. (1991). *Objectivity, Relativism and Truth. Philosophical Papers*, vol. I. Cambridge: Cambridge University Press.

Veyne, Paul. (1971). *Comment on écrit l'histoire*. Paris: Éditions du Seuil.

von Wright, Georg Henrik. (1971). *Explanation and Understanding*. Ithaca, NY: Cornell University Press.

11

INTERPRETATION AS HISTORICAL, CONSTRUCTIVISM, AND HISTORY

TOM ROCKMORE

In recent years, "interpretation" has been taken to refer *inter alia* to the understanding of art works of all kinds, including literature; the construal of legal texts or the law; as descriptive of knowledge in the social sciences; and as a synonym for hermeneutics. The latter, which is sometimes depicted as the art or theory of interpretation, is currently understood in at least three main ways: first, to construe the sacred texts; second, following Dilthey, to refer to the method or methods of the human or historical sciences, which rely on understanding, as opposed to the natural sciences, which depend on explanation; and, third, following Heidegger, to refer to the grasp of something as something. As used here, "interpretation" will be understood as synonymous with "hermeneutics." It will be further understood as a source of knowledge, perhaps, after the apparently irremediable decline of epistemological foundationalism, the main modern epistemological strategy, as the leading source of knowledge. In this sense, there is no difference in principle between epistemology and interpretation, since the former is merely a form of the latter.

This chapter will center on a historical approach to interpretation, with special reference to historical knowledge, or knowledge of history. The widespread tendency to approach epistemology as concerned with knowledge of an independent object as it is influences the tendency to regard interpretation as providing different views of a single stable object, which supposedly remains invariant.

The view that to know is to know the way the world is remains remarkably constant in the philosophical debate from Parmenides, apparently its first known source, through Plato, where it receives canonical form in the *Republic*, up to the present. This conceptual model is common to Cartesian rationalism, to classical forms of empiricism (F. Bacon, Locke), and above all to realism. Michael Devitt, presently one of the most important realists, links truth to realism, by which he means a cognitive grasp of the mind-independent world as it is, since a true theory is one that gets it right about independently existing entities, or things that exist in independence of the mental (see Devitt 1991, 197). This model is further important at present in so-called objectivism, an approach (see Chalmers 1982, 113–33) to philosophy of science featured in Popper (1972), Lakatos (1976), and Musgrave (Lakatos and Musgrave 1974). It is again central to Putnam's internal realism (now abandoned by that author), according to which different theories relate to one common world (1981, 49–74). And it is present in Kuhn's idea that the same stimuli are interpreted differently to yield different data (1977, 309n.), and in physicist Stephen Weinberg's critique of Kuhn for denying that science ever gets closer to the way things are (Weinberg 1998).

I regard this model as deeply mistaken. I further believe that any theory of knowledge, hence any theory of interpretation, needs to take into account the lessons of Kant's much-neglected Copernican revolution. As I see it, Kant makes two points that should structure all discussion of knowledge, hence our understanding of interpretation. On the one hand, as Kant points out, we do not know that we know the way the independent world is, since there is no way to know that we know independent objects. This is very different from the currently popular weak form of scientific realism, according to which the external world exercises an empirical constraint on knowledge (McDowell 1994, 1996). On the other hand, the condition of knowledge is not that we discover what is already there, but rather that we in some way "produce" or, perhaps better, "construct" what we know.

Kant's Copernican revolution in philosophy is often mentioned, but rarely discussed in detail and, to the best of my knowledge, has never been refuted. If Kant is right, then any theory of knowledge, including interpretation, necessarily presupposes a "constructivist" approach. Yet Kant can scarcely be said to provide an adequate account of how the subject "constructs" its cognitive object, which, in a famous passage, he describes as an activity hidden in the depths of the human soul (1962, B 181, 183). A central task of later philosophy, one that occupies Hegel, Marx, Dilthey, and many others, is to understand how human beings "construct" the human world by which we are shaped and which we in turn shape as a condition of knowing it. In this chapter, I will apply a Kantian "constructivist" approach to historical knowledge understood as interpretation. One result of this approach is to show that because we must reconstruct the past in order to know it, we cannot recover the past as it happened or know it through natural laws, although it does not merely become another kind of fiction.

Knowledge as Historical

If the cognitive object is not a mere given, but a "construct," then knowledge is historically relative, or relative to a perspective or point of view that pertains in a given time and place. Knowledge is always human knowledge, hence dependent on, never independent of, the nature and cognitive limits of finite human beings. It seems obvious that, as products of their historical moment, society, and culture, human beings are shaped by their surroundings and, through them, by the preceding historical tradition, which durably influences us in ways no one fully understands. The preference in a given culture for one type of music rather than another, the identification of a particular palette of colors and not others, the meaningfulness of a whole range of conceptual issues, even our perceptions, depend on the influence of the historical past as mediated through the present historical moment.

Few observers question the obvious relation between artistic taste (or the capacity to discern the aesthetic features of objects, especially beauty) or the appreciation of literary merit and the cultural surroundings. On this basis we routinely understand the preference for, say, Shakespeare rather than Robert Service, Greek rather than Roman art, the Beatles rather than rap, and so on.

The claim made to explain artistic, literary, or aesthetic taste encounters considerable resistance as soon as attention is drawn to a possible link between human cognition and the cognitive limits of finite human beings. Efforts by such writers as Descartes, Bacon, Marx, Nietzsche, and Freud to set limits to human cognition are counterbalanced by a widespread tendency to deny any cognitive limits through two main strategies. On the one hand, there is a widespread approach to knowledge that gives no consideration to the knowing subject, which was even more prevalent in ancient philosophy. This strategy was revived in this century in Husserlian phenomenology, which maintains that things show or reveal themselves to us. On the other hand, it is widely believed that under specifiable conditions, all, or at least some, human beings are capable of surpassing time and place. Descartes, for instance, contends that our cognitive capacities suffice to reach apodictic knowledge.

The most determined effort to make out this claim is featured in epistemological foundationalism, the leading modern strategy for knowledge. Foundationalism goes all the way back to ancient Greek philosophy. In some interpretations, Plato and Aristotle qualify as foundationalists. Like Greek intuitionism, for which it is the main modern alternative, epistemological foundationalism is intended to provide knowledge beyond time and place. Modern proponents of epistemological foundationalism from Descartes to Davidson routinely claim to know the way the world is, as distinguished from the way it merely appears to us. Yet foundationalism of all kinds simply founders on the representationalist reef, or the inability to show that representations really represent.

Prospective Interpretation

Ever since early Greek philosophy, many writers have tried to make the argument for knowledge merely on epistemic grounds, which are somehow magically disconnected from the cognitive limitations of real human beings. The cognitive limitations of human beings were already clear to Plato, who, in the *Republic*, suggested that on grounds of nature and nurture perhaps a few selected individuals, "men of gold," might be capable of "seeing," or directly intuiting, independent reality. Yet since there is no plausible account of how finite human beings know in nonfinite or infinite ways, there is no alternative to understanding knowledge of all kinds, including that following from interpretation, as historical, hence, as inextricably bound up with human history.

History is temporal, but time is not historical. Things, but not people, are in time; people are in history. But since people are historical beings, there is an obvious uncertainty concerning the future of our cognitive claims. There is simply no way to know whether the views we now hold will still appear viable in the future. Human history is replete with ideas which, like the fabled works of Ozymandias, seemed destined to stand forever but were later abandoned. Natural science currently passes for the most reliable source of knowledge. Yet if the past is a reliable indication, many, perhaps most, of the scientific views we now cherish will be later abandoned.

A striking example is the Christian worldview embodied in Ptolemaic astronomy, an astronomical theory that was progressively abandoned in the wake of what is usually called the Copernican astronomical revolution. From, say, the time of Ptolemy to the time of Kepler and Galileo, it was simply inconceivable to all but a few hardy astronomers that this astronomical conception, hence the associated worldview, would ever be abandoned. To be sure, the very idea of a scientific revolution, hence the existence of the Copernican revolution, is now under attack (Shapin 1996). It may be that, if there is no abrupt break with prior views, what is currently understood as the Copernican revolution is merely the result of incremental change over time. It is also known that the Copernican theory was anticipated in ancient times by Aristarchos of Samos. Yet it hardly makes a difference whether the Copernican revolution took place incrementally over many years, as now seems likely, or in a single decisive break with prior thought, since in both cases the result is to transform the modern world, including our views of ourselves and our relation to nature.

The importance of the Copernican revolution is difficult to overestimate. It has perhaps the best claim to be the single defining event that brought about the modern world (Pavlenko 1997). One can speculate that had the Copernican revolution not occurred, then neither the revised conception of human beings as at the root of their own world and themselves, which resulted from the French Revolution, nor, perhaps, even the French Revolution itself, would have occurred. For both depended on the unforeseen and literally unforeseeable crumbling of the Christian worldview at the beginning of modernity as a consequence of the Copernican astronomical revolution.

Retrospective Interpretation and Historiography

Among recent writers, no one has done more than Gadamer to emphasize the link between interpretation and history (Gadamer 1988). If interpretation depends on the influence of the past tradition on the present, then it cannot be the same before and after the great turning points of world history. The world as we know it is fundamentally different now from what it was before the Copernican revolution (Koyré 1958).

The historical character of interpretation applies to knowledge of the past, which has often been understood in ahistorical ways, as in the German neo-Kantian effort toward the beginning of the twentieth century to understand the transcendental conditions of a science of history; in Husserl's transcendental analysis of history; in Heidegger's concern to recover the problem of being as it was originally posed in early Greek philosophy; in Sartre's effort, in his biography of Flaubert, to reconstruct or, in his terminology, to capture entirely at least a single life; and in Ranke's desire to grasp history as it actually occurred. In different ways, these and related efforts aim to cognize the independent historical past, or historical past in independence of our view of it; they lead to a choice between knowledge of the past as it was, similar to the grasp of the way the world is, as the very model of what it means to know history, or to historical skepticism as the price of failing to know history as it actually occurred.

As in other forms of knowledge, so for history the proposed choice between grasping independent reality and skepticism seems mistaken. Just as we never know that we know the way the world is, we also never know that we know history as it occurred. The latter can at best be a regulative ideal, but it cannot be constitutive. At best we know only a reconstruction of history, which is never more than a representation of the historical past, and which changes with the perspective on which it is based (Aron 1969, 1981).

There is an obvious distinction between merely collecting facts and weaving them into a coherent narrative, and the very different task of understanding the significance of that narrative. The writing of history always requires more than a mere recital of facts about the past. There is an exact parallel between the inability to grasp the way the independent world is and the inability to grasp the past as it was. Those who think we can grasp the past as it was are tacitly committed to a solution of the problem of representation.

By "representation" I will mean here the problem of the objective depiction of the independent external world as it is. The problem of representation, which goes back to early Greek philosophy, is addressed in Plato's famous criticism of artists and poets. In modern philosophy, the problem is clearly posed, perhaps for the first time, by Kant. In his famous letter to Herz, Kant notes that claims for truth and knowledge require an understanding of the relation of the representation to the object (1967).

Posed in this way, the problem of representation is insoluble, since we cannot know that representations represent, nor how. There is no way to know that a given view of an object correctly represents it other than as it appears, as distinguished from the way it is. Short of getting outside ourselves to determine how the world is in itself – in other words, short of making good on the correspondence theory of truth – there is no way to compare our view of the world to the world, hence no way to make good on the claim to know the way the world is, which thus remains no more than an empty assertion. Claims to provide a correct representation of the independent world either rest on a misunderstanding, feature a different understanding of the object of knowledge,[1] or are asserted dogmatically. An example of the latter is provided in Putnam's natural realism, his new name for direct realism, whose claims to know he does not even attempt to justify (1994).

A historical narrative is no more than a representation of the historical past as it appears to us through our reconstruction of it. There is no way to know that we know how it relates to the independent historical past in itself, which necessarily remains unknown. Our only access to history is through our reconstruction of the historical record through whatever is transmitted from an earlier to a later period, which should not be conflated with the independent historical past. The latter is no more than a posit; no practical maneuver can ever allow us to identify the independent historical past.

I believe we never know the past as it was, but only know it as it is reconstructed by us. Interpretation is necessary precisely because we cannot know history directly, say, through a neutral grasp of the historical facts, but can only know it through one or another reading of the historical record. Yet if we could not know the historical past through narrative reconstruction, then interpretation of it would obviously be superfluous.

Facts and Historical Facts

All efforts to recover the historical record depend on what are called facts. Facts and historical facts raise similar conceptual issues. If there are ascertainable neutral or independent facts – facts independent of any particular theoretical framework, facts that have the same status for all observers in all times and places – then there are independent historical facts as well; but the nonexistence of such ascertainable independent facts undermines any theory of historical knowledge based on knowledge of the independent facts.

[1] Husserl, who regards the denial that perception in fact grasps things themselves as nonsensical, has in mind the grasp of the empirically real, although he denies that the phenomenon stands for an independent real outside experience, hence denies its representative function – which is precisely the point at issue. See Husserl 1962, §43, 122–24.

As concerns facts, five points should be made. First, there are no independent facts as such that can be ascertained in isolation from any
perspective. Since facts are facts for a perspective and not facts in independence of it, Davidson's effort, inspired by his interpretation of Quine
and Tarski (the former more than the latter), to dismiss the very idea of a
conceptual scheme is mistaken (Davidson 1991). For conceptual schemes,
like natural languages or scientific paradigms, provide the indispensable
framework within which we can grasp data. Davidson's suggestion is
intended to shore up knowledge by jettisoning what he regards as the third
and last dogma of empiricism in order to avoid skepticism. Yet to accept
his approach would only produce skepticism because of an inability to
pick out relevant empirical data, that is, data relevant to the favored
conceptual scheme. More generally, even the most sophisticated induc-
tivist approach to natural knowledge, such as that developed in the Vienna
Circle program, which arguably culminates in Carnap's probabilist analysis (1962), must always fail, since it depends on the capacity to ascertain
facts prior to and apart from any conceptual framework (Chalmers 1994,
1–12).

Second, the familiar claim to distinguish between what is often called
a given and its interpretation, for instance, in the distinction between
sensation and perception, incorrectly substitutes a theoretical distinction
for what occurs in experience. This claim is difficult, since, as Hegel
points out in his analysis of sense certainty, there is nothing resembling an
uninterpreted given, and as Sellars maintains, there is not even a given
(Sellars 1991). Conscious experience is confined to the contents of
consciousness, including first-order perceptions and second-order perceptions, or meta-reflections about them. We never actually experience sensations – we only infer them in order to understand the conceptual difference
between the "external" input and what we ourselves contribute to the
percept. This inference is necessary since otherwise all knowledge claims
would be claims about self-knowledge. There is no way to subtract our
contribution from perceptions to leave only sensations, hence no way to
grasp what is really out there as opposed to what is given in experience,
no way even to know that there is in fact a given.

Third, this point is relevant to understanding the relation of so-called
facts to reality and to independent reality. Putnam's internal realism, like
Kuhn's conception of scientific paradigms, depends on a view of facts
indexed to conceptual schemes, which in turn further refer to an independent real. There is no significant distinction between Kuhn's view that
different views interpret the same stimuli differently and Putnam's view,
influenced by James's idea of the really real, that one and the same independent world can be interpreted differently.[2] Kuhn is concerned to defuse

---

[2] Putnam distinguishes between external realism and internal realism. See Putnam
1981, Chapter 3: "Two Philosophical Perspectives," 49–74.

the controversy arising from his famous claim that scientists favoring different theories literally live in different worlds (1970, 118). Putnam is concerned to bolster the claims that science is about the same independent external world. Both defend a tacit notion of cognitive objectivity. Yet we never know there is a common world out there; that there is one is at best an epistemological posit. What we call "nature" cannot simply be taken as an invariant independent given, since it is in fact a historical construct deriving from the view that prevails at any particular moment. If this claim is correct, then not only are there no ascertainable neutral facts, since "facts" always and necessarily depend on a particular framework, but independent reality is itself no more than a construct.

Fourth, like historical facts, the way that history is reconstructed is never neutral but always depends on the interpretive perspective. It seems obvious that there is no single way to reconstruct the historical record, but many different ways, hence many different readings of historical texts, or historical events. A recent example is the concern to present the feminist perspective.

The way one or a series of events is interpreted often depends on prior interpretations. An interpretation of the French Revolution in the wake of François Furet would be very different from interpretations dominated by the Marxist historiography he wanted to counter. The difference, although great, is not so great as to deny the idea, common to all interpretations, of the series of events from 1789 to the coup d'état on the 18th Brumaire 1799, which, in putting an end to the *ancien régime*, radically changed the social, political, juridical, and religious structures in France. Yet in virtue of the different emphases, the different readings of the French Revolution concern similar, but irreducibly different series of historical events bearing the same general title: the French Revolution.

Fifth, the possibility of different readings of historical events bearing the same general title implies the incorrectness of any effort to determine what, in Kantian terminology, can be called the transcendental conditions of history. This undertaking engaged the combined effort of a series of German neo-Kantians (including Windelband, Simmel, Lask, Rickert, M. Weber) at the end of the nineteenth century to elucidate the general conditions of the possibility of history and historical knowledge whatsoever (Rockmore 1992, 55–77). But if there is no single view of history, hence no single history, there can be no elucidation of the most general conditions of history and historical knowledge. There are only different views of history, hence different reconstructions of it, accordingly, different accounts of its real conditions.

Historical Texts, Historical Interpretation

Interpretation, including historical interpretation, is not confined to historians, or historians of philosophy and other disciplines. Many others, including literary critics, art critics, and certain types of scientists (such as archeologists, paleontologists, experimental physicists, and so on), either interpret texts or interpret data assimilable to texts. If by "texts" is meant "independent documents," and by "facts" is meant "independent facts," then I believe that strictly speaking there are neither facts nor texts, but rather a complex relation between human beings who interpret, various interpretive perspectives, and the facts on which interpretation is based and through which it is supported.

History provides a useful example. Historians deal with what they call the historical record, consisting in what is available from documents, what can be gleaned from archives and earlier historical studies, what can be assembled through interviews with historical actors, and so on. We do best to take a constructivist, rather than an empiricist or a skeptical, approach to historical knowledge. What we call the past is literally "constructed" by us in the form of a narrative concerning one or more events, such as the French Revolution, the signing of the Magna Carta, and so on. The writing of history, which obviously requires the historian to select what is meaningful in order to construct an appropriate narrative, never merely consists in the assembling of the empirical facts, whatever one means by this term. In the writing of history, what is meaningful clearly depends on the perspective adopted. It follows that the historian does not simply "read" an independent historical record, since there is none, but rather only "reads" a historical record written by the historian himself.

It is tempting to suppose that knowledge of the past, like all kinds of knowledge that require a grasp of what is as it is, requires a grasp of what was as it was. According to this view of the matter, history is knowable in the same way and to the extent that anything at all is knowable. This idea is the presumed basis of claims by a great many writers, including historians, philosophers, philosophers of science, social thinkers, and others, to know the past as it in fact was. Yet if historians must literally constitute history as a condition of interpreting it, then they cannot know it as it was, but only as it appears to them to have been.

This point is obviously relevant to Heidegger's obsessive concern with being. Unquestionably, the interpretive traditions that grow up around a text over time can tend to obscure it. Heidegger's proposed "destruction" of the history of ontology is intended to contribute to recovering the so-called ontological question as it was originally, supposedly "authentically," raised in early Greek philosophical texts. Heidegger, who seems to assume that what he wishes to recover was already constituted at an earlier date, further assumes that events, historical objects, theories, and philosophical questions are comparable to, say, a painting obscured by a patina, which, through the appropriate chemical process, can simply be removed to reveal the original colors. Yet although a painting can only be "understood" in historical perspective, it is not like a historical process, and its patina is not the same as a historical tradition. As Gadamer points out, since all interpretation occurs out of our historical moment, by implication Heidegger's ahistorical view of the interpretation of ontology incorrectly presupposes that we can grasp what is already constituted in independence of our present historical moment (Rockmore 1993–1994).

Interpretation and Historical Knowledge

The limits of historical interpretation are the same as the limits of interpretation in general. Any account of interpretation needs to distinguish between truth in interpretation and the truth of any particular interpretation. I hold that interpretation cannot be true, although it can be false. An interpretation cannot be true since, except for special cases, which are probably very rare, almost any text admits of more than one reading. As Quine points out, translation is indeterminate, since reference is indeterminate. Yet, as usually understood, "truth" implies the possibility of a single correct interpretation, which correctly grasps an object, as in the correspondence view of truth. If a truth claim requires that there be at most a single reading of a given text, then, like the proverbial single true reading of *Hamlet*, its possibility must be denied. Yet interpretations can certainly be false, as when a particular reading fails to find support, or at least what is regarded as adequate support, in the text. In practice, we are confronted with the possibility of a multiplicity of readings of a particular text, each of which has at least some supporting evidence drawn from the particular version of the text.

These related, but different readings constitute the traditions that grow up around different texts, such as the different interpretations of Plato's corpus, the different ways of understanding the big bang, the different readings of quantum mechanics, or the different construals of President Clinton's behavior, lately much in the news, in the West Wing of the White House.

It would be a mistake to infer that if different interpretations are possible, none of which is true, all interpretations are on the same level, since none is better than the other. This objection, which is sometimes brought against relativism, as in the silly claim that any view is as good as any other view, rests on an obvious caricature of the doctrine. It does not follow, if more than one interpretation is possible but none is true, that all are equally plausible. To rank interpretations, we require criteria allowing us to choose between them, such as explanatory richness, or the capacity to account for more rather than fewer items in a given text or series of events. In principle the absolutely best, fully adequate interpretation, a regulative idea probably never reached in practice, would not only be better than its competitors, but would finally, wholly adequately, and fully explain everything to be explained.

Historical Interpretation and Historical Knowledge

I want now to defend this modest claim against three possible objections due, respectively, to what I will call the positivist approach to historical phenomena, the form of historical skepticism following from a denial of the positivist approach, and the obviously related question concerning cognitive objectivity.

The general idea that knowledge claims, hence historical knowledge claims, are interpretive can be contrasted with recent positivist approaches to history and historical knowledge arising independently out of the Vienna Circle, Marxism, and Foucault. As concerns history, these and related approaches are characteristic of the general effort to grasp history directly by bypassing interpretation, without recourse (for explanatory purposes) either to specific historical actors, such as Napoleon, or to deeper explanatory principles, as in Marx, Nietzsche, and Freud, and so on. In eschewing interpretive frameworks, historical positivism is the historical equivalent of various forms of natural scientific inductivism, which, in assuming the existence of independent facts, uses them as the basis of theoretical constructs, in relation to which they are regarded as independent.

With respect to history, the Vienna Circle unity of science movement culminated in Hempel's famous paper in which he treated history as a science like the prototypical science of physics, a science *primus inter pares* and the basis of physicalism, and suggested that there must be historical laws in history. According to Hempel, there are general laws in history and in natural science. By "general law" Hempel means a universal statement capable of being confirmed or disconfirmed on empirical grounds. In denying that history is concerned with the description of particular events rather than general laws, Hempel contends that

> general laws have quite analogous functions in history and in the natural sciences, that they form an indispensable instrument of history research, and that they even constitute the common basis of various procedures which are often considered as characteristic of the social in contradistinction to the natural sciences. (1949, 459)

This view has been much criticized from many angles by Marxists and non-Marxists alike. A paradigmatic Marxist criticism is provided by Rakitov, who, after noting the guiding assumption that explanation in the historical and the natural sciences is identical, claims that Hempel's covering law model does not allow for the specific character of historical explanation and historical knowledge in general (Rakitov 1987, 249). Rakitov, who maintains that Hempel's theory manifests what he calls the profoundly antiscientific orientation of Western philosophers and historians, namely, their antipathy to objective laws and hypotheses in the structure of historical knowledge, contends that historical materialism alone grasps the real historical laws which Hempel's bourgeois critics deny (Rakitov 1987, 250).

A third form of historical positivism, in opposition to global histories, but under the influence of attention to lengthy periods featured in the French *annales* approach, is provided in Foucault's epochal conception of history as composed of discontinuous forms of organization without authors, or so-called *epistemes*. On this basis, Foucault studies history as the history of different practices organized, as becomes clear in his later books, around forms of power (1969). The result is an approach, like structuralism, to which Foucault's theory bears an unclear relation, that is non- or a-anthropological (1969, 26). This approach is intended to grasp the *énoncé* just as it is without ever asking what is manifested through it. According to Foucault, clinical, economic, natural-historical, psychiatric, and other forms of discourse merely group together types of *énoncés* (1969, 141). From this perspective, a practice is defined as "the general system of the formation and transformation of *énoncés*" (1969, 171).

Like inductivism, positivism of all kinds seeks to surpass interpretation by seeking a direct basis in experience. These and other forms of historical positivism turn away from the subject, a pattern apparent as well in structuralisms of all kinds, in the later Heidegger, and in the *annales* approach to history (the *longue durée*) in order to focus directly on the given. This approach is doubly controversial. First, it is unclear that there is or even could be anything like a given in the sense positivism presupposes since, as already noted, Hegel's critique of sense certainty and Sellars's attack on the so-called myth of the given undermine this line of argument.

Second, it is clear that, like inductivism, historical positivism cannot avoid a tacit appeal to theory, which intervenes in two ways. On the one hand, theory intervenes with respect to what counts as a fact – which is determined by the theory, since, as noted above, there are no neutral facts ascertainable outside of theories. On the other, theory intervenes with respect to the choice among the available facts picked out by the theory. Since there are always more facts than can be taken up, which facts among others are relevant is a function of a given theory. Hence, even the most positivist approaches to history cannot avoid interpretation. It follows that historical positivism in all its forms fails on its own merits.

Rorty, de Man, and Historical Skepticism

I believe that most, perhaps all, knowledge claims, in particular our claims about the past, are interpretive in character. In practice, I see a steady reliance, not on knowledge of the independent real, the obsessive theme of philosophical epistemology from Parmenides through Plato to the present, but rather on interpretation of the contents of experience, which is often misdescribed as the independent real. It might be objected that to limit interpretation, hence historical interpretation, would have the unfortunate consequence of inviting skepticism about knowledge in general, and as concerns history, skepticism about history, or historical knowledge. Versions of this skeptical claim, in effect a form of conceptual blackmail, are raised independently by Richard Rorty and literary critic Paul de Man.

As part of his polemic against any meaningful form of epistemology, Rorty desires to prevent any effort to recover theory of knowledge by other means, such as hermeneutics, understood as interpretation (1979, 315). If "epistemology" means "knowing the way the world is in independence of us," then, as already noted, it can have no successor, since there is no way to know that we know the way the world is. In this sense, Rorty agrees with Kant's view that we cannot know an independent object. But that does not imply that meaningful discussion of knowledge, something Rorty has never abandoned, is impossible.

Rorty loads the dice, as it were, in his favor, in distinguishing sharply between epistemology and hermeneutics. He dismisses the latter as the mere conversation of mankind, simply kibitzing among the intellectual *haut gratin*, which has no epistemological weight. In Rorty's view, interpretation is not and is not even potentially a source of knowledge.

The obvious alternative is to hold that what we call knowledge is no more than a reading, construal, or interpretation, in effect, a theory of what is given in experience. Such a theory, as Quine reminds us, is never forced on us by what is given in experience, hence never deduced from it (1961). It constitutes no more than our best view of the matter, based on the information at our disposal, of what is given in experience. If, on the contrary, "epistemology" means no more than the interpretation of the contents of experience, an interpretation that is justified, to the extent that such justification is possible, by the standards in use in a given cognitive domain, then epistemology as hermeneutics is indeed the legitimate successor to epistemology as it has usually been understood.

Whereas Rorty sees hermeneutics as a struggle against commensurability, or the idea that there is a set of rules that will settle disputes by allowing rational agreement (1979, 316), I hold that epistemological interpretation depends on the present strategies at our command in the cognitive disciplines and on the invention of new strategies whenever necessary. Skepticism dependent on doubt, the radical type featured in Descartes, cannot be assuaged, since we cannot know that we know the way things are. But through the process of normal debate we can by all means hope to agree about views that will hold, if not for all time, at least for a time, by the proper use of the best techniques currently at our disposal. The result is and is intended to be an endless conversation, but also more than that, since it is the source of what knowledge we can have at any given point in time. Unlike Rorty, who sees epistemology and hermeneutics as approaches that are not in competition but are mutually supportive (1979, 346), I view hermeneutics as sharply opposed to epistemology as it is usually understood and as Rorty understands it, but as indistinguishable from epistemology when the latter is redefined on interpretive grounds.

A related objection is raised by de Man in his attack on the familiar distinction between history and fiction. In a discussion of Derrida's reading of Rousseau, de Man remarks that in any text there is always a confusion between fact and fiction (1986, 12). In a discussion of Blanchot, he writes: "Fiction and the history of actual events converge toward the same nothingness; the knowledge revealed by the hypothesis of fiction turns out to be knowledge that already existed, in all the strength of its negativity, before the act of consciousness that tries to reach it" (1983, 75).

As I read de Man in these passages, he is complaining about the regrettable tendency to confuse fact and fiction, in short, to take fiction for fact. This is something that can never be imputed in good conscience to one's critics, but only to psychotics who lose their hold on what we call reality. Yet like Derrida, who, in a way inconsistent with his attack on the meaningfulness of philosophy, employs words with standard philosophical precision in order to deconstruct definite reference, de Man, who desires to cast doubt on this distinction, is caught in an obvious performative contradiction. For one can only complain about the failure to recognize that fiction is only fiction if one acknowledges the distinction between history and fiction, which de Man is at pains to deny. In other words, de Man is hoist with his own petard.

Conclusion: Historical Interpretation and Cognitive Objectivity

I close with a comment about cognitive objectivity. The problem of cognitive objectivity is the same for historical interpretation as for interpretation in general. In both cases, we only know that we know what we "construct" through the cognitive process as a condition of knowing the historical world or the world in general. What we mean by "objectivity" can no longer mean the grasp of the independent object. It cannot simply mean the verification of such claims, for instance, by testing them against further experience, construed as providing an empirical restraint, since claims to know can always be verified in at least a minimal manner for the obvious reason that the particular framework invoked also generates evidence for them.[3] Cognitive objectivity can only mean the "construction" of knowledge claims according to standards currently acceptable in a given historical moment to members of the discipline – for historians, by standards acceptable to historians; for physicists, by standards acceptable to physicists; and so on. As concerns cognition, including historical

---

[3] For this claim, see Hirsch 1979.

cognition, or knowledge of the historical past, there is no escape from relativizing our knowledge claims to the historical moment.

References

Aron, Raymond. (1969). *La philosophie critique de l'histoire*. Paris: Vrin.
——. (1981). *Introduction à la philosophie de l'histoire: Essai sur les limites de l'objectivité historique*. Paris: Gallimard.
Carnap, Rudolf. (1962). *Logical Foundations of Probability*. Chicago: University of Chicago Press.
Chalmers, A. F. (1994). *What Is This Thing Called Science?* Indianapolis: Hackett.
Davidson, Donald. (1991). "On the Very Idea of a Conceptual Scheme." In *Truth and Interpretation*, 183–98. Oxford: Clarendon Press.
de Man, Paul. (1983). *Blindness and Insight: Essays in the Rhetoric of Contemporary Criticism*. Introduction by Wlad Godzich. Minneapolis: University of Minnesota Press.
——. (1986). *The Resistance to Theory*. Foreword by Wlad Godzich. Minneapolis: University of Minnesota Press.
Devitt, Michael. (1991). *Realism and Truth*. Princeton, NJ: Princeton University Press.
Foucault, Michel. (1969). *L'archéologie du savoir*. Paris: Gallimard.
Gadamer, Hans-Georg. (1988). *Truth and Method*. Translated by Garrett Barden and John Cumming. New York: Crossroad.
Hempel, Carl G. (1949). "The Function of General Laws in History." In *Readings in Philosophical Analysis*, edited by Herbert Feigl and Wilfrid Sellars. New York: Appleton-Century-Crofts.
Hirsch, E. D., Jr. (1979). *Validity in Interpretation*. New Haven, CT: Yale University Press.
Husserl, Edmund. (1962). *Ideas: General Introduction to Pure Phenomenology*. Translated by W. R. Boyce Gibson. New York: Collier.
Kant, Immanuel. (1962). *Critique of Pure Reason*. Translated by N. K. Smith. New York: St. Martin's.
——. (1967). *Philosophical Correspondence, 1759–99*. Translated and edited by Arnulf Zweig. Chicago: University of Chicago Press.
Koyré, Alexandre. (1958). *From the Closed World to the Infinite Universe*. New York: Harper and Brothers.
Kuhn, Thomas S. (1970). *The Structure of Scientific Revolutions*. Chicago: University of Chicago Press.
——. (1977). *The Essential Tension: Selected Studies in Scientific Tradition and Change*. Chicago: University of Chicago Press.
Lakatos, Imré. (1976). *Proofs and Refutations*. Edited by J. Worrall and E. Zahar. Cambridge: Cambridge University Press.

Lakatos, Imré, and A. Musgrave, eds. (1974). *Criticism and the Growth of Science*. Cambridge: Cambridge University Press.

McDowell, John. (1994, 1996). *Mind and World*. Cambridge: Harvard University Press.

Pavlenko, A. N. (1997). *Evropeiskaja Kosmologija, Osnovannija Epistemologicheskovo Povorota*. Moscow: Intrada.

Popper, Karl. (1972). *Objective Knowledge*. Oxford: Oxford University Press.

Putnam, Hilary. (1981). *Reason, Truth and History*. Cambridge: Cambridge University Press.

———. (1994). "Sense, Nonsense, and the Senses: An Inquiry into the Powers of the Human Mind" (Dewey Lectures 1994). *Journal of Philosophy*, 91, no. 9, 445–517.

Quine, W. V. O. (1961). "Two Dogmas of Empiricism." In *From a Logical Point of View*, 20–46. New York: Harper and Row.

Rakitov, Anatoly. (1987). *Historical Knowledge: A Systems-Epistemological Approach*. Translated by H. Campbell Creighton. Moscow: Progress Publishers.

Rockmore, Tom. (1992). *Irrationalism: Lukács and the Marxist View of Reason*. Philadelphia: Temple University Press.

———. (1993–1994). "Heidegger, Übersetzen und Philosophiegeschichte." *Existentia*, 3–4, nos. 1–4, 625–30.

Rorty, Richard. (1979). *Philosophy and the Mirror of Nature*. Princeton, NJ: Princeton University Press.

Sellars, Wilfrid. (1991). "Empiricism and the Philosophy of Mind." In *Science, Perception and Reality*. Atascadero, CA: Ridgeview.

Shapin, Steven. (1996). *The Scientific Revolution*. Chicago: University of Chicago Press.

Weinberg, Steven. (1998). "The Revolution That Didn't Happen." *The New York Review of Books*, 45, no. 15 (October 8), 48–52.

12

RELATIVISM AND INTERPRETIVE OBJECTIVITY

JOSEPH MARGOLIS

The following is an argument in favor of a heterodox account of interpretation. I assume there is no point in speaking of objective interpretation without explaining what it is about the nature of things that fits them for interpretation and how we may be said to know that particular interpretations do indeed fit interpretable things objectively. That's all.

I

If, ideally, the right description of the world were largely constrained by the terms of causal explanation, and if causal laws reliably invoked the necessary and universally sufficient physical structures of nature, and if whatever was real entered into causal interactions, then it might be argued that the "proper logic" of nature must be bivalent. One might also suppose that in addition, a full description of the world sometimes requires and justifies our relying on an interpretation of (that is, a weaker conjecture about) some set of describable entities, because, say, we lacked the full evidence for a comprehensive description and because we supposed interpretation could be rigorously confined to such an auxiliary function. Then it might again be reasonably argued that, apart from the contingent interests, limited perspectives, and diverging information of particular investigators, an objective account of those structures would yield, at most, a single inclusive right interpretation. That is the heart of what is now called "objectivism" (see Bernstein 1983; Putnam 1980) or, as I prefer, "Cartesian realism" – viewed dismissively from the vantage of the achievement of post-Kantian philosophy. The idea is fanciful, of course, because there is no known compelling reason for restricting description or interpretation along these lines and, moreover, because even if we embraced it, we would not know how to proceed conformably.

Nevertheless, I yield the point for the sake of a better lesson, namely, that even on these utopian suppositions, it makes no sense to declare what the logical constraints on description and interpretation should be without considering the actual nature of the phenomena in question. I put it to you that the overwhelming bias in the sciences and the interpretation of art and history and language and human life in general (to the extent the latter are even conceded to approach the proper discipline of a bona fide science) favors an unrelenting bivalence, with almost no hesitations about the nature of all the possible objects that could be described or the possible recalcitrance of interpretable structures.

The plain assumption is that physical nature fits a bivalent logic to perfection and that the norm in the physical sciences should or must be the right norm for the interpretive disciplines as well. That is an unearned advantage, to say the least. The idea that, for anything that is genuinely real, an objective characterization of it (whether descriptive or interpretive) must converge toward a single finding of what "it is" is hardly more than a casual hostage to an impoverished imagination. It may be true, but no one has ever shown that it is. I see no principled difference, here, between theorizing, a priori, about the appropriate "logic" of high-level *explanantia* among the physical fundaments of the universe and about the structures of garden-variety literary texts and histories. For example, if speculations like Paul Feyerabend's (1962) and Thomas Kuhn's (1970) about epistemological incommensurabilities in the physical sciences (specifically explanatory and evidentiary incommensurabilities) had proved valid (as in the notorious Priestley/Lavoisier controversy) – they are of course regularly dismissed but (in my opinion) have never been rightly answered in a principled way[1] – the bare admission would alter our philosophical tolerances in a trice.

The most candid no-nonsense statement of the canonical conviction regarding interpretation in the arts – call it "Fregean" if you wish, though as far as I know Frege never explained the meaning of the discrepancy between the apparent laxity of the logic of natural-language discourse and the ideal rigor of a carpentered language presumably addressed to the same world but now constrained without distortion by an exceptionless bivalence – appears quite unceremoniously in Monroe Beardsley's well-known theory (1970). I have no wish to take up Beardsley's specific argument here – I suppose I have done so too many times already – but Beardsley's comfortable pronouncement affords the easiest way to fix our intuitions on the issue. Beardsley lays down a number of "principles" – I should say "postulates," since, though he believes them to be well-nigh incontestible, he nowhere tries to prove that they cannot be reasonably opposed without paradox or self-contradiction.

I need cite only two of Beardsley's would-be principles to make my point. One, "the Principle of Autonomy," holds

---

[1] I have discussed the matter in an as yet unpublished paper, "Incommensurability Modestly Recovered," presented at a conference, "Incommensurability (and related matters)," University of Hannover, Hannover, Germany, June 13–16, 1999.

that literary works are self-sufficient entities, whose properties are decisive in checking interpretations and judgments. (16)

About the other, Beardsley says the following:

> I hold that there are a great many interpretations that obey what might be called the principle of "the Intolerability of Incompatibles," i.e., if two of them are logically incompatible, they cannot both be true. Indeed, I hold that *all* of the literary interpretations that deserve the name obey this principle. (44)

Take notice, please, that the first sentence of the second principle is entirely uncontroversial, without particular reference to interpretation, and that the second sentence introduces a quite disputatious notion, expressed as a personal conviction rather than a reasoned finding. Certainly, two incompatible descriptions or interpretations cannot both be *true*; but it hardly follows from that that all seemingly valid or confirmable interpretations (those "that deserve the name") either obey the bivalent rule or, if they do not, should be appropriately forced to. It is surely conceivable that what, on a bivalent logic, would count as "incompatibles" may, on the adoption of a many-valued logic, be counted as valid (no longer "incompatible"), as among those interpretations "that deserve the name" – because (on an argument easily supplied) they answer to the supposed real nature of what is being interpreted.

Beardsley never satisfactorily demonstrated why we should not concede the laxer practice (that is, the logically laxer practice that might ultimately prove epistemically more rigorous); in particular, he never showed that, or why, the *nature* of literary texts (or of other kinds of artworks, which he did not examine in an explicitly analogous way, or even histories, which he viewed as subject to objective constraints much like those he supposed affected literature) precluded the laxer policy. But we may concede openly enough that, up to his own conviction that literary texts were "autonomous" and "independent" entities that behaved, logically, very much the way physical objects do – except of course that they possess (as physical objects do not) semiotic or linguistic properties, or "meanings," that are somehow really "in" the works in question – Beardsley does not fail to link his views on the logic of interpretation with his own "metaphysics."

Contemporary discussants are not always as careful as Beardsley. For instance, Robert Stecker (1997, 228n. 11) holds that a relativistic treatment of interpretation (which, on my own view, would require invoking a many-valued logic) is *always* able to be recast, without loss, in the terms of a bivalent logic (see also Barnes 1988). But Stecker nowhere addresses the question of the "nature" of interpretable *denotata* on which his claim might be tested. And Michael Krausz (1993, 62–65), exploring the logic of interpretation, claims to be "agnostic" about the "ontology" of artworks, though not about the social "practices" (presumably distinct from artworks) in which their interpretable features are said to be discerned. Krausz does not, however, explain the relation between the two or how, precisely, the two "spaces" may be segregated. I could name a great many other well-known discussants of related matters who tell us in no uncertain way why, a priori, descriptions, interpretations, analyses of a realist cast *must* conform to an exceptionless bivalence. I feel sure, though, that many of them would not be entirely satisfied with their own answers once they were obliged to explain why "reality" could not possibly be otherwise than they suppose. I ask only for candor here.

But that's not the whole of the story. Doctrines of Beardsley's sort, all the usual "objectivisms" in fact, fail to come to terms with what may be called the first line of considerations affecting any would-be metaphysics – which is not at all what the authors mentioned choose to address. Before we can say whether we must opt for a bivalent logic wherever we claim to be addressing the real world objectively, we surely must take care to review at least the conceptual resources we call on pertinently and with assurance. And there, the facts stare one in the face: we literally have no way to vouchsafe the epistemic conditions on which (alone) *anything* like Beardsley's principles could ever be shown to be necessary or necessarily true. The supporting arguments would show at a stroke the deep importance of the interpretive question for all versions of realism – not, I should add, in a merely auxiliary role. That question cannot rightly be resolved without a very large canvass of our fundamental views about reality and knowledge: Beardsley – and Stecker and Krausz – are doubtless willing to share their deepest convictions with us, but they are noticeably stingy about sharing any supporting arguments. There's room for disagreement, no doubt; but you will find that, in all the best-known analyses of realist description and interpretation, there are almost none that are willing to consider the possibility of departing from a metaphysics like Beardsley's or the inviolability of the bivalent rule about reality.

I am not recommending that we adopt a skeptical or "agnostic" or anarchical stand of any kind. No: there "is" a real world and we know a great deal about it – possibly not enough, however, to settle the question before us. Yielding on the matter of *what*, precisely, an objective knowledge of all the parts of the real world might entail has nothing to do with subversive uncertainties about the robustness of the world itself. The world would not become less robust if relativism were convincing. Certainly it would not mean that "anything goes" or every judgment is as good as any other. (That is only the apocalyptic tale.) But it might well mean that the ubiquity of bivalence may be fairly challenged. To *know*, say, that Brahms's Fourth Symphony can be validly performed in several "incompatible" ways (speaking "bivalently") is not the troubling question: everyone admits it. The question, rather, is: If (metonymically) that were so, what would it mean to admit that it was? What must the world be like, and how should our cognitive capacities conform, if interpretation has realist standing despite the fact that it could not in principle secure the inviolability of a bivalent logic of interpretation? That is a question almost never rightly canvassed.

I am moving very slowly here because long experience has taught me that wherever these matters can be misunderstood, they will be if we don't take care. I put it to you that it is entirely conceivable – perhaps even a stronger conjecture than any that runs contrary to it – that incompatible interpretations of a particular artwork or history may, without paradox, be shown to be coherent, to be entitled to realist standing as such, and to be reconcilable with a metaphysics and epistemology (and logic) that do not threaten any well-established part of our best inquiries. I am persuaded that such a theory *can* indeed acquit itself favorably in contest with any known alternative. You cannot ask for more than that.

Doubtless, it would require a very considerable overhaul of our usual metaphysical and epistemological convictions. I am aware of that. I also believe that ordinary discourse does have incipient proclivities of these sorts (despite Wittgenstein's demurrer), and I would not deny that they go overwhelmingly against my recommendation. But that leads me to say more pointedly that I have no intention of providing a full-blown theory of interpretation here. (I have tried to do that elsewhere.) What's needed is a clear sense of the philosophical rationale for going against the crowd. I fancy that the genuine force and good sense of the arguments backing relativism in interpretive matters are not actually very well known. That single fact, I hope, will catch a little of your patience in what might otherwise be a dreary matter.

I admit a great many knowledgeable discussants will have none of this. Let me mention, therefore, two additional views which, in somewhat different ways, capture the prevailing antirelativist sentiment of the canonical "realists." I want to fix very clearly the familiar doctrine that I oppose and deem demonstrably arbitrary. Nicholas Rescher, for one (1999), commenting, I may say, on my own view, affirms very confidently: "Questions about the structure of reality admit only of resolving answers within the true/false dichotomy, even where they have a degree-like position in the certainty spectrum" (159). I take that to mean that on the question whether, say, the cat is on the mat, the answer must accord with the logical dichotomy of true and false, but that on the question of the "evidentiation" of such an assertion, the answer "is subject to relativistically degree-like qualification" (153). But how does Rescher know that all questions about "the structure of reality" behave bivalently? The other matter he raises is not really a question about relativism at all; it speaks only to the relativity of evidence, and thus to probabilizing the semantics of truth regarding what we believe.

Here, in tandem, is Hilary Putnam's conjecture (McCormick 1999), which raises – implicitly – a very different question from Rescher's, which

Putnam nowhere answers but which affects the matter of bivalence, the fate of relativism, and the self-evidence of Rescher's dictum:

> That the sky is blue [Putnam says] is causally independent of the way we talk; for, with our language in place, we can certainly say that the sky would still be blue even if we did not use color words. . . . And the statement that the sky is blue is, in the ordinary sense of "logical independence," logically independent of any description that one might give of our use of color words. . . . In any sense of "independence" I can understand, whether the sky is blue is independent of the way we talk. (92–93)[2]

Putnam nowhere says what that sense is – the sense in which the sky's being blue *is* independently blue and can be known to be blue (*as it is independently*).

You may suppose Putnam merely wishes to deny any "magical" connection between reality and belief or discourse about reality. Fine. But notice, please, that he adds – with confidence – that what he's saying *is* in conformity with "any sense of 'independence' I can understand." But what of the sense of "independence" in which the sky's being blue *is* independent of my saying so here and now (against the "magical" option), but *is not* independent in any sense completely unrelated to the specific concepts and categories and theories that we invoke in saying that (the famous philosophical option that has taken close to two hundred years, running from Descartes to Hegel, to get clear about)? *That* is the option that must be aired if the contest between (say) objectivism and relativism could ever be satisfactorily put to rest.

Rescher notes that realist discourse cannot but be bivalent. Putnam holds that the world is determinately what it is independently of whatever we say or think, though (as he also says in the same passage), without language, there would be no *truths* to that effect! How then does he know that, apart from the language in which we express our beliefs, the world is determinately such that, for instance, the sky's being blue really obtains; or that, given our particular language, our supposing that the sky is blue answers to what really obtains in the world "independently" of that; or that

---

[2] I take these citations from Peter McCormick (1999). I have not been able to locate their original source, but they conform with Putnam's characteristic themes – in particular, with the following: "To deny, as I do, that there is a 'ready-made world' is not to say that we make up the world. . . . But I have long argued that to ask which facts are mind independent in the sense that nothing about them reflects our conceptual choices and which facts are 'contributed by us' is to commit a 'fallacy of division.' . . . To try to divide the world into a part that is independent of us and a part that is contributed by us is an old temptation, but giving in to it leads to disaster every time" (1992b, 58). I add this clarification to confirm McCormick's citation and to offset any impression that I am unaware of the carefully crafted way in which Putnam says what he does. Still, I think that the force of what he says depends on whether we can fix *any denotatum* objectively. Putnam is more sanguine here than his own argument can support.

our objective judgment must accord (in the relevant sense, that is, against relativism) with bivalence?

These are very old chestnuts – which I believe *can* be smartly "answered." I am not pressing them here, except for their strategic value. I mention them, not to launch an endless skeptical tirade but to give point to my warning that policies like Beardsley's, Stecker's, and Krausz's regarding interpretation and Rescher's and Putnam's in a wider setting trade on well-entrenched prejudices that none of them could possibly defend; and that, as a result, their matter-of-fact insistence on the adequacy or necessity of adhering to bivalence (or the inadmissibility of invoking a "relativistic logic") hangs in the balance. Well, then, exasperation asks, how would *you* answer?

I should begin by distinguishing between these two very different concerns: (1) what it means to speak of the nature of the real world "independently of language and thought" as opposed to how we characterize the world as it "appears to us" in experience and in accord with our concepts and categories and (2) whether, if a bivalent logic fits and serves standard parts of realist discourse, it is still possible that a relativistic logic also fits competitively some part of the realist phenomena that bivalence claims exclusively for its own, or fits even better and more convincingly parts of the realist domain that standard bivalent treatments noticeably slight or ignore. Strategies associated with question (1) try to answer Descartes's question favorably for bivalence; strategies associated with (2) abandon (1) in the Cartesian sense and simply address the comparative advantage of bivalence and a relativistic logic in inquiries already internal to our realist admissions. The first leads to skepticism, which, I suggest, all of my exemplars risk invoking; the second does not.

Here, I agree entirely with Putnam: regarding (1), any effort to distinguish a priori or in any evidentiary sense between what is "independent" and what is "mind-dependent" would be nonsense. But if that is so, then neither Rescher nor Putnam can defend the views I've cited, on pain of reviving Descartes's original paradoxes, or else, no answer can be given that did not treat that distinction as a *constructivist* solution (that is, a solution offered in a logical space in which the epistemic difference between "independent" and "mind-dependent" had no a priori standing – was, instead, an artifact of that same space). If all that were true, then, assuming ordinary consistency, *there would be no prior ground on which (2) could be judged to be an illicit question.* That's all that relativism, incommensurabilism, historicism, and similar outlaw doctrines require in order to place a clean foot in the philosophical door. Few discussants would admit the point, but I know no way of defeating it. The recovery of relativism – the reconciliation of realism and relativism – depends on such maneuvers. That is the tiresome truth that we need patience to appreciate: it's the shortest way to grasping the force of a relativistic treatment of interpretation.

II

There are many arguments of the kind I have just given that might serve as what I am calling "first considerations," that rightly take precedence over the questions Beardsley and Rescher and Putnam address, and that, once posed, block our accepting at face value the presumptive answers all three give (in particular the alleged necessity of abiding by bivalence in realist discourse). They block them, I say, because the issues Putnam and the others raise (and answer) pretend to outflank any number of first considerations *or* preclude all those deviant realisms that my own first considerations might help to show to be conceptually eligible. I say "my own," but what I mean of course are the first considerations Hegel and the abler post-Kantians had shown us were well-nigh ineluctable if we mean to avoid any vestigial forms of "Cartesian realism" (or "objectivism," as the current idiom prefers). My point is simply that, at a first approximation, relativism stands with the post-Kantians and its contemporary opponents do not.

Let me put this in a tidier way. Here are six theorems that I claim to draw from post-Kantian first considerations, of which, I admit, I have provided no more than a passing glimpse:

(1) Intransparency: No realism can escape the inherent paradoxes and contradictions of "Cartesian realism" (spanning pre-Kantian philosophy from Descartes to Kant and, on a reasonable interpretation, extending to Kant himself) if it does not reject the a priori standing of a *relational* account of cognizing subjects and "independent" cognized objects (or intermediary representations of same) intended to ensure an undistorted *correspondence* between belief and world.

Hence, (2) Constructivism: Whatever realism we are able to defend (regarding the "independent" world) must be *constituted* in the logically trivial sense of affirming (1) and must, as a consequence, construe the cognizing *relation* between subjects and objects (presupposed and entailed in admitting truth-claims) as a critical and revisable artifact *internal* to the "space" of that construction, precluding thereby all possibility of privileged or apodictic access to the "independent" world or to the conditions for knowing same.

(3) Symbiosis: The "independence" or "mind-independence" of physical nature is not compromised by (1) or (2), but the ontic independence of *anything said* to be real is, on pain of contradiction, *epistemically* dependent on, or inseparable from, whatever may be affirmed and confirmed "objectively" – which, therefore, must itself be similarly constructed in accord with (2).

Hence, also, (4) Holism: There is no principled priority or separability of metaphysical, epistemological, semantic, logical, or psychological (mental or subjective) analyses bearing on realist or legitimative questions; but that is benignly compatible with a constructivist (and "internal") account of relationships between subjects and objects.

But if that is so, then (5) Presuppositionlessness: Whether a bivalent or a relativistic logic (or any other logical provision) suits our realist claims best or adequately in this or that sector of the world depends on what we take to be the actual nature of the phenomena of that domain. If we assume elementary coherence and consistency, there can then be no a priori disqualification of relativism, incommensurabilism, historicism, or similar doctrines from any vantage that presupposes the falsity of (1).[3]

And finally, (6) Constructive realism: The argument that runs from (1) through (5) is not tantamount to idealism (the supposed "mind-dependence" of the "real" world) but only the denial that there is any valid a priori disjunction between the sense of "realism" and the sense of "idealism" that accords with the "Cartesian" tradition.

All this may strike you as only distantly related to the question of defending relativism or a specifically relativistic treatment of the interpretation of any part of the real world. But I assure you these distinctions count among the ineliminable first considerations on which the vindication or defeat of relativism finally depends. The trouble is – as my exemplars confirm – these linkages are regularly ignored. Furthermore, what I have offered here is no more than a small sample of such first considerations. It would take me too great a labor to defend all those I would wish to bring to the assessment and resolution of the questions drawn from Beardsley, Stecker, Krausz, Rescher, and Putnam. (I have addressed them elsewhere in greater detail.) But I can add any number of further theorems that are derivable from the six I have just introduced and that would strengthen our sense of the question-begging tactics of the views I've sampled – and so bring relativism closer to philosophical respectability.

I suggest, in short, that the best accounts of interpretive rigor are systematically suppressed or dismissed as a result of a certain deep prejudice (mostly innocent) about the nature of "reality" that is almost never explicitly defended, and that that enabling prejudice has been with us from ancient times. I find myself obliged, therefore, to retrace a bit of philosophical history in order to reintroduce a neglected option in a better light.

The complaint should not be a surprise. For if, say, you scan Aristotle's *Metaphysics* Gamma (without any doctrinal preference in hand), you will certainly find, there, a master strategy that might easily be thought to vindicate proceeding directly to answer questions like those posed by my specimen figures – implicitly subversive of the dialectical priority of my own first considerations. Aristotle, of course, was not a "pre-Kantian," but he did subscribe to First Philosophy and he did speak about what was necessarily true about reality as such. Furthermore, the pre-Kantians, even those contemporaries (*our* contemporaries) who straddle the pre-Kantian

---

[3] The baldest violation of theorem (5) that I am familiar with in the current literature – in fact, of the entire set – is afforded by Michael Devitt (1991).

and Kantian worlds and who have been partly inoculated by post-Kantian vaccines – Putnam (1980, 1994) and John McDowell (1996), for instance – look to Aristotle for a clear sense of how bivalence may be vouchsafed as the "logic" of realism. In this attenuated sense, Aristotle violates my first considerations.

Favoring (in the *Metaphysics*) what he takes to be the intractable constraints of a bivalent logic in realist contexts, Aristotle fortifies his claim by championing at least the following: (1) necessities *de re* and *de cogitatione* (reaching up to bivalence); (2) the ontic invariance of the structures of reality; and (3) the inseparability of the semantic and meta-physical standing of the principles of noncontradiction and excluded middle that are said to govern all forms of valid knowledge. (I concede here that in other texts, Aristotle takes a laxer view.) All three of these claims are incompatible with the theorems I have advanced; and, one way or another, my exemplars favor something akin to Aristotle's view of biva-lence. But, unlike Aristotle, they do so chiefly by ignoring or overriding the priority of those first considerations. (They could not otherwise proceed as they do.)

Aristotle does not arbitrarily reverse the order of the argument: he moves instead to legitimate it (by his own lights) by the seeming self-evidence of First Philosophy, which is to say, by subscribing to (1)–(3) without going beyond their apparent inviolability. The important points for my present purpose are that none of my exemplars can rightly avail himself (on his own doctrine) of Aristotle's strategy; that Aristotle's own strategy could never pass muster by current views of philosophical rigor; that First Philosophies fatally require the apodictic certainty of the invari-ance of the real; and, therefore, that the stalemate of the tactics of each of my exemplars (too briefly introduced, it's true) reassigns their particular claims to a provisional limbo that awaits the results of one or another set of first considerations not unlike those I've offered. There's a large gain for very little labor.

I should perhaps say more pointedly that my six theorems are meant to collect the strongest lessons of the entire early modern period of philoso-phy that runs from Descartes to Hegel – and that on the argument I have in mind, it is very likely that no convincing analysis of the conditions of description and interpretation, or of the nature of "independent" reality, could justifiably exempt itself from the constraints I've tallied. I argue in one step, therefore, that it cannot be shown that relativistic descriptions or interpretations of real entities must violate the ontic or epistemic constraints known to be necessary to any valid form of realism. You see here why the question of the logic of interpretation cannot possibly be a simple matter. To be perfectly honest, I cannot recall any sustained discus-sion of relativism (apart from the one I am in the process of advancing and have often defended) that either considers the recovery of post-Kantian themes or demonstrates its indefensibility despite acknowledging the force of those same themes. The only argument against relativism that I know depends entirely on its alleged incoherence, and that is clearly unconvincing (see Margolis 1991).

None of the considerations advanced, however, actually confirms the validity of any version of relativism. That's the beauty of proceeding as I have. All of my first considerations contribute nothing but reasons for leveling the contest between relativism and its better opponents – precisely by disqualifying (for cause) all would-be realisms of the "objectivist," "God's Eye," "neutral," "Cartesian" sorts – that cannot be defended anyway. What is extraordinary is how robust relativism will seem (both metaphysically and epistemologically) once these privileged views are effectively retired. Thus, if you say reality must have an unchanging structure, I ask you why you believe that its denial (the doctrine of the flux) is either incoherent or self-contradictory. If you say one cannot, rationally, violate the principle of noncontradiction, I say it is a purely formal schema that must be interpreted or supplied with some determinate semantic content to be applicable at all – and that it cannot then serve as a necessary rule or disqualify a relativistic treatment of interpretation. If you say excluded middle must be exceptionless in realist contexts, I remind you (at the very least) that, say, Michael Dummett's (1978) intuitionistic provision is not at all paradoxical or self-contradictory.[4] If you say that all realist discourse must conform with the principle of bivalence, I ask you how you know that there are, or could be, no entities in our world that can be shown to escape (or would need to be relieved of) that restriction. There is no ground mentioned by any of my exemplars on which the affirmation of my theorems, or my challenge to the doctrines drawn from Aristotle, can be shown to be unconditionally untenable – or necessarily false. That's all that's needed!

Once you see this, you see that there must be many similar findings that contribute to the eligibility, *not* (or not yet) to the actual confirmation, of relativism: for example, the fact that there is no known criterial or principled or algorithmic way to fix reference, denotation, numerical identity, reidentification, haecceity; or that, failing Platonism, there is no way to fix predicative similarity criterially or algorithmically; or that there is no way to fix the precise context in which referential, predicative, or (otherwise) assertoric claims may be correctly interpreted or tested; or that the precision and exactitude of every supposed cognizing competence will be ineluctably affected by the logical laxities just adduced; or indeed that we cannot claim to have any conceptual resources by which to ensure that all serious inquiries of a realist cast *must* converge toward any uniquely valid account of "what there is." The point is that concessions of even these very general sorts may be quite enough to vindicate relativism's viability. That comes as a surprise.

---

⁴ Contrast Wolterstorff (1980).

Here, for example, I agree with Hilary Putnam (1992a), who straight-forwardly affirms that "the metaphysical notion of 'all objects' [that is, the idea that *all* real objects are in principle denumerable] has no sense" (120). The admission is of considerable importance. For Putnam does not go on to consider that if, adding to his assertion, it is true that we cannot account for referential and reidentificatory success by nonconstructivist means, or, indeed, that there is no way to account for predicative success except (again) by consensual (constructivist) means, then we may find ourselves suddenly without any grounds at all for pressing any of a large number of standard objections against the pertinence, viability, even the preferability, of a relativistic account of description and interpretation – in (at least) certain sectors of inquiry. Or if we admit (contrary to Putnam's view) that relativism need not be formally paradoxical or self-contradictory, then we may find that there are remarkably few grounds left (if there are any at all) on which to oppose a policy of reasonable parity between relativistic and nonrelativistic interpretive practices. It is a little startling to discover just how much of a burden is lifted once reasonable first considerations are put into play.

III

Here, I must enter an important qualification. Up to this point, the argument favors a constructive realism – that is, assuming intransparency (in the sense given), all perceptual and experiential reports may be said to be implicitly (constitutively) *interpretive*. This is *not* to affirm or deny that we also interpret (in another sense of the word) whatever perceptual or related data we happen to concede as data: we do indeed interpret them (in that second, as yet unspecified sense). It's only that what we count as an uncontested or objective datum is already, merely as such, an indissoluble hybrid that (on an argument in accord with my first considerations) cannot but be insuperably dependent on our organizing and orienting concepts – assignable inferentially, of course, only retrospectively, constructively, conjecturally, and by comparing the effects of alternative conceptual schemes on perception and experience. In principle, the issue is not unlike that of comparing Priestley's and Lavoisier's alternative conceptions of the perceived world, though it is more global in its sweep.[5] Still, it is very much to the point to remark that an interpretive attribution of the (consti-

---

[5] I may say that Kuhn (1970, Section X) was quite explicit (and persuasive) about the importance of rejecting a disjunction between neutral data and the interpretation of those data, as in the quarrel about "swinging stones" (Aristotle) and "pendulums" (Galileo). If neutrality or neutral data cannot be vouchsafed – as by my theorem (1) – then it is difficult to avoid something close to Kuhn's incommensurabilism (despite Kuhn's own unhappiness about that outcome); but to admit that is to be well on the way to vindicating a strong form of relativism.

tuting) kind plays its own important role in interpretive disputes involving another (the second, as yet unspecified) kind of interpretation – as indeed the Priestley/Lavoisier dispute and the Aristotle/Galileo dispute compellingly confirm. Otherwise, the first sort of "interpretation" would hardly count for much.

What I am suggesting is that what we *describe* as perceptual data are already, under the post-Kantian picture I am invoking, *interpretively* formed. We do not, therefore, interpret them in the sense of forming a first judgment about their obtaining: for if, in any context, they are our ground-level data, they cannot be viewed as "interpretations" of something else, in the sense in which, as we say, we interpret what we have already posited in descriptive terms. To say nevertheless that those data *are* "interpretations" is to theorize (in second-order terms) that they are "constituted" (in a certain way) *as* the objective data that they are (descriptively). We do, furthermore, interpret what, antecedently, we *have posited as* such original data – for instance, with the drift of history. That is precisely what Kuhn and Feyerabend had hit upon, and what discussants like Michel Foucault (1970) and Hans-Georg Gadamer (1975) have featured in their own particular forms of historicism.

Thus, *if* (and *since*) Kantian transcendentalism fails and violates at least item (1) of my original tally – though it may be reasonably replaced by an analogous symbiosis (eschewing a priorism) expressed in terms of diverse, historically contingent forms of conceptual enculturation – perceptual belief may be fairly characterized *as* "interpretive," though in an admittedly unfamiliar sense. It is unfamiliar, I suggest, because most discussants are effectively wedded to one or another form of Cartesian realism: witness my exemplars! The sense of interpretation that I recommend could not be viewed *relationally* in any primary epistemic regard – see theorem (1) – and would certainly signify more than the innocent sense conceded in theorem (2). In fact, the "interpretive" aspects of original perception and experience could only be unearthed inter- and intra-societally, and over historical time, by comparing the inferred effect of divergent conceptual schemes on different reportorial and explanatory practices. This is what is missed in Putnam and McDowell.

It's clear enough, of course, that Kuhn's and Feyerabend's evidentiary incommensurabilism, as well as Hans-Georg Gadamer's implicitly hermeneutic relativism,[6] depends essentially on what I may now call interpretation in the "constituting" sense. I mean the sense in which we concede that the characterization of what, in every society (or subsociety), is treated as objective in the way of reported data is (on a theory) also viewed, *without disturbing the other*, as "interpretively" formed by the enculturing processes of that particular society – and hence the sense in

---

    [6] Gadamer's position (1975) is very much influenced by Heidegger's notion (1996, Division Two) of the historicized, culturally preformed conditions of understanding.

which it is impossible to claim to have arrived at an assuredly *neutral* account of such data, free of any "construction," which we may *then* interpret for this or that purpose.

This is Kuhn's and Feyerabend's explicit view, of course. I frankly cannot see how this kind of claim can be disqualified as being not as reasonable a conjecture as any that might oppose it – assuming, always, that it need not succumb to the insurmountable paradoxes usually attributed to it. But if that is conceded, then a distinctly relativistic treatment of cognitive and "evidentiating" processes will have been admitted as a definite option. That possibility, you must appreciate, would not have been possible except for one or another of my first considerations.

The standard objection against this option – which is irrelevant to the case before us and preposterous in its own right – holds that any such thesis must (of necessity) exhibit the same self-defeating weakness attributed to Protagoras's doctrine in Plato's *Theaetetus*: namely, that "true" means "true-for-x" – that is, that "true" defines truth relationally with regard to some would-be agent x – which, to be sure, does yield a self-defeating paradox.[7] The point is, the definition of truth in the case before us need not be relational in the self-defeating sense, even though it *is* true (if it is true) that our cognitive and conceptual powers are contingently formed under the enculturing processes of one or another society. There is indeed a conceptual *relationship* between what is evidentiarily pertinent to our truth-claims and the cultural conditions under which our "data" are (interpretively) constituted in the way they are, but that has nothing, as such, to do with any *relational definition* of "true." The objection now looks like a complete non sequitur or a bad joke. (If it is a bad joke, though, it is a very old one!)

Nevertheless, it cannot be denied that it represents a very widespread and peculiarly stubborn conviction. More to the point, theorists like Putnam (1992b) and Richard Rorty (1991) are quite willing to admit the "cultural relativity" of our concepts, though they both fail to see that (and why) their own concessions (difficult to refuse, of course) lead directly – by way of first considerations – to a viable form of "cultural relativism." I believe they cannot escape.

But I am getting ahead of my story. To pick up the main thread again, we must distinguish between two senses of "interpretation": one, the "constituting" sense just sketched, and the other, what may be called the "ampliative" sense, the (second) sense (hinted at before) in which any admitted data and phenomena and objects posited in the first sense (if that sense be allowed) may then be subject (for particular purposes) to an explication of their meaning or significative or semiotic structure, or their evidentiary bearing in a would-be explanatory theory, or something of the

---

[7] The standard view has been updated by Myles Burnyeat (1976) and is, in effect, seconded by Putnam (1992a, 1992c).

sort. The ampliative sense is usually thought to be open to objective stand-ing: that is, to take truth-values in much the same sense as are judgments in other inquiries that are not thought to be interpretive in this regard. Part of what the contrast signifies, then, is the nonparadoxicality of speaking of judgments as both descriptive and interpretive. Notice, of course, that what are posited (descriptively) as initial "data" may well change under chang-ing theories of the interpretive "constitution" of perception and experience. That is certainly the import of the alleged "paradigm shift" regarding the pendulum that Kuhn makes so much of. I see no difficulty there; in fact, it may even enhance the prospects of certain forms of relativism.

More to the point, there are at least two very large collections of cases in which one or another form of relativism – or, better, of relativistic inter-pretation – may be offered as a viable theory of judgment, ranging over one or another kind of inquiry. One collection concerns certain cultural diversities having epistemic import; the other, metaphysical distinctions regarding certain kinds of entities and their assignable natures. I believe these two sorts of cases collect the important varieties of interpretation that have been most disputed. If so, then we have gained a nice economy.

Broadly speaking, relativisms of the incommensurabilist and historicist sorts (Kuhn's and Feyerabend's and, say, Foucault's) tend to favor an analysis of what I'm calling interpretation in the constituting sense, whereas relativisms attributed to art-critical, literary, legal, moral, histori-cal, and similar judgments tend to favor the metaphysical peculiarities of cultural entities and cultural phenomena (artworks, documents, and histo-ries, for instance) and regularly arise in what I am calling interpretation in the ampliative sense. But I would certainly not deny – in fact I would insist – that relativisms of the second sort often involve epistemic complications bearing on interpretations of the constituting sort. I find such an admission required, for instance, in explicating Foucault's account of *Las Meninas* (1970). Also, attributions of the first sort may well – often – implicate interpretations of the second sort, as Kuhn's and Feyerabend's claims make clear.

IV

I have, in the process of laying out my interpretive scheme, attached a somewhat fuller sense of relativisms of the epistemic sort (incommensu-rabilism, say, or historicism) that depend on forms of cultural relativity collecting divergent perceptions and beliefs and the like that are capable of affording a first-order ground for relativisms of a specifically eviden-tiary and methodological cast. But I have yet to provide a comparable picture of interpretations of the second kind – ampliative interpretations that would be able to support one or another form of relativism. Let me turn to sketching some of the important factors that bear on the defense of relativistic interpretations of the second kind.

Ampliative interpretation is, of course, more widely discussed than the other. But it is the other, I suggest, that has occasioned the greatest opposition to so-called "interpretive *tertia*" – intervening conceptual schemes that theorists like Donald Davidson (1986) and Richard Rorty (1986) have, as "naturalists" (I should say "Cartesians"), inveighed against; for the (new) naturalists are unconditionally opposed to *epistemic intermediaries of any sort* between cognizer and cognized. On the argument I have already offered, all that is needed to offset this objection is that such intermediaries (which the post-Kantian conception requires) *not* be construed relationally in the sense disallowed by theorem (1). I should add as well that the ubiquity of ampliative interpretation – and its complications along relativistic lines – is undeniably due to the unavoidability of interpretive *tertia* in the sense here intended.

Part of what we need is not specifically keyed to vindicating relativism directly, though it will be hospitable to relativism's better fortunes. I have, for instance, drawn attention to the fact that, in both referential and predicative matters, there is no prospect of finding an algorithm that could be counted on to secure or legitimate success of either sort. Haecceity is not a discernible property of any kind, and Platonism is either a conceptual delusion or utterly inaccessible in any human way. Furthermore, all matters of context and relevance bearing on truth are inherently informal (logically), so that we cannot be forced to a bivalent rule on the strength of the rigors of linguistic behavior alone.

Relativism seems to fit our linguistic and evidentiary practices as well as any opposed conceptual policy. Identification and reidentification, fixity of meanings, tolerance regarding generalizations of every kind, the perception of rational connections in abductive and inductive conjecture, cannot be called on to disallow any relativistic treatment of truth-values that is otherwise admitted to be, on independent grounds, coherent and self-consistent.

But these are of course matters that bear on the presumptive "metaphysics" of natural-language discourse. Hence, if relativism is to be defeated, we shall require an argument much more strenuous than those that are usually trotted out. Certainly, nothing drawn from Plato's *Theaetetus* or Aristotle's *Metaphysics* Gamma – or, indeed, from Putnam or Rorty – will be sufficient.

I am prepared to argue – though I shall not do so here – that if, in fact, the following conditions obtain, then it is probably impossible not to concede a general parity between relativism and the usual bivalent conceptions of objective judgment ranging over description, interpretation, and explanation:

1. conditions akin to my six theorems, which catch up the work of the post-Kantian tradition
2. the deep logical informality of the resources of natural-language

discourse regarding reference, predication, context, meaning, relevance, rational hypothesis, and nondeductive inference, more or less
along the lines already sketched, which (if pressed) I should characterize as Wittgensteinian in spirit (though Wittgenstein would certainly
not favor my application of *"Lebensform"* and "language-games"
[1953])
3. widespread (first-order) cultural relativity affecting perception, belief,
modes of reasoning, theories, values, conceptual schemes of at least a
partially overlapping sort – contra Davidson (1984) and in sympathy,
for instance, with Hacking (1982) – as both Putnam and Rorty conge-
nially affirm
4. the formal coherence of a relativistic "logic" by which claims and judgments that on a bivalent logic would be or would yield incompatibles
can be shown to be (formally) consistent by suitably replacing or
supplementing bivalence, in context, with a many-valued logic, which
I shall briefly spell out below.

Put in the most compendious way, I argue that once something like
(my) theorem (1) is conceded, relativism cannot fail to be philosophically
eligible, viable, even advantageous in at least some important sectors of
inquiry – and that this is particularly true in interpretive matters. You see
this already in my suggestions regarding the recovery of incommensurabilism in the natural sciences, which (I remind you) brings what I have
called interpretation in the constituting sense to bear on ampliative interpretations of an explanatory sort. The point, there, is not to insist that
(say) the Priestley/Lavoisier quarrel must be interminable, but rather that
where such disputes are resolved, they are resolved in a constructivist way
that does not (and could not) demonstrate that bivalence or a methodology favoring bivalence must have exclusive sway. There's no known
reason why all such incommensurabilities must be resolvable disjunc-
tively. For all we know, the difficulty of interpreting the quantum world
may lead to an insuperable (but entirely benign) incommensurabilism. In
any case, the resolution of pertinent incommensurabilities of these
explanatory sorts may be managed on grounds that are not primarily
evidentiary – or bivalent – and may (as far as we can see) involve questions of conceptual taste that need not lead to anything like a knockdown
disconfirmation. What relativism opposes is the modal presumption: it is
content to find its best bed wherever that may lie.

But we are searching among the standard ampliative cases for "metaphysical" distinctions that might support a relativistic theory of interpretation. Here, the most likely feature to fasten on is the very one that,
paradigmatically, renders certain kinds of *denotata intrinsically interpretable*, namely, their inherently possessing (as the kinds of things they
are) any of a family of properties that I shall call *Intentional* (see Margolis
1995a). This family includes linguistic, "lingual," semantic, gestural,

semiotic, significative, symbolic, meaningful, representational, expressive, rhetorical, institutional, rulelike, intentional, purposive, historical, traditional, stylistic, genre-bound, and other similar properties. I should perhaps explain that I call certain actions or activities "lingual" if their Intentional properties presuppose linguistic competence but do not involve actual speech or the actual use of language – for example, making love, preparing a meal, dancing, and creating a sculpture. And I equate the "Intentional" and the "cultural," so that interpretation (in the ampliative sense) is primarily, or paradigmatically, addressed to cultural entities and phenomena.

By that I do not mean that physical nature cannot be interpreted. If I believed that, I should not have been able to offer the Priestley/Lavoisier controversy as an instance in which interpretation in the constituting sense affects the fortunes of ampliative explanation in the natural sciences. But you surely see that the normal way in which interpretation plays a role in the physical sciences is in explanatory contexts where perceptual data are ampliatively *interpreted* (and often redescribed, in the constituting sense) as evidence for confirming and disconfirming some explanatory theory about why the data are as they are said to be. That is in fact what the Priestley/Lavoisier example confirms. The phenomena of nature are *not* "intrinsically" interpretable, as are the artifacts of the cultural world; but insofar as they are subsumed under this or that explanatory theory – or insofar as they are described in accord with a vocabulary favorable to one such theory or another – they may be viewed as interpretable, by way of an obvious "courtesy."

This is not to oppose Kuhn's rejection of epistemological neutrality with regard to perceptual data, for Kuhn's thesis concerns what I am calling interpretation in the constituting sense – and is directed, there, against what I have called Cartesian realism. But there could not be a quarrel of the sort Priestley and Lavoisier shared unless there were, in some effective way (however attenuated), agreement about a run of data that (on the occasion) are *not* in dispute. Those data are, of course, still subject to Kuhn's constraint and may well enter into further disputes of the kind Priestley and Lavoisier's instantiates (Galison 1997, Chap. 1). (Notice, please, that this admission does not disallow Kuhn's or Feyerabend's sorts of incommensurabilism, as Davidson seems to suppose.) As far as I can see, there are no other large categories of interpretive activity comparable in importance to these two, that is, concerned primarily with truth-claims (Margolis 1995b).

About "cultural entities," I shall say little beyond what I need in order to make my case: perhaps no more than that they intrinsically possess Intentional properties and that those properties are indissolubly "incarnate" in physical or material properties. One instance is the way in which the representational property of the pietà relating Mary and Jesus is incarnate in the physical properties of the marble Michelangelo worked into a sculpture (the *Pietà*), which is *not* (as such) a property of the physical marble itself. It is a property only of the cultural artifact, the sculpture. By parity of reasoning, I say that the sculpture is indissolubly "embodied" in the block of marble Michelangelo worked, but cannot be reduced to the physical block since the one possesses, and the other lacks, Intentional properties. The sculpture "emerges" (sui generis, in the way cultural entities come to exist) through the work of a pertinent activity, exists as such, and can be discerned as such only by the cognizant members of an apt society (of selves) who are themselves suitably encultured to be able to make and appreciate such things. In this way, I avoid all awkward dualisms, provide an ontology fitted to intrinsically interpretable things, but do not foreclose on my options regarding the logic of interpretation.

It is easy to see that to admit entities and properties of these sorts is to admit an entire run of phenomena that are largely ignored in canonical metaphysics and that do not occur in the natural world except in human cultures. There, we pertinently find (among such entities) either ourselves (or the members of similar societies) or what we (or they) have "uttered," that is, produced, made, created, or brought about by linguistic or lingual means – artifacts or artifactual phenomena nominalized as *denotata* (for example, the performance of a Mozart sonata) that intrinsically invite and support some form of ampliative interpretation. My point, here, is that all the "artifacts" of the cultural world may, in principle, be viewed predicatively, as the "utterances" of apt agents (human selves), or entitatively, as nominalized *denotata* apt for interpretation. We interpret ourselves by interpreting our utterances: deeds, actions, creations, makings, work, speech, histories, even dreams; or we interpret all of these directly, where they can be stably nominalized and are worth viewing thus. Here, differences between events and things count as no more than a subordinate consideration (Wolterstorff 1980).

I freely admit that there are all sorts of puzzles that would need to be resolved if one were to offer this small fragment of a theory in a suitably developed form: for instance, regarding what the sense is in which we ourselves (selves or persons) are also "cultural" artifacts of some kind (not mere members of *Homo sapiens*). I am prepared to answer (Margolis 1995a), but we do not need the details here. I am offering little more than a rationale for a very large argument.

I trust you see that we have circled back to Beardsley's theorems. It should be clear that Beardsley's insistence on bivalence is directly due to the fact that he believes there is *no significant metaphysical difference* between (say) literary texts and physical objects! I admit straight off that *if* objective discourse about physical nature did not require (or would not benefit from admitting) a role for relativism (or relativistic interpretation), and *if* literary texts (or other artworks or histories and the like) were "entities" similar in all essentials to physical entities, then, finally, there would be no need to invoke relativism. But the idea that there *are* entities that *possess* (among their attributes) meanings or Intentional natures (which Beardsley's own theory requires) – which we can discern objectively – cannot possibly fail to pose methodological and epistemological disputes that are sui generis and must be met. The telling weakness in Beardsley's account is simply that he dismisses the obvious problem. Nor does Stecker, Krausz, Rescher, or Putnam consider the possible metaphysical complication of cultural entities. I have already made clear that a cognate difficulty is certain to arise in the effort to explain physical phenomena (which lack Intentional properties) when such phenomena are examined (causally) under epistemic terms that yield in the direction of items (1)–(4), listed just above.

Anyone who has tried to make sense of a reasonably complex or puzzling painting (say, Picasso's *Guernica*) or an equally complex and puzzling story (say, Kafka's *The Trial*) is perfectly aware that such "entities" possess (what I am calling) Intentional properties, but that it is not at all apparent what an objective analysis (or ampliative interpretation) of them would or must yield. The problem is not entirely different from that of the Priestley/Lavoisier dispute but is much more diffuse and lacks the realist constraints of the other. In the combustion case, we are able to call on predictive and technological considerations associated with causal processes and successful invention (think of testing the atomic bomb for the first time). In the Intentional cases, we have only the supposed regularities and legibilities of the very structures we are interpreting to rely on. We cannot escape the deeper circularity of our ampliative practice.

Given constraints (1)–(4) plus the metaphysical complications I am beginning to address, it is hard to see *why* anyone would deny that it may in principle be true that no uniquely valid interpretation is possible, but that the work or *denotatum* in question may be objectively interpreted nonetheless. Why not? For the life of me, I cannot find a single compelling argument against it – or against the idea that among the valid interpretations we might produce there may be some that, on a bivalent logic but not on a relativistic logic, would be or would yield incompatible findings ("incongruent" interpretations, as I prefer to term them). That is, I cannot find a single compelling argument against the practice, *if* the practice has (as it obviously does) serious public and professional support and if relativism is not formally incoherent or self-contradictory. I see no grounds for ruling the possibility out, and I note that much of our practice would make bright sense on its adoption.

Now then, I do claim that entities that have Intentional "natures" are not at all like physical exemplars. They *do* support an ampliative practice very different from the perceptual description of ordinary physical objects (for example, "The cat is on the mat" or "The sky is blue"), except where physical "descriptions" are clearly interpretively assigned in accord with larger quarrels   between   opposed   explanatory   theories   (as   in   the

Priestley/Lavoisier case). But that only enlarges the scope of possible application.

V

I draw your attention finally to a decisive distinction – I regard it as a metaphysical difference – between the specification of physical properties and of Intentional properties, which, once confirmed, provides a ground for even deeper differences between the two sorts of property. Consider only that if we are describing an ordinary perceptible physical property – color or shape, say – it is normally the case that the description can be made more determinate by way of adding further (relevant) intensional specifications. For example, "red" may be made more specific by being qualified as "scarlet" or "rose" – or, even further, as "a scarlet like that of . . . rather than of . . ." or a "faded rose" or something of the sort. *But that kind of specification normally does not obtain among Intentional properties.*

Physical description tends to permit itself to form linear arrays of increasingly determinate intensions. This encourages the idea that intension varies inversely with extension and (I believe) lends plausibility to our favoring the adoption of an invariant rule of bivalence in the objective description of "reality." (But see Putnam 1975.) The idea is that a property *is* in some important sense determinate; hence, increasingly determinate specifications of an intensional kind may be taken to be matched by increasingly extensional restrictions of it. Also, of course, predicates or predicables are inherently general, in the sense of "divided reference" – in the sense that if they are validly predicated of anything, they may be predicated of indefinitely many different things. Predicates or predicables, therefore, are both relatively *determinate*, without ever being completely *determined* (without ever becoming incapable in principle of being made more determinate), and, also, *determinable*, in the sense of being able to be made more determinate (see Peirce 1931–1935, 5–448 and n. 7). This does not hold among Intentional properties.

Intentional properties are not always viewed as "descriptive," perhaps because of the common prejudice that, among physical things, descriptions obey the bivalent rule in the manner already stated and in accord with the determinate/determinable notion just sketched, whereas the assignment of Intentional properties is not likely to behave in that way. It is partly for this reason that we think of the specification of a "meaning" or significative structure as interpretive rather than descriptive, though very little hangs on that distinction (assuming "constructive realism" in the sense earlier affirmed).

More important is the idea that if we are characterizing the Intentional properties of something, those properties will not form an array conformable with the determinable/determinate pattern that holds among physical properties. No seemingly more determinate intension of a given *Intentional* predicate can be counted on to yield a further extensional determination *of the property designated.* (I am not, of course, affirming that among non-Intentional predicates, intension and extension vary in any fixed way.)

Interpretation, we say, must be *juste, not* more or less correct by linear approximation. Every Intentional characterization is rather like a holist punctum: it applies validly (if it is valid at all), *not* in any graded way, but aptly, all at once, singularly, in the sense of a good fit one on one. If we do add to a given characterization, we must take care to explain the sense in which we are indeed holding fast to *the same* determinable (not any physically determinate) Intentional property. For, indeed, large differences in interpretive attribution are likely to be thought to signify a change in interpreted *denotatum* (again, on the model of physical exemplars). The truth is, however, that such predicative swings are not at all unusual when the properties in question (Intentional properties) are *determinable but not determinate* (in the sense of "determinate" that is thought to obtain among physical properties).

That would explain why the spread of ampliative interpretations among Intentional *denotata* – however startling (think of the possibilities of something like the interpretation of Kafka's *The Hunger Artist*) – is quite possible without (1) entailing interpretive changes of a constituting kind that (as in Feyerabend's cases) involve a change in *explanandum* (or, possibly, a change, by redescription, in evidentiary properties) and (2) without subverting a fair (constructivist) sense of interpretive objectivity. Krausz and Stecker, for instance, incline toward the suspicion of a change in *denotatum* under a relativistic practice. But that is entirely gratuitous. There may be any number of "incongruent" interpretations of a suitably rich artwork or history that are all apt (in the punctuated holist sense suggested) and that are, accordingly, incapable of being ordered, logically, in the way of linearly arrayed intensions. If so, it would be more than difficult to reconcile the practice with an exceptionless bivalence.

There's a decisive difference there. Physical properties appear to be determinate in the sense of being increasingly determinable in a linear way as far as their determinateness is concerned. Intentional properties, on the other hand, are not determinate in that way at all; they are *determinable* only in being open to being interpretively *determined* – where what counts as an objective determination depends primarily on the consensual rigor of a particular society's ampliative practice. (Think of New Testament interpretations.) Too great a laxity will subvert the sense of interpretive rigor altogether; too great an insistence on fixed meanings will risk the sense of any pertinent public method. Bivalence is not likely to mark a sensible choice across that divide. But if not, then, plainly, the interpretation of Intentional artifacts is likely to favor some form of relativism.

Meanings and significative structures cannot be more precisely fixed than are denotation and predicative generality. But for compelling reasons already briefly mentioned, both must be inherently informal. In hermeneutic (romantic) accounts, literary meanings are said to be governed by authorial intent – or, better, to accord with the fixed genres of literary production with which authorial intent must itself conform. But it is reasonably clear that genres cannot possibly be inviolably fixed, because they must change to accommodate the evolving exemplars of a living literature (see Hirsch 1967; Margolis 1992). This would allow, of course, for a constructive and historicized account of interpretive objectivity, but it could never, then, convincingly preclude a relativistic account.

Finally, if cultures are inherently historical, in the sense in which the Intentional import of societal life changes with changes in its collective experience – changes that must continually affect, even alter, the interpretation of its own past, its Intentional (not its physical) past[8] – then whatever may count as objective in the way of interpreting, ampliatively, the *determinable* structure of its own artifacts will, in principle, have to accommodate that same historical drift. And then, once again, relativism will be found to fit our practice better than bivalence.

You must realize that once one subscribes to theorem (1) and makes concessions in the direction of any of the other conditions I've collected, objectivity (of any kind) will have to be construed in constructivist terms. It will, then, have to be construed interpretively and in a way that will not be able to preclude relativism. (That is, constructivism or constructive realism is not, or need not be, a form of idealism – in the sense the Cartesians rightly reject.) Once one abandons the "Cartesian" account of realism, *what* will count as objectivity cannot fail to be an artifact of what we view as our cognitive competence. The "metaphysical" oddities of Intentional *denotata* are not introduced ad hoc for the sake of relativistic prejudice; nor, indeed, are the informalities of reference and predication. But when we bring these two matters together, under constructivist terms, we find ourselves forced to concede the reasonableness of the relativist's outlook. If that's not so, then please explain how relativism can be convincingly disqualified (if it is not formally paradoxical or self-contradictory).

I have tried to show how the epistemological informalities of evidentiary "redescription" in the physical sciences entail the rejection of (Cartesian) "neutrality" (à la Kuhn) and how, as a result, they lead to the inexorable challenge of incommensurabilist versions of relativism. Opponents of incommensurabilism, Davidson (1984) and Putnam (1992c) in particular, go to great lengths to ensure the incoherence of incommensurabilism itself, because they cannot possibly gain their point by working through the actual

---

[8] This goes contrary to Danto (1985).

epistemological puzzles. For, as we've now seen, the complications that arise in the sciences as a result of fruitful first-order semantic incommensurabilities directly affect the (ampliative) *interpretation of physical nature itself*, that is, affect its characterization in a way in which there can be no principled disjunction between description and interpretation.

Now it turns out, quite apart from *epistemological* possibilities (the ones Kuhn and Feyerabend have exploited), that there are distinct *metaphysical* oddities as well, among the things of the cultural world, which appear to be particularly congenial to relativistic treatment. To admit them is to oblige ourselves to ask whether and how they could possibly support an objective (ampliative) practice that did not yield strongly in a relativistic direction. I argue that if you admit (1) the ubiquity of (first-order) cultural relativity affecting both Intentional and non-Intentional distinctions, (2) the inherent informality of fixing meanings, (3) the sense in which we are (in interpreting Intentional things) trying to understand ourselves and our "utterances," (4) the different senses in which the determinable/determinate distinction applies to the Intentional and the non-Intentional, and (5) the effect of the historical drift of our best hermeneutic efforts on attempting to fix the Intentional determinately, then, assuming objectivity must take a constructivist form, it is hard to see how one could escape some robust form of relativism.

Beardsley, I remind you, insisted on treating a critic's efforts to specify the meaning of a poem as descriptive of that poem's properties in a sense essentially indistinguishable from that of the description of physical properties. But given the indefensibility of (Cartesian) "neutrality" and the ubiquitous function of the "constituting" sense of interpretation under constructivism, there can be no principled disjunction between description and interpretation. More than that, to admit the consensual sense in which "meanings" are objectively determined, as well as the hermeneutic effect of the historical drift of collective experience, is to admit that "meanings" cannot be "located" (by way of intentions) "in" an author's mind or (by way of analogy with physical properties) "in" a poem.

Intentional properties are determinately *imputed* to this or that particular *denotatum*: the rigor with which that may be done reflects what we mean by the objectivity of so doing. There is no undue laxity there. But there is no way to "examine" the words of a poem apart, in the way in which a physical object can be "inspected." (That is essential to the notion of cultural "utterance": for, ultimately, we examine ourselves in cultural space, or what we examine in physical nature we cannot examine without examining ourselves.) Words "mean" whatever they can be "objectively" judged to mean – *by* consulting (in the consensual sense I have borrowed from Wittgenstein) whatever can be rightly *imputed to them*, within the general terms of our linguistic fluency.

We rely on our cultural fluency – which, under the pressure of history, may yield (consensually, not criterially) changing attributions even to the same *denotatum* (think of *Hamlet*). We *cannot* rely on fixing the Intentional properties of, say, a particular poem in fixing the denotation of that poem. That, also, is an ontological peculiarity of Intentional entities. The very idea that an interpretation functions as (what I've called) a "holist punctum" (*un mot juste*) is itself a miniature application of the idea that imputations of meaning to particular *denotata* presuppose the benign holism of cultural life itself. (That, of course, is what is meant by the "hermeneutic circle.")

It remains to be said that a relativistic and a bivalent "logic" can be compatibly applied in interpretive contexts, provided only that we abide (in whatever ad hoc manner we choose) by suitable relevance constraints that preclude assigning mixed truth-values to the same claims. It is easy to see that *descriptive* and *interpretive* judgments may be conveniently sorted in this way. But nothing need be lost: whatever is judged "descriptive" could easily be viewed as interpretive in another setting.

In short, as far as I can see, there are no resources a bivalent model of interpretation could claim as its own that are precluded in a relativistic account, but the reverse is certainly not true.

References

Barnes, Annette. (1988). *On Interpretation*. Oxford: Basil Blackwell.

Beardsley, Monroe C. (1970). *The Possibility of Criticism*. Detroit, MI: Wayne State University Press.

Bernstein, Richard J. (1983). *Beyond Objectivism and Relativism: Science, Hermeneutics, and Praxis*. Philadelphia: University of Pennsylvania Press.

Burnyeat, Myles. (1976). "Protagoras and Self-Refutation in Plato's *Theaetetus.*" *Philosophical Review*, 85.

Danto, Arthur C. (1985). *Narration and Knowledge*. New York: Columbia University Press.

Davidson, Donald. (1984). "On the Very Idea of a Conceptual Scheme." In *Inquiries into Truth and Interpretation*. Oxford: Clarendon.

——. (1986). "A Coherence Theory of Truth and Knowledge." In *Truth and Interpretation: Perspectives on the Philosophy of Donald Davidson*, edited by Ernest Lepore. Oxford: Basil Blackwell.

Devitt, Michael. (1991). *Realism and Truth*. 2nd ed. Princeton, NJ: Princeton University Press.

Dummett, Michael. (1978). *Truth and Other Enigmas*. Cambridge: Harvard University Press.

Feyerabend, Paul. (1962). "Explanation, Reduction, and Empiricism." In *Scientific Explanation, Space and Time*, edited by Herbert Feigl and Grover Maxwell. Minnesota Studies in the Philosophy of Science, vol. 3. Minneapolis: University of Minnesota Press.

Foucault, Michel. (1970). *The Order of Things: An Archaeology of the Human Sciences*. New York: Vintage.

Gadamer, Hans-Georg. (1975). *Truth and Method*. Trans. Garrett Barden and John Cumming. New York: Seabury Press.

Galison, Peter. (1997). *Image and Logic: A Material Culture of Microphysics*. Chicago: University of Chicago Press.

Hacking, Ian. (1982). "Language, Truth and Reason." In *Rationality and Relativism*, edited by Martin Hollis and Steven Lukes. Cambridge: MIT Press.

Heidegger, Martin. (1996). *Being and Time*. Trans. Joan Stambaugh. Albany: State University of New York Press.

Hirsch, E. D., Jr. (1967). *Validity in Interpretation*. New Haven, CT: Yale University Press.

Krausz, Michael. (1993). *Rightness and Reasons: Interpretation in Cultural Practices*. Ithaca, NY: Cornell University Press.

Kuhn, Thomas S. (1970). *The Structure of Scientific Revolutions*. 2nd ed. Chicago: University of Chicago Press.

Margolis, Joseph. (1991). *The Truth about Relativism*. Oxford: Basil Blackwell.

———. (1992). "Genres, Laws, Canons, Principles." In *Rules and Conventions: Literature, Philosophy, Social Theory*, edited by Mette Hjort. Baltimore: Johns Hopkins University Press.

———. (1995a). *Historied Thought, Constructed World: A Conceptual Primer for the Turn of the Millennium*. Los Angeles: University of California Press.

———. (1995b). *Interpretation Radical but Not Unruly: The New Puzzle of the Arts and History*. Los Angeles: University of California Press.

McCormick, Peter. (1999). "Interpretation and Objectivity." In *Interpretation, Relativism, and the Metaphysics of Culture: Themes in the Philosophy of Joseph Margolis*, edited by Michael Krausz and Richard Shusterman. Amherst, MA: Humanity Press.

McDowell, John. (1996). *Mind and World*. Cambridge: Harvard University Press.

Peirce, Charles Sanders. (1931–1935). *Collected Papers of Charles Sanders Peirce*. 6 vols. Ed. Charles Hartshorne and Paul Weiss. Cambridge: Harvard University Press.

Putnam, Hilary. (1975). "The Meaning of 'meaning.' " In *Philosophical Papers*, vol. 2. Cambridge: Cambridge University Press.

———. (1980). *Reason, Truth and History*. Cambridge: Cambridge University Press.

———. (1992a). "Irrealism and Deconstruction." In *Renewing Philosophy*. Cambridge: Harvard University Press.

———. (1992b). "A Theory of Reference." In *Renewing Philosophy*. Cambridge: Harvard University Press.

Putnam, Hilary. (1992c). "Wittgenstein on Reference and Relativism." In *Renewing Philosophy*. Cambridge: Harvard University Press.

——. (1994). "Sense, Nonsense, and the Senses: An Inquiry into the Powers of the Human Mind" (The Dewey Lectures 1994). *Journal of Philosophy*, 91.

Rescher, Nicholas. (1999). "The Limits of Cognitive Relativism." In *Interpretation, Relativism, and the Metaphysics of Culture: Themes in the Philosophy of Joseph Margolis*, edited by Michael Krausz and Richard Shusterman. Amherst, MA: Humanity Press.

Rorty, Richard. (1986). "Pragmatism, Davidson and Truth." In *Truth and Interpretation: Perspectives on the Philosophy of Donald Davidson*, edited by Ernest Lepore. Oxford: Basil Blackwell.

——. (1991). "Solidarity or Objectivity." In *Philosophical Papers*, vol. 1. Cambridge: Cambridge University Press.

Stecker, Robert. (1997). *Artworks: Definition, Meaning, Value*. University Park: Pennsylvania State University Press.

Wittgenstein, Ludwig. (1953). *Philosophical Investigations*. Trans. G. E. M. Anscombe. Oxford: Basil Blackwell.

Wolterstorff, Nicholas. (1980). *Worlds and Works of Art*. Oxford: Clarendon.

Notes on Contributors

F. R. Ankersmit is professor for intellectual history and historical theory at the University of Groningen. His publications include *Narrative Logic: A Semantic Analysis of the Historian's Language; History and Tropology: The Rise and Fall of Metaphor*; and *Aesthetic Politics: Political Philosophy beyond Fact and Value*. He edited, together with H. Kellner, *The New Philosophy of History* and has published many books and essays in Dutch.

Noël Carroll is the Monroe C. Beardsley Professor of Philosophy at the University of Wisconsin-Madison. His most recent publication is *A Philosophy of Mass Art*.

Jorge J. E. Gracia is Samuel P. Capen Chair and SUNY Distinguished Professor in the Department of Philosophy of the State University of New York at Buffalo. He is author of ten books, including *A Theory of Textuality: The Logic and Epistemology; Texts: Ontological Status, Identity, Author, Audience; Philosophy and Its History: Issues in Philosophical Historiography*; and *Individuality: An Essay on the Foundations of Metaphysics*. He has edited books on metaphysics, medieval philosophy, and Hispanic philosophy and is currently working on a book titled *Can We Know What God Means?: The Interpretation of Revelation*.

Michael Krausz is the Milton C. Nahm Professor and Chair of the Department of Philosophy at Bryn Mawr College. The author of *Rightness and Reasons: Interpretation in Cultural Practices* and the co-author of *Varieties of Relativism*, he is currently completing *Limits of Rightness*. In addition, he is contributing editor to nine volumes on such topics as relativism, rationality, interpretation, cultural identity, metaphysics of culture, creativity, interpretation of music, and the philosophy of R. G. Collingwood.

Peter Lamarque is Ferens Professor of Philosophy at the University of Hull. He is co-author, with Stein Haugom Olsen, of *Truth, Fiction, and Literature: A Philosophical Perspective*; author of *Fictional Points of View*; and editor of *Philosophy and Fiction: Essays in Literary Aesthetics*. He edits *The British Journal of Aesthetics*.

Joseph Margolis is Laura H. Carnell Professor of Philosophy at Temple University. His most recent books include *Interpretation Radical but Not Unruly*; *Historied Thought, Constructed World*; and *What, After All, Is a Work of Art?* He is completing a book on art and culture and a book on American philosophy.

David Novitz is Reader in Philosophy at the University of Canterbury, New Zealand. He is author of several books and many articles in the philosophy of art.

Stein Haugom Olsen is Chair and Professor of Humanities and Director of the School of General Education at Lingnan University, Hong Kong. He is the author of *The Structure of Literary Understanding*; *The End of Literary Theory*; and (with Peter Lamarque) *Truth, Fiction, and Literature: A Philosophical Perspective*. He has also published more than thirty articles on literary theory, literary criticism, and aesthetics. Among his most recent articles are "Spontaneity in Art Appreciation," in *Interpretation and Its Boundaries*, edited by Arto Haapala and Ossi Naukarinnen, and "Why Hugh MacColl Is Not, and Will Never Be, Part of Any Literary Canon," in *The Quality of Literature: Studies in Literary Evaluation*, edited by Willie van Peer.

Tom Rockmore is a professor of philosophy at Duquesne University. He has published widely, particularly on Hegel and Heidegger. His most recent books include *Heidegger and French Philosophy*; *On Hegel's Epistemology and Contemporary Philosophy*; and *Cognition: An Introduction to Hegel's Phenomenology of Spirit*. He is currently completing *Epistemology as Hermeneutics: Knowledge after Foundationalism*.

Paul Thom is Dean of the Faculty of Arts at the Australian National University. His research areas are aesthetics, Greek philosophy, history of logic, metaphysics, and theories of interpretation. His publications include *For An Audience: A Philosophy of the Performing Arts*, as well as numerous articles. His book *Making Sense: A Theory of Interpretation* is in press.

Cecilia Tohaneanu is a senior research fellow at the Romanian Academy's Institute for Social Theory. She is the author of *Epistemologia Istoriei: De la mitul faptelor la mitul Semnificatiilor* (*Epistemology of History: From the Myth of the Facts to the Myth of the Meanings*).

Index